Also available at all good book stores

9781785316470

9781785313929

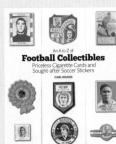

9781785315602

9781785317927

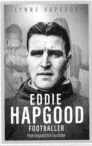

9781801500494

9781801500487

9781801501149

9781801500524

9781801500586

FOSSE
V LUFFS

NIGEL FREESTONE

FOSSE
V LUFFS

LEICESTERSHIRE'S
FORGOTTEN
FOOTBALL RIVALRY

First published by Pitch Publishing, 2022

Pitch Publishing
A2 Yeoman Gate
Yeoman Way
Worthing
Sussex
BN13 3QZ
www.pitchpublishing.co.uk
info@pitchpublishing.co.uk

ISBN 978 1 80150 061 6

Typesetting and origination by Pitch Publishing
Printed and bound in India by Replika Press Pvt. Ltd.

Contents

1

Introduction to Victorian Football

THE INTER-COUNTY footballing rivalry between Leicester Fosse – the forerunner of Leicester City – and Loughborough Town at the end of the 19th century, although short-lived, was as intense as any in modern English football. Loughborough, known as the Luffs, played an important role in the history and development of the Fosse and hence Leicester City FC. Club rivalry stemmed predominantly from their geographical proximity. The Fosse were the dominant club in the town of Leicester, while Loughborough were the biggest and most successful club in the county of Leicestershire, so each encounter was seen by both clubs and sets of supporters as a battle for footballing supremacy in Leicestershire.

Prior to discussing encounters between Leicester Fosse and Loughborough on the field, we need to acclimatise to the period and better understand the game played during the Victorian era. Hopefully, this chapter will cover all you need to know to get into football of the 1880s and 1890s. This will be of benefit as we chronicle the intense rivalry between the Fosse and the Luffs from their formation in the early 1880s to the demise of the latter at the very beginning of the 20th century. The story is full of drama, controversy, excitement, and passion, and peppered with sadness.

Introduction to 19th-Century Football

Although football had been played in one form or another for hundreds of years in Britain, it was not until the Victorian period that clubs formed and rules were codified. The Factory Act of 1850, among other things, stated that all work must stop at 2pm on Saturdays. This meant that the working class had 'free time' for recreational activity, which was unheard of for 'ordinary people'.

Free time could also mean trouble. Groups of young men on the streets being a nuisance or propping up a bar was likely to become something of a Victorian problem, and indeed that happened.

The first football clubs were started by churches through the emergence of Muscular Christianity, a movement that encouraged participation in sport to develop Christian morality, physical fitness, and 'manly' character. Promoting abstinence from the demon drink and clean living were also high on the religious agenda. Leaders worked with factory owners hoping to encourage healthy pursuits, which would be beneficial to the Church and employers alike. Football clubs were formed from Church groups (such as Aston Villa, Bolton Wanderers, Birmingham City, Leicester Fosse, Southampton and Tottenham Hotspur), factory groups (Manchester United – from the Lancashire and Yorkshire Railway depot at Newton Heath, as the club was first known; Arsenal from

Royal Arsenal in Woolwich, known as Woolwich Arsenal; West Ham United who were formerly Thames Ironworks; Coventry City who were first Singers FC, having been founded by employees of the Singer bicycle company), or existing sports clubs (such as Loughborough Town from Loughborough Athletics Club, and Derby County from Derbyshire County Cricket Club).

The Rules

Football has been played in England for over 1,300 years, with each region or county or school having its own unique set of rules. This severely limited the number of potential opponents and hindered its growth. The Cambridge Rules, drawn up in 1848 at a meeting of Eton, Harrow, Shrewsbury and Winchester public schools at the University of Cambridge, were highly influential in the development of subsequent codes, including association football. They were not universally adopted and other rules, most notably those of the Sheffield Football Club, were written nine years later in 1857, which led to the formation of the Sheffield FA in 1867.

The Football Association first met on 26 October 1863 at Freemasons' Tavern, on Great Queen Street in London, and over several meetings across a period of three months produced the first comprehensive set of rules. Blackheath withdrew from the FA over the removal of two draft rules at the previous meeting: those allowed running with the ball, and hacking. Other clubs followed and instead of joining the Football Association, they were instrumental in the formation of the Rugby Football Union in 1871. The Sheffield FA played by its own rules until the 1870s, with the FA absorbing some of its rules until there was little difference between the games.

The FA Cup, the world's oldest football competition, has been contested since 1872, while in the same year the first international football match took place, between England and Scotland. England is also home to the world's first football league, which was founded in Birmingham in 1888 by Aston Villa director William McGregor.

The following are the rules in place when Leicester Fosse were founded in 1884:

1. The limits of the ground shall be, maximum length, 200 yards; minimum length, 100 yards; maximum breadth, 100 yards; minimum breadth, 50 yards. The length and breadth shall be marked off with flags and touchline; and the goals shall be upright posts, eight yards apart, with a bar across them eight feet from the ground. The average circumference of the association ball shall be not less than 27 inches and not more than 28 inches.

2. The winners of the toss shall have the option of kick-off or choice of goals. The game shall be commenced by a place kick from the centre of the ground in the direction of the opposite goal line; the other side shall not approach within ten yards of the ball until it is kicked off, nor shall any player on either side pass the centre of the ground in the direction of his opponents' goal until the ball is kicked off.

3. Ends shall only be changed at half-time. After a goal is won the losing side shall kick off, but after the change of ends at half-time the ball shall be kicked off by the opposite side from that which originally did so; and always as provided in Law 2.

4. A goal shall be won when the ball has passed between the goal posts under the bar, not being thrown, knocked on, or carried by any one of the attacking side. The ball hitting the goal, or boundary posts, or goal bar, and rebounding into play, is considered in play.

5. When the ball is in touch, a player of the opposite side to that which kicked it out shall throw it from the point on the boundary line where it left the ground. The thrower, facing the field of play, shall hold the ball above his head and throw it with both hands in any direction, and it shall be in play when thrown in. The player throwing it shall not play it until it has been played by another player.

6. When a player kicks the ball, or throws it in from touch, any one of the same side who, at such moment of kicking or throwing, is nearer to the opponents' goal line is out of play, and may not touch the ball himself, nor in any way whatever prevent any other player from doing so until the ball has been played, unless there are at such moment of kicking or throwing at least three of his opponents nearer their own goal line; but no player is out of play in the case of a corner kick or when the ball is kicked from the goal line, or when it has been last played by an opponent.

7. When the ball is kicked behind the goal line by one of the opposite side it shall be kicked off by any one of the players behind whose goal line it went, within six yards of the nearest goal post; but if kicked behind by any one of the side whose goal line it is, a player of the opposite side shall kick it from within one yard of the nearest corner flag post. In either case no other player shall be allowed within six yards of the ball until it is kicked off.

8. No player shall carry, knock on, or handle the ball under any pretence whatever, except in the case of the goalkeeper, who shall be allowed to use his hands in

defence of his goal, either by knocking on or throwing, but not carrying the ball. The goalkeeper may be changed during the game, but not more than one player shall act as goalkeeper at the same time; and no second player shall step in and act during any period in which the regular goalkeeper may have vacated his position.

9. In no case shall a goal be scored from any free kick, nor shall the ball be again played by the kicker until it has been played by another player. The kick-off and corner flag kick shall be free kicks within the meaning of this rule.

10. Neither tripping, hacking, nor jumping at a player, shall be allowed, and no player shall use his hands to hold or push his adversary, or charge him from behind. A player with his back towards his opponents' goal cannot claim the protection of this rule when charged from behind, provided, in the opinion of the umpires or referee, he, in that position, is wilfully impeding his opponent.

11. No player shall wear any nails, except such as have their heads driven in flush with the leather, or iron plates, or gutta-percha on the soles or heels of his boots, or on his shin-guards. Any player discovered infringing this rule shall be prohibited from taking any further part in the game.

12. In the event of any infringement of rules five, six, eight, nine or ten, a free kick shall be forfeited to the opposite side, from the spot where the infringement took place.

13. In the event of an appeal for any supposed infringement of the rules, the ball shall be in play until a decision has been given.

14. Each of the competing clubs shall be entitled to appoint an umpire, whose duties shall be to decide all disputed points when appealed to; and by mutual arrangement a

referee may be chosen to decide in all cases of difference between the umpires.

15. The referee shall have power to stop the game in the event of spectators interfering with the game.

Definition of Terms

Place kick: the ball is kicked when lying on the ground, in any position chosen by the kicker.

Free kick: the ball is kicked when lying on the ground. No opponents are allowed within six yards of the ball, but players cannot be forced to stand behind their own goal line.

Hacking: intentional kicking of an opponent.

Tripping: the throwing of an opponent by use of the leg, or by stooping in front of him.

Knocking on: when a player strikes or propels the ball with his hands or arms.

Holding: includes the obstruction of a player by the hand or any part of the arm extended from the body.

Handling: playing the ball with the hand or arm.

Touch: the part of the field, on either side of the ground, which is beyond the line of play.

Carrying: moving more than two steps when carrying the ball.

Some notable differences from the modern game include:

- There was no crossbar. Goals could be scored at any height.
- Although most forms of handling were not permitted, players were allowed to catch the ball but could not run with it or throw it. A so-called 'fair catch' was rewarded with a free kick (this still exists in Australian Rules football, rugby union and American football).

- Any player ahead of the kicker was deemed offside (similar to today's offside rule in rugby union). The only exception was when the ball was kicked from behind the goal line.
- The throw-in was awarded to the first player (on either team) to touch the ball after it went out of play. The ball had to be thrown in at right-angles to the touchline (as today in rugby union).
- There was no corner kick. When the ball went behind the goal line, there was a situation somewhat like rugby: if an attacking player first touched the ball after it went out of play, then the attacking team had an opportunity to take a free kick at goal from a point 15 yards behind the point where the ball was touched (somewhat similar to a conversion in rugby). If a defender first touched the ball, then the defending team kicked the ball out from on or behind the goal line (equivalent to the goal kick).
- Teams changed ends every time a goal was scored.
- The rules made no provision for a goalkeeper, match officials, punishments for infringements of the rules, duration of the match, half-time, number of players, or pitch-markings (other than flags to mark the boundary of the playing area).

The following amendments were made to the Rules during the period of Leicestershire football derby games.

- 1887: the goalkeeper may not handle the ball in the opposition's half.
- 1888: the drop ball is introduced as a means of restarting play after it has been suspended by the referee.
- 1889: a player may be sent off for repeated cautionable behaviour

- 1890: a goal may not be scored directly from a goal kick.
- 1891: the penalty kick is introduced, for handball or foul play within 12 yards of the goal line. The umpires are replaced by linesmen. Pitch markings are introduced for the goal area, penalty area, centre spot and centre circle.
- 1897: the laws specify, for the first time, the number of players on each team (11) and the duration of each match (90 minutes, unless agreed otherwise). The halfway line is introduced. The maximum length of the ground is reduced from 200 yards to 130 yards.

The penalty kick, introduced out of frustration to combat cynical fouls committed to prevent a goal, was launched at a meeting of the International FA Board held in the Alexandra Hotel in Glasgow on 2 June 1891.

The four British associations agreed, 'If a player intentionally trip or hold an opposing player, or deliberately handle the ball within 12 yards from his own goal line, the referee shall, on appeal, award the opposing side a penalty kick, taken from any point 12 yards from the goal line under the following conditions – all players, with the exception of the player taking the penalty kick and the opposing goalkeeper, who shall not advance more than six yards from the goal line, shall stand at least six yards behind ball; the ball shall be in play when the kick taken; a goal may be scored from the penalty kick.'

It must be remembered that football began in England's top public schools and was played by gentlemen. Since a gentleman would never deliberately foul an opponent, penalty kicks were disdained by gentlemen amateur teams of the period. If awarded against them, the goalkeeper would leave the goal unguarded while the opposition took the kick, and if they were awarded a penalty, they would deliberately miss it. The legendary Corinthians player C.B. Fry wrote, 'It is a standing insult to sportsmen to have to play under a rule which assumes that players intend to trip, hack or push their opponents, and behave like cads of the most unscrupulous kidney.'

The kick could be taken from any point 12 yards from the goal line and the goalkeeper could narrow the angle by advancing up to six yards off his line. On 14 September 1891, Billy Heath of Wolves scored the first penalty awarded in the Football League, against Accrington at Molineux, early in the second half of a 5-0 victory for his team. In some sources, it is reported that Leicester Fosse also scored with a penalty against Notts County on the same day. Another Wolverhampton Wanderers player, Harry Allen, became the first man to miss a league penalty just five days later, shooting over the bar against West Bromwich Albion.

Officials

Team captains initially ran the game. It was not until the early 1870s that referees appeared on the touchline, to act both as timekeeper and to settle disputes when the two captains could not agree. By the time the Fosse and Luff encounters began, two umpires, one appointed by each team, replaced the captains. Referees took complete control of games in 1891, when the umpires were relegated to the touchline, effectively becoming linesmen. Neutral linesmen were first used on a regular basis in 1898/99, but only for 'important' games.

Even during Victoria times referees were much maligned characters. Forced to get changed in a shed or pub requiring them to walk long distances to and from the ground, or in a tent adjacent to the pitch, without any security or protection of themselves or their belongings, they were subjected to verbal and sometimes physical abuse during and after the game. Many clubs were reluctant to pay the referee, who at the end of the game was required to seek out a club official to ask for his fee. Often because not he could not find anyone, he would have to write a letter to the club secretary a few days later requesting a cheque to be forwarded to his home address. Adcock's 1905 handbook, entitled *Association Football*, states that the standard pay for referees for an 'ordinary cup tie' was 10s 6d. A society for referees was established in London in 1893, and by the end of the century membership of the 27 societies in England reached 773. To ensure consistency in all regions the overall responsibility for refereeing was passed to the FA.

Montague Sherman, in his 1887 book *Athletics and Football*, neatly summarises the role of officials, 'Each side has its own umpire, who is armed with a stick or flag; the referee carries a whistle. When a claim for infringement of rules is made, if both umpires are agreed, each holds up his stick, and the referee calls the game to a halt by sounding his whistle. If one umpire allows the claim, and the referee agree with him, he calls a halt as before; if the other umpire and referee agree that the claim be disallowed, the whistle is not sounded. Two of the three officials must therefore agree in allowing the claim or the whistle is silent, and players continue the game until the whistle calls them off. Both umpires and referee, therefore, must lose no time in arriving at a decision, or so much play is wasted.'

Excerpts from the Football Association's 'clarification rules' memorandum, which contains several pointers for umpires and linesmen; hopefully help further in bringing 19th century football to life:

1. The kick-off must be in the direction of the opposition goal line, and therefore, all back kicking is illegal; and, secondly, that the other side shall not approach within TEN yards of the ball until it is kicked off.
2. Goals cannot be scored until the whole of the ball has passed over the goal line. The ball is also in play until the whole ball has passed over the touchline.
3. A player is always offside if he is in front of the ball at the time of kicking unless there are three or more of his opponents nearer the goal line. A player is never offside if there are three or more players nearer the goal line than himself at the moment the ball was last played. A player cannot be offside if the ball was last played (i.e., touched, kicked, or thrown) by one of his opponents or by one of his own side who at the time of kicking is nearer his opponents' goal then himself. Law 6 further enacts that a player being offside shall not in ANY WAY WHATEVER interfere with any other player.
4. A goalkeeper is allowed to use his hands in defence of his goal. The committee do not consider a goalkeeper to be in defence of his goal when he is in his opponents' half of the ground.
5. No player shall wear any nails, excepting such as have their heads driven in flush with the leather, or iron plates, or gutta-percha on the soles or heels of his boots or on his

shin guards. Any player discovered infringing this rule should be prohibited from taking further part in the game.
6. In the event of an appeal for any supposed infringement of the rules, the ball shall be in play until a decision is being given. Umpires should remember how very important it is for the proper working of this rule that their decisions should be given as quickly as possible.

Ownership and Management of Football Clubs

Early football clubs were run by committees elected by its members. Management committees oversaw the running of the club, signed players and were responsible for team selection. Sometimes secretary-managers were appointed to carry out these duties. The club secretary was often an old or former player and would try to entice opposition to his team's home ground that would attract a larger than usual crowd. This often involved promising them a percentage of the gate money.

Mismatching was not uncommon, resulting in scores of more than 10-0. Crowds got bored with watching either their team thrash a hopelessly outclassed opposition, or would leave the ground in their droves long before the end of the game if their team were losing by more than four or five goals with 20 minutes to go. Top teams would often field severely weakened sides or send teams to more than one location on the same day.

Towards the end of the 19th century, as clubs and businesses sought to exploit the huge popularity of the game, the Football Association allowed Football League clubs to form limited companies. However, they restricted the profits that could be issued to shareholders to a maximum of five per cent of the shares held. In addition, club directors could not be paid. So, in essence, clubs operated as not-for-profit businesses.

The Football Association aimed to ensure that clubs met the social and cultural needs of the communities they represented, while still permitting a fair rate of return to their owners. Leicester Fosse would later take advantage of this to help themselves out of a financial crisis. With hindsight, if Loughborough had adopted a similar strategy, they might still be a footballing force today.

A maximum wage was also introduced to stop clubs from increasing salaries as a means of retaining players. Gate receipts, the only significant source of revenue at the time, were split between the competing clubs, with a small percentage going to a central fund for redistribution to all Football League clubs. The idea was to ensure that smaller town clubs would not be at a disadvantage to those from large towns and cities with larger fan bases.

The Game

Football at the end of the 19th century was a brutal game, once described as 'the terror of mothers, the dread of the timid and the joy of athletes'. Although 'hacking', kicking an opposition player beneath the knee, an integral part of the pre-Football Association game, had been banned, players could charge or interfere in any manner that did not involve tripping, hacking, or using hands to hold or push. A young Coalville player was even charged in 1878 with the manslaughter of an Ashby player following a 'charge'.

The violent nature of football attracted the attention of the world-renowned medical journal, *The Lancet*. In 1885, it published an article entitled 'The Perils of Football', which collated all the footballing accidents, both association and rugby union codes, reported by newspapers during the 1884/85 season. It made grim reading with numerous broken legs, arms, ankles, collar bones, cuts, players having to retire as a result of their injuries, and, tragically, some subsequent deaths.

Although the list does not represent total amount of the season's football casualties, it amply demonstrates the exceptionally dangerous nature of the game. No other popular game had the same amount of peril attached to it. *The Lancet* urged both Rugby Football Union and the Football Association authorities to reform. *The Lancet* did state that the nature of the reforms 'is not for us to decide, but we would venture to call the attention of the Rugby Union and the Association authorities to collaring and charging, respectively'.

The article and recommendations appear to have had little effect, for during the 1888/89 season there were no fewer than eight fatalities and numerous injuries from lockjaw and brain fever through to limb amputations and ruptured kidneys. Shrewsbury Town player John Henry Morris died aged 23 on 12 November 1893 from an internal haemorrhage following a kick in the abdomen by William Evans in an ill-tempered cup tie against Madeley Town at Shrewsbury. A verdict of 'accidental death' was returned. Evans had to be escorted from the coroner's court by the police and was 'followed to the railway by an excited crowd'.

Another football fatality occurred less than two weeks later. William Bannister of Chesterfield Town had collided with the inside-right of Derby Junction at the Recreation

Ground on 4 November 1893. Better known as 'Wash', Bannister appeared to recover rapidly and when he took up his place at the back again, he was loudly applauded. After the match, however, Bannister collapsed and was taken home. Dr William Booth and Dr Robinson were called in, and after careful examination they found that Bannister had ruptured his kidneys but believed that he might pull through. However, just as he appeared to be on the mend, he slipped on a stone, fell and re-opened the wound. A relapse set in, he gradually grew worse, and tragically died. The consensus of players, officials and medical staff was that there was no one to blame. Rough play did not cause the injury; instead it was the simplest collision.

In March 1896, following a clash of heads, Teddy Smith, playing for Bedminster against Eastville Rovers in the Gloucestershire Cup semi-final, suffered severe concussion. After a short period of rest, he bravely carried on playing, but was forced to leave the field and by the next morning he had died from his injuries. Loughborough Town suffered a fatality, as we shall see later, with many players across Leicestershire having to endure life-changing injuries as a result of playing the kicking game.

Team tactics were simple: dribble the ball straight down the middle of the field. There was little sideways movement of the ball. This often meant using sheer physical force to move through, rather than around, the opposition. When the opposition successfully stopped an individual forward, another member of the onrushing group followed up to force the ball on by dribbling or kicking to team-mates who were close by. Mass 'scrimmages' occurred as loose balls were pounced upon when dribbles were cut short by hacks and fouls.

Although passing of the ball occurred, it generally was a last resort and took only two forms – very short passes exchanged by forwards running together in pairs or small groups, and long forward punts by backs for the pack of forwards to chase. The sweeping pass to the wing, or longer lateral or even backward passes designed to set up subsequent forward attacks, were unknown in this era.

In many respects the game was more similar to rugby league than modern football. Teams lined up and played with a goalkeeper, two or three backs and half-backs, and the rest of the team as a tightly packed swarm of forwards. This style of football changed slowly during the 1870s into one based around teamwork and cooperation. Developed by Queen's Park in Scotland, the so-called 'combination' or 'passing' game was rapidly adopted with considerable success by English clubs Liverpool, Aston Villa, Blackburn Rovers, Fulham, Arsenal, Southampton, and Derby County. The playing style involved a combination of dribbling and passing, offering a great advantage over the rudimentary style of football. It seems strange that until then, the idea that a ball could be deliberately passed to a team-mate in a better position had barely been considered. By cooperating and working together as a team, giving them the upper hand.

Teams typically employed the 2-3-5 'pyramid formation', which dominated the game for 60 years, until a more technical, defensive approach, when Arsenal developed the 'W-M', essentially a 3-4-3. For the first time, a balance between attacking and defending was reached. One of the backs often acted as a minder or bodyguard to the goalkeeper, protecting him from excessive barging and acting as a last line of defence. The other roamed further upfield to break up attacks. The offside rule at the time required three defenders to be between the recipient of the ball and the goal. Therefore, it was tactically sound to utilise the second back to play higher to spring an offside trap far from goal. Backs with big kicks were highly sought after to both clear the ball away and to launch attacks. When defending, the two backs would watch out for the opponents' outside- and inside-forwards, while the half-backs (midfielders) would watch for the other three forwards.

As today, the midfield was the engine room of the team, taking the ball from the opposition and launching attacks. The central half-back had a fundamental role in both coordinating attacks, as well as marking the opponents' centre-forward, generally considered to be their most dangerous player. The forward line comprised outside and inside wing men who would combine to make rapid progress down the less muddy wings and create chances for other forwards. The role of the centre-forward was to get on the end of crosses from his wing men and essentially to be in the right place at the right time to score. It was this formation that gave rise to the convention of shirt numbers.

The Victorian goalkeeper's role was quite different from that of today's keeper. Until 1912 he was permitted to handle the ball anywhere in his own half of the field. Few goalkeepers managed to take full advantage of this, as they had to bounce the ball every two steps to continue running. This was almost impossible on muddy and uneven pitches.

Goalkeepers could be legally charged by burly opposing forwards and if knocked over the goal line while carrying the ball they would concede a goal (point). This meant that the goalkeeper generally stayed close to goal, preferring to fist or punt the ball high up the field instead of catching the ball.

Just to confuse matters, the goalkeeper wore the same kit as his team-mates. Gloves only started to be worn in the 1890s. The law changed in 1894 when charging was only permitted while goalkeepers were in possession of the ball. In 1866, Darlington's Charles Craven identified the attributes and skills required to be a goalkeeper, 'A good goalkeeper should not be less than 5ft 6 in. in height (the same in girth if he likes), active, cool, and have a good and quick eye. He should be a safe kick. In clearing the ball, he should strike up in the air, so that the ball does not meet an opponent and rebound. He sometimes has eight yards to cover in next to no time, and as it is quicker to fall than to run, he should practice throwing down himself. When this art is acquired (and it cannot be done without practice) he will find it fairly useful.'

During the period Fosse and Luffs met, football did noticeably change from dribbling and scrimmages to a passing game, with even the odd goal being scored from a header.

Players

It must be remembered that association football began as an amateur game. A rule had been in effect since 1881 and stated, 'Any member of a club receiving remuneration or consideration of any sort above his actual expenses and any wages lost by any such player taking part in any match, shall be debarred from taking part in either cup, inter-association, or international contests, and any clubs employing such player shall be excluded from this association.'

Throughout the early 1880s the issue of professionalism would simply not go away. The Football Association had several disputes with northern clubs, including Bolton Wanderers, Blackburn Rovers and Darwen who had all signed Scottish players professionally. Many northern clubs retained two sets of 'books', with one set of true accounts and another book detailing fabricated accounts that would be presented to the Football Association if the need were to arise. It was common practice for players to be paid from gate receipts, prior to the club declaring the gross takings on matchday. Local tradesmen were often used by clubs to 'employ' players. In reality these players had their wages paid by the clubs themselves. Many of these practices had become very well established; for example, excessive payments had been given for time taken off work (broken-time payments), paying players for 'one-off' or ad hoc games and myriad other financial inducements, all of which were implemented to ensure that particular players represented a particular football club.

The Football Association embraced 'amateurism' promoted by Corinthian FC and other clubs founded by alumni from top public schools. The difference between the southern amateur clubs and the professional teams from the north came to a head in 1884 when Preston North End played Upton Park in January 1884 in the FA Cup. Preston were accused of professionalism, which they admitted. Billy Sudell, who masterminded Preston's rise to the pinnacle of

English football, admitted the practice was commonplace. He said, 'Professionalism must improve football because men who devote their entire attention to the game are more likely to become good players than the amateur who is worried by business cares.' Feeling they had little option, Preston withdrew from the competition.

At least 30 other clubs, mainly from the north of England, quickly followed suit, and threatened to set up a rival British Football Association if the FA did not allow professionalism. The FA relented, and in July 1885 professionalism was formally legalised in England. Professionals had to be registered and there were strict conditions, on paper at least. The main condition was that professionals were required to either be born, or have been in residence for two years, within six miles of the ground or headquarters of their club. Preston, however, was a long way from London and the rule was difficult to police and was abandoned in 1889. Professionals were also not able to play for more than one team a season without special permission of the FA. Though English clubs employed professionals, the Scottish Football Association still banned them. Many Scottish players consequently moved to England to ply their trade. Preston North End's 'Invincibles' team, who won the 'Double' of the FA Cup and the inaugural Football League championship in 1888/89, fielded no fewer than ten Scottish professionals.

Although Leicester Fosse and Loughborough players from 1889 onwards were classified as professionals, most did not earn enough to support themselves. They supplemented their income by working for a local employer. Lesser-known players received a pittance. This meant that through a mixture of employers refusing to allow players to take time off, illness or fecklessness it was not unusual even for top teams, particularly away from home, to be short of one or more players, or to acquire substitutes from the crowd.

Training

Training was not part of the 'gentlemanly' ideal. Intense training was considered to be 'poor form'; 'Practising too much undermined natural grace and talent … gentlemen were not supposed to toil and sweat for their laurels.' Due to the aggressive and physical nature of the game, players who could kick long and were robust were favoured over those with ball skills or speed. Robert Crompton, the Blackburn Rovers full-back and England international, was described in the following terms, 'Physically Bob Crompton is one of the finest examples of the native-born professional player. Standing 5ft 9in, and weighing 12st 7lb, he is splendidly developed, and a fine figure in shirt and knickers … He can charge with effect, however, on occasions, but he is something more than a mere rusher … His kicking is naturally powerful-probably his punts are the biggest things in league football … Perhaps he balloons the ball rather too much for the perfect back, and when attacking his feeding passes often have too much powder behind them.'

Meanwhile, Herbert Smith, the captain of Reading, was once described as follows by a former team-mate, 'In watching the figure of Herbert Smith on a football field one is tempted to exclaim, "There stands a man!" As a specimen of English manhood, one might search far and wide for his equal. It may be that in these days purely physical qualities are extolled too much, but a fine man, a perfect human animal will always command respect. To watch Smith at play, to see him run, to witness the play of his muscles, makes one feel proud of one's kind. He is a type of perfectly developed manhood.'

Given the emphasis on brute strength and idea of Muscular Christianity promoted by the Church, many early professional football clubs employed professional athletes or ex-boxers. Training sessions rarely developed ball skills and typically involved 'the use of heavy clubs and dumb-bells to 20 minutes' skipping, ball-punching, sprinting, and alternating with an eight- or nine-mile walk at a brisk pace'. An unnamed former English international, writing in the early 20th century, bemoaned the lack of skills development in training, 'There is no running about or dribbling, feinting, passing with the inside or outside of the foot, trapping or heading the ball and placing it with the head like you do with your feet, judging distances etc; indulged in at all.'

In an article entitled 'The Day's Work', Mr W.I. Bassett, a former England international who played for West Bromwich Albion for 16 years, gave a detailed account of the manner in which a professional footballer was trained, 'The bulk of the trainers vary in their methods … Monday is often a *dies non*. Many clubs allow the men to do as they like on that day, providing that there is no midweek engagement. On the Tuesday morning they get to the ground at ten o'clock and the trainer takes them for a good walk into the country. They probably cover five or six miles, and do it at a fair pace. This is the form of training

I cordially approve of ... plenty of good fresh air. Should the morning not be conducive to pleasant walking, then the trainer orders alternative exercise.

'One of the greatest full-backs of the day is in the habit of skipping every morning; practically he does little else, and he is always in the pink of condition. It makes for increased agility, it improves the wind. Most of our leading clubs have a well-equipped gymnasium.

'Another player will have a long turn with the Indian clubs, and others will punch the ball for an hour ... Some of our leading pugilists are very fine ball punchers ... Then there is running exercise. Most of the players will run round the ground a few times or many, according to the amount of exercise each are deemed to require. This was the only real training I ever did. Then there is sprinting exercise ... The men indulge in short bursts at top speed. But I fancy I hear the reader ask, what about learning to play football? Once a week, and once a week only, the men have ball practice ... the men simply kick in ... My own opinion is that men get nothing like as much actual work with the ball as they need.'

The Pitch

Although some private pitches may have been used, most football clubs began on public parks, which began to appear in Britain from the 1860s onwards. In Leicester, for instance, Abbey Park (1882), Victoria Park (1883) and Spiney Hill Park (1885) all opened within three years of each other. The best-known private sports grounds in Leicestershire during the 1880s were the cricket grounds on Wharf Street, Aylestone Cricket Round (Grace Road),

Belgrave Cycle, all of which were in Leicester, Coalville's Fox and Gosse Cricket Ground and Loughborough's Hubbards Athletics Ground.

Pitch markings when Fosse played their first game in 1884 simply comprised a four flags to mark the corners of the playing area. The goalposts were eight yards apart – precisely the same distance as they need to be today. In general, there was nothing to indicate the edge of the pitch, nor the end of it. Pitches were just patches of grass wherever they could be found. Only when clubs had their own homes was it possible to lay down pitch markings. Bollards or a rope fencing along the field edges were used to help players know where they could not go beyond and to keep the spectators close to the action.

When it was decided that players could no longer be offside from a throw, for example, it wasn't necessary for there to be markings on the pitch to denote that. But when the rules were changed in 1887 to ban goalkeepers from handling the ball in the opposition's territory, referees clearly could not enforce the new law without knowing the location of the halfway point of the field of play.

The biggest change resulted from the introduction of the penalty kick four years later in 1891 to punish players other than the goalkeeper for handling the ball within 12 yards of the goal line. Equally, a penalty could also be awarded for foul play within the area, meaning that referees needed to be able to see exactly where that area began and ended. That was why pitch markings were introduced, dictating where both the goal area and penalty area were located as well as the location of the centre spot and the centre circle.

In many ways, markings were more similar to what a modern supporter would expect to see in rugby than on a football pitch. The halfway line and centre circle would be familiar, but the penalty area was indicated by a dotted line across the width of pitch 18 yards from the goal line. The 12-yard line was put in place, with penalty-takers able to strike the ball from anywhere along that line. The goalkeeper's area wasn't the box that we are used to today; instead it was in a shape that can really only be described as looking like a pair of breasts. It began a couple of feet on either side of the goalposts and curved up to meet in the middle of the goal, but rather than meet as a full curve, it came together as the lines do at the top of a Valentine's Day heart. Why? In 1891, the goal kick was formalised in the rules, which stated, 'The ball … shall be kicked off … within six yards of the goal post nearest the point where the ball left the field of play.'

The football pitch began to take on a shape far more similar to what we're used to in this day and age, though it had enough differences to mean that a modern fan wouldn't be 100 per cent confident of what they were looking at if they saw it. It would take another 11 years for the humble football pitch to begin to look like the one that you'll come across today, whether you head to the King Power, Wembley or the Camp Nou. The penalty area became the rectangular box that we know and love, while the six-yard box flattened down and became something of a hybrid between the 'boob' area and the line at the 12-yard mark that was in place previously. One further change was made. After suggestions from various other European football associations, an arc was added to the penalty area.

Balls and Boots

The tanned leather balls of the Victorian era typically comprised six panels of three strips each, with the seams tied together with laces. These balls were notoriously heavy and could double in weight in wet conditions as they sucked up rainwater like a sponge, making them hard to kick let alone control or run with on heavy pitches. Heading was almost impossible in wet conditions and caused headaches and could even knock a player unconscious. To make matters worse, the brown balls were difficult to see for spectators, let alone the players in the mud.

Footballs were relatively expensive. In the late 1870s they were being advertised for 8s 6d, which was equivalent to almost a week's wage for an unskilled worker. As a consequence, footballs were prized and well looked after, laces routinely replaced, and the leather regularly dubbed. In some parts of the country footballs could be hired at 1s for a game. Clubs did not have multiple balls and should a ball burst, then that would often result in the premature end of the game.

Before the early 1890s, football boots were not in use. Heavy work boots, often with reinforced toes, were worn instead, but they were not ideal for running in, or controlling a ball with. Players according to the 1863 rules were not allowed to wear footwear with 'projecting nails, iron plates, or gutta percha on the soles or heels of his boots'. Consequently, players struggled in wet and icy conditions to stay upright. Around 1891 a revision to the rules allowed boots to utilise small bars or studs leading to the manufacture of specific footwear for playing football. Made from thick leather, they were laced up at the ankle for better protection.

Shin guards or shin pads, developed in 1874 by the Nottingham Forest captain Stan Weller Woddowson from cut-down cricket pads, were fastened with leather straps, on the outside of stockings below long knickerbockers. By the end of the 19th century, the pads had become smaller and were being worn inside the stockings. The rule that knickerbockers must cover the knees of players was dropped by the Football Association in 1904 and as a result player wore much shorter 'knickers'.

Almost all teams wore shirts of a contrasting colour or design to their knickerbockers. Loughborough wore black-and-white-striped shirts and either white or dark blue knickerbockers. The Fosse, meanwhile, adopted a range of short designs from black with a blue sash across the chest to blue and maroon quarters before finally settling on the colours of blue and white. The Football League ruled in 1890, two years after its formation, that each member club had to register the colour and pattern of their shirts, to avoid clashes. Presumably, this resulted in arguments between clubs and was later abandoned. Instead, teams had to ensure that a second set of shirts in a different colour was available for all games. In the event of a colour clash, the home team was initially required to change colours.

The away side usually travelled to the game by tram and/or train and had to carry kit and other provisions with them. In 1921 this rule was amended, requiring the away team to change. As stated earlier, goalkeepers wore the same shirts as outfield players. This meant that match officials struggled to identify goalkeepers among a ruck of players. Yet another change to the rules, in 1904, stated that the goalkeeper must wear a different-coloured shirt from their team-mates. There were just two colours initially allowed – scarlet or royal blue. Green was added as a third option in 1912, which became so popular that up until the 1970s almost every goalkeeper played in green. In the Victorian era, goalkeepers generally wore a heavy woollen garment more akin to a jumper than the shirts worn by outfield players.

Supporters

As the Covid pandemic has clearly demonstrated, 'Football is nothing without fans,' to quote the great Jock Stein. The first spectators of Leicester Fosse, Loughborough Town and all other teams were non-playing members, their families, and friends. As clubs played each other, and the popularity of football rapidly increased, inherent rivalries developed, with spectators becoming supporters.

The popularity of football rapidly increased during the late-Victorian period and clubs became an integral part of their local communities. Factory workers finished at 2pm on a Saturday and flocked in their thousands to watch football in the industrialised north and Midlands. It is hardly surprising that football appealed to the working classes. Anyone, regardless of size or strength, could play football, unlike rugby, and matches were completed within a relatively brief timeframe, unlike cricket. Football was within the reach of everyone, a truly democratic game, which rapidly exerted an appeal of 'gigantic dimensions' in working-class communities: it was a game of remarkable simplicity that was enjoyable to both watch and play.

As crowds grew in size and intensity, they began to influence the outcome of games. They generated noise and passion and at times an intimidating atmosphere. It was not unknown for the crowd, literally separated from the players by a rope, to interfere with the game, by tripping players as they ran by with the ball. There were no goal nets in the early years, so the rope went right along the goal line – the main reason the goal net was invented in 1890s. Spectators would throw mud, apple cores, orange peel and anything else that came to hand at opposing players, and sometimes their own as well verbally abuse them.

Large gatherings of men, some fuelled by alcohol, others by the excitement of 'rough' play would use coarse, threatening language that triggered rowdy and violent behaviour. A search of newspaper reports of the era revealed numerous incidents of violence and crowd trouble at matches. Examples include former Aston Villa man Archie Hunter writing that 'hats, sticks and umbrellas were flying in all directions, almost darkening the air' as trouble broke out after his club won the Birmingham Challenge Cup in 1880; in 1888, Everton's Alec Dick struck Albert Moore of Notts County 'in the back in a piece of ruffianism', leading the fans to charge the field at the end of the game with Dick being struck by a stick, although he was later suspended for the remainder of the season for his initial offence; and two seasons later, fans of The Wednesday 'were on the ground and went for the referee' after a game. It was reported that the referee was threatened and, 'Despite some mud throwing, he got into the dressing tent without being molested'. The Wednesday supporters then 'vent their spleen at the visitors, who had a shower of stones, bricks, etc., thrown at them.

There were also incidents of fans attacking railway officials, damaging trains, and pitched battles outside grounds. Football authorities tried to clamp down by punishing players and closing grounds down.

Leicestershire supporters also misbehaved. In response to a report by the Leicestershire Football Association in 1899 aimed at eliminating these unsavoury aspects of football, one fan wrote to the *Leicester Mercury* urging Loughborough Town's management committee to do 'all they can to keep the game so that no self-respecting man may hesitate to bring male or female members of his family'. Loughborough's first cup final was disrupted by supporters of a rival team, their home ground was closed by football authorities on no fewer than three occasions as a punishment for crowd misbehaviour and a Leicester Fosse fan was physically assaulted by a well-known Derby player following an FA Cup tie. These incidents and many more interesting events will be discussed as we begin to chronicle the story of the rivalry between Leicester Fosse and Loughborough Town FC.

Excerpts of match reports and newspaper archives are included to help tell the story, although some of the language used by football correspondents at that time may seem strange, so here is a short glossary to help you:

- Citadel – goal
- Combination – football based around teamwork and cooperation. It would gradually favour the passing of the ball between players over individual dribbling skills which had been a notable feature of early association games
- Custodian – goalkeeper

- Flag kick – corner
- Leather – ball
- Point – goal
- Screamer – impressive long-shot goal
- Screw – shot that curves or bends
- Scrimmage – goalmouth scramble. Newspaper reporters were often unable to identify the scorer and would report simply that the goal had been scored 'from a scrimmage'

2

Friendlies and County Cup Games

LEICESTER WAS in a period of prosperity, expansion, and improvement throughout the latter part of the 19th century. The town's population rapidly increased from 68,000 in 1861 to just over 142,000 in 1891 and by 1911 it had reached 227,000. The town's chief industries were dominated by hosiery and footwear manufacture, which had largely shifted from domestic to factory production. As prosperity increased, the town's infrastructure developed. New gas works were constructed on Aylestone Road and continually expanded throughout the 1880s to cope with the increase in demand. Electricity was not supplied to the town until the mid-1890s and, even then, only to the commercial and business quarter in the centre of the town. The electricity works were situated by the gas works on the Aylestone Road site.

Public transport was provided by Leicester Tramways Company. The company's first tram service, opened in 1875, was between Leicester and Belgrave, and in the following year two further services, along London Road and Humberstone Road, began operating. In 1878, the Victoria Park line was extended along London Road to Knighton Road, and further routes along Aylestone Road in the south and to Woodgate in the north were added. Further expansion of the tram system did not take place until 1901 and motorised omnibuses did not appear until the 1920s. Many of Leicester's landmarks were constructed during the second half of the 19th century, as wealthy Victorians made their mark on the town – London Road railway station (1840), the clock tower (1868), King Street (1850), Corah and Sons – St Margaret's Works (1866), Town Hall (1876), Grand Hotel (1897) and Western Park (1899).

Life on the streets and in the public houses of Victorian Leicester was violent. Newspapers of the time feature innumerable cases of assault. Men who could fight were highly respected within their community. Hundreds of men would gather on open land or abandoned buildings to watch prize fighters as well as informally organised contests to settle disputes. In 1887, a 34-year-old plasterer, Arthur Taylor of Sanvey Gate, died from injuries received in a fight with Samuel Fowkes (27), of Barston Street. The incident was the outcome of a long-standing dispute between the two after Taylor had cut open Fowkes's head with a pewter pot the previous year. A meeting in the Star Inn led to agreement to fight the matter out on the Pasture, where they met after closing time. A witness reported that a crowd gathered to watch a fight of many rounds, which lasted for around 40 minutes. Two to three minutes before its conclusion, Taylor exclaimed, 'You. You have given me one; you have kicked me.' Fowkes was quick to deny the accusation. Afterwards, Taylor 'gave over', proposing a wager for a further fight, which Fowkes refused. At the assizes, Fowkes was found guilty of manslaughter, but received only the seemingly lenient sentence of two weeks hard labour as the judge found it 'a fair stand-up fight'. Leisure activities, for those who could afford them, centred around the church, music halls, public houses and 'pre-modern' sporting activities.

One the distinguishing features of 'pre-modern' sport was the central place of cruelty to animals, and/or of contests involving animals. There was a great affection for dog sports in 19th century Leicester. As late as 1886, the *Pall Mall Gazette* reported, 'The Leicester rough is ... greatly addicted to small white dogs and small brown rats.' A newspaper noted in 1881 that there was a rat pit in Soar Lane, owned by a Mr Terry, which was 'patronised by dog fanciers from the nobleman down to the nailer'. Other sporting activities popular in Leicester included dog fighting, pigeon flying, 'running naked', prize fighting and pitch and toss. The rules of many pastimes and games, some of which had previously been played with a variety of unofficial laws for several centuries, were officially codified in the early and middle years of the 19th century. As a result, local clubs and societies were formed across a broad range of sports including cricket, boxing, tennis, and golf as well as horticultural societies. Attempts to formally organise and regulate dog racing, another popular pastime, such as a series of dog handicaps staged at Belgrave Road Ground in 1881, were unsuccessful.

With the rise of commercial attractions, notably cycling in the late 1870s and cricket and football in the 1880s and '90s, these sports become less prominent, or acquired 'legitimate' forms – long-distance pigeon racing, boxing, etc. Leicester acquired several of its major sports clubs and sporting institutions during this period – Leicester Fosse (1884), Leicester Football Club (1880), Leicester Athletic Society (1868), the Belgrave Athletic Sports and Races (1870) and the Stoneygate School Athletic Sports (1867). The rapid growth of sport was reflected by the local press. Weekly newspapers gave only occasional coverage to sport in 1873, usually items on specific events in the 'Local Notes' column. By 1883, the *Leicester Daily Post* carried half a column of sporting news every day, which had increased by 1893 to up to two pages, with fixture lists, previews, and results of local and national events. The *Leicester Mercury* had a Saturday evening football edition. Such extensive coverage continued to be the norm until 1914, although by 1903, local clubs had joined the Football League and cricket's County Championship, and the Tigers (Leicester Football Club, the leading rugby club) acquired a national reputation. Several attempts were made to establish a Leicester sporting paper, but as elsewhere, the effectiveness of the local daily and weekly press reduced the potential audience, and none lasted for very long. The prominence of sport in the press, and complaints by churchmen and others that sport took up too much of people's attention, indicate that, by 1900, sport had acquired a far more salient place in the consciousness of large sections of the population.

However, it was cycling, rather than football or cricket that attracted the biggest crowds in Leicester throughout most of the 1870 and 1880s. The only exception was the cricket match against Australia in 1878. Even then, the first-day crowd of 12,000 at Aylestone Road was no bigger than that which gathered for the 25-mile bicycle championship of the world in 1884. *The Cyclist* observed in July of that year that the visit gave the ground a 'more animated appearance than is usual for cricket matches'. In 1886, the county cricket club brought in only 2.3 per cent of total revenue as against 32.4 per cent from admissions and season tickets and 49.1 per cent from the sale of refreshments.

The centres of Leicester and Loughborough are just 12 miles apart. Travel between the two towns throughout the Victorian period was by horse-drawn carriage, stagecoach, or train. Leicestershire's first turnpike road was a section of the main road between London and West Scotland, now the A6, built in 1726. This road bisected the county from south to north passing through Market Harborough, Leicester, and Loughborough. Toll houses were located at the ends of each section. The section between Leicester and Loughborough had a toll houses at Belgrave, and Quorn. The Quorn toll house was later moved to the junction of the turnpike with Woodthorpe Lane on the edge of Loughborough. Initially the road was surfaced with gravel and small stones, but by the end of the 18th century granite chippings from Mountsorrel were utilised. The section between Mountsorrel and Quorn was paved with granite setts. A fast public stagecoach service was inaugurated from Leicester to London in 1766.

Journey time for the 98 miles was typically 12 hours. Coaching inns were built along the route, and the old coach gateways can still be seen at the Three Swans (originally known as the Swan) and the Angel Hotel in Market Harborough. In 1822 the whole road was re-laid with tarmac, and the volume of traffic began to increase, until the advent of the railway in the 1840s. The Turnpike Trust was wound up in 1878. Without the extensive rail network and regular trains, professional football would not have been possible, as it allowed teams and their supporters to travel by train across the country.

Loughborough, by comparison with Leicester, was a small town with a population in 1888 of 11,000, which increased to 25,000 over the following decade. Robert Taylor's bell foundry, John Taylor and Co and the Falcon works, which manufactured steam locomotives and later motor cars before being taken over by Brush Electrical Machines, were all established in the town during the industrial revolution. In 1897, Herbert Morris set up a factory at the Empress Works in Moor Lane which became one of the foremost national crane manufacturers by the mid-20th century. There was also significant municipal investment in the town's infrastructure, with the construction of a new sewage works in 1895, waterworks in Blackbrook and a power station in Bridge Street in 1899. The corporation took over the Loughborough Gas Company in 1900.

There appears to have been little popular interest in football in Leicester before the spread of the modern game in the last decades of the 19th century. Based on the reporting of association football by local newspapers alone, football appears to have spread southwards from Yorkshire and Nottinghamshire through Loughborough, Sheepshed (now Shepshed) and Coalville to the county town. The Great Leicestershire Cricket and Football Club of the 1840s is widely cited as one of England's earliest football clubs, but little is known about it. Although a rugby stronghold, the town of Leicester certainly had teams playing the association rules following the codification of the game in the late 1860s. It wasn't uncommon for a team to play different versions of 'football', depending upon the opposition.

The first reported football games in both towns were staged by public schools during the early 1870s. Leicester-based teams included and Leicester Athletic Football Club, patronised by gentry and leading townsmen, and established by the Leicester Athletic Society. The public school teams of Field House, Wyggeston School, and Leicester Grammar all played on Victoria Park (Racecourse). Leicester Athletic Society Football Club regularly attracted what were described as large attendances (no figures were given), but the sport remained informally organised and a minority event. Football tournaments were well established by the mid-1880s. Long Eaton Rangers took the first prize of £3 10s, and Kegworth the £1 10s as runners-up in a football contest participated in by four Kegworth teams, and others from Long Eaton, Castle Donington, and Hathern in August 1886. Other attractions for the large crowd were roundabouts, shooting galleries, and Sunday amusements. A greasy pole was also successfully climbed for the prize of a leg of mutton. The following month, Sheepshed FC won the first prize of £3 in a 'Football Contest' at Hugglescote. There can be no doubt, however, that football was considerably more popular in the north of the county than in Leicester. The selection of early newspaper reports given at the end of this chapter provides a flavour of the games played.

Leicester Fosse Football Club was formed during the spring of 1884 by a group of Old Wyggestonians and members of a Bible class run by Reverend Parsons at the now demolished Emmanuel Chapel in New Parks Street. When the Fosse were formed, there were over 50 teams in Leicester and the surrounding county playing rugby, the handling code. Two Leicester 'kicking code' football clubs, Old Victoria and Hill Street, had recently folded, with Leicester Town, Wyggeston School and Mill Hill House keeping the flag flying for the 'kicking game' in Leicester. Leicester Fosse thus came into existence in an atmosphere of complete apathy towards association football. So complete was the apathy into which the club was born, that when the Midland Railway Company organised a trip from Leicester to Derby for the FA Cup semi-final between Queen's Park and Blackburn Olympic, there were hardly sufficient supporters to fill a single carriage. Seventeen-year-old Frank Gardner was elected as club secretary and treasurer of the Fosse. The driving force behind the club, he came up with the name Leicester Fosse, was instrumental in forming the Leicestershire Football Association in 1886, bought in the era of fee-paying spectators, and helped sign the club's first professional player as well as playing in the team that won the Leicestershire Senior Cup in 1880. By the time his eight-year stint as secretary had ended, Leicester Fosse were playing in the Midland League, had 12 professional players, and had moved to Walnut Street (Filbert Street). It can be safely said that without Frank Gardner there would not be Leicester City FC.

Leicester Fosse's first game, on 1 November 1884 against Syston Fosse, was played on a field close to where Midland Railway's Leicester-to-Burton line crossed what is now Fosse Road South, where it meets Westleigh Avenue. The venue was close to where most of the team, all aged around 16 and

17, lived. Members paid nine pence each towards a ball and the same amount in subscriptions. A carpenter was paid 14s for a set of roughly finished goals and side posts that were gaily decorated in amber and black colours.

Fosse, led by captain W. Johnstone, wore black jerseys with a blue diagonal sash, and won 5-0 with goals from Hilton Johnson (two), Arthur West (two) and Sam Dingley. Remarkably, the *Melton Mercury Oakham and Uppingham News* covered the game. They published the positions of the players to illustrate the influence of rugby on team formation and tactics. By January 1885, the Fosse were playing on Victoria Park, the Fosse Road field having been taken over for road development and a building scheme.

The newspaper's report, printed on 6 November 1884, told the story, 'This match was played under association rules, on Saturday, on the private ground of the Fosse F.C. Syston won the toss and chose to play downhill. The first half of the game the play was pretty even, but the home team had the better of it, some near shots for goal being made and before half-time A. West put the ball through for the Fosse F.C. After half-time the Fosse played up well again, and despite the resistance of the Syston backs West again scored. Some sharp play followed the kick-off, S. Dingley scoring another goal for the home team. Soon after H. Johnson ably assisted by the Fosse forwards, scored a goal. Afterwards several more shots were made but did not succeed; until just before time when H. Johnson sent the ball through the Syston goal once more, leaving the Fosse victorious by five goals to nil.

'For the Syston team T.S. Rowley, A.E. Simpson, F. Belshaw, and Clarke rendered good service, while H.

Johnson, A. West and Lewitt in the forwards, and W. and E. Johnson in the backs showed up well for the Fosse. Sides: Fosse: E. Smith (goal). F. Burdett (three-quarter-back), E. Johnson, W. Johnson, F. Gardner (half-backs); forwards: Johnson, Lewitt (right wing), A. West, F. Bromwich (centres), A. Ashby, Dingley (left wing). Syston Fosse: T. S. Rowley, A.E. Simpson, F. Belshaw, W. Belshaw, Clarke, Walton, C. Burdett, J. Toone, B. Toone, F. Noon, and J. Plant.'

The following week, Fosse played their second game, a 1-1 draw against Wyggeston School on Victoria Park. Used as a racecourse from 1806 to 1883, Victoria Park formally opened as a public park in 1882 and was laid out in 1883 with wide expanses of grass, crossed by mainly straight paths lined with trees, small play areas and ornamental shrubbery, and with trees along the outer boundaries. Most of the mature trees were planted between 1884 and 1904. In 1887 the park was enclosed by ornamental iron railings, which mostly brought to an end the practice of grazing animals, although horses, cows, and sheep were regularly seen until the early 1890s.

The Italianate-style Racecourse Grandstand located where the Granville Road public car park currently stands at the southern end of Regent Road, which could hold 800 spectators, became a changing pavilion for cricket, rugby union and football teams. Sadly, it was irreparably damaged during World War II by a landmine and had to be demolished.

The Fosse shared the park with a host of other sporting clubs. Victoria Park became the Fosse's home ground for the next three seasons (1884–1887). It was perhaps in keeping with Leicester's sporting traditions that Victoria Park played an early part in the history of the Fosse, since it was here that the great W.G. Grace 'smote lusty sixes', Fred Archer rode many winners, and Jem Mace fought in a boxing booth. Up to 2,000 spectators would congregate in Victoria Park on a Saturday afternoon to watch a variety of games of both football codes, although it has to be said that the vast majority watched rugby, with football attracting just a handful of loyal spectators.

During their inaugural season, Fosse also played the odd game under rugby union rules. The list of friendlies included encounters with Mill Hill House, St Marys, Syston St Peters, and Melbourne House. It was a very promising first season, as they won seven and drew three of their 13 games, scoring 19 and conceding just eight goals. Two games are thought to have been 12-a-side and a further fixture, against Syston Fosse, was abandoned due to heavy rain, while Fosse were leading 1-0. At the end of the season, the new club made a surplus of one shilling and tuppence.

Leicester Fosse used the West Bridge Coffee House, and later the East Gate Coffee House overlooking the clock tower in the centre of Leicester, for team selection and tactics. Subscriptions were raised to three shillings per annum for 1885/86, plus a one shilling joining fee. At the end of their second season, the Fosse were two shillings and a ha'penny in the red. Fixtures were still predominantly against local sides Belgrave, Mill Hill House, Leicester Town, and St Marys, among others, although they did travel to play Market Harborough in February 1886. On the pitch they performed well, losing just one of the 11 games played during 1885/86 season, against Mill Hill

House, a team of teachers who were probably at the time the best side in Leicester. They scored almost two and a half goals per games and conceded just four throughout the season. In Loughborough, the Athletics Club established its own football section. They achieved some prominence in November 1878 when they played a fixture under electric lights – at a time when the town was lit entirely by gas.

THE ELECTRIC LIGHT

ON THE

LEICESTERSHIRE CRICKET GROUND

(LATELY POSTPONED).

ARRANGEMENTS have now been completed with an eminent Firm of Electricians, who have guaranteed to exhibit the

ELECTRIC LIGHT

on the above Ground on BOXING NIGHT and following Night, December 26th and 27th.

SEVEN LIGHTS

will be shown, and a number of interesting Experiments will take place during the Evening.

A FOOTBALL MATCH and BICYCLE SPORTS will take place, full particulars of which will be announced in next week's papers.

Admission 6d.

A large Marquee will be erected, and accommodation provided for Ladies and Gentlemen visiting the Ground. Admission 1s.

As part of that floodlight night, a bicycle race was held with cash prizes for the winners. On 28 Novemeber 1878,

FOOTBALL MATCH AND BICYCLE RACES
BY
ELECTRIC LIGHT :

ON WEDNESDAY Evening. November 27th, a
FOOTBALL MATCH between the Leicester
Alert F.C. and the Loughborough F.C., will take place
on Bromhead's Cricket Ground. Loughborough.

On the same Evening. Prizes will be given for a
ONE-MILE HANDICAP BICYCLE RACE (open to
all Amateurs). 1st Prize value £3 : 2nd Prize value
£1 10s : 3rd Prize value 10s. Entrance Fee 2s. 6d.
Entries, giving name. address. colours. and height of
machine, to be sent to T. B. CARTWRIGHT. Forest
road. Loughborough. on or before Monday. November 23rd.

The Ground will be illuminated with a GRAND
DISPLAY of the ELECTRIC LIGHT. by Messrs.
Welch and Scott. Electrical Engineers. Manchester,
with two Siemens' Machines', producing lights equal to
12,000 Candles.

Admission to the Ground. One Shilling. and Six-
pence.

Bicycle Races commence at 7 o'clock; Football
Match commences at 7.30 p.m.

the *Loughborough Advertiser* revealed the outcome, 'Shortly
after seven o'clock, a one-mile bicycle race was commenced.
There were 11 entries for the event, but only five put in an
appearance. These were W.A. Thompson, 180 yards start;
J. Grudgings, 150 yards; G.H. Upton, 130 yards; J.H.
Taylor, 20 yards; and W. Wood (Whitwick), scratch. After
a good race, Wood was the winner by nearly a lap, Taylor
being second, and Grudgings third.'

As for the floodlit football, with Loughborough
playing against Leicester Alert FC, the newspaper
reported, 'Loughborough won the toss, and the kick-
off was made by Perkins, the first goal being obtained

by J. Cartwright. After a spirited game in which the splendid kicking of Gulliver, Bromhead, and the capital dribbling of Turner, were remarkably conspicuous, the Loughborough team won, they having scored five goals to none. The Loughborough team comprised Messrs. Pickering, T.B. Cartwright, J. Cartwright, J. Perkins, G. Bromhead, W. Cockayne, T. Mills, W. Harris, T. Bowley, G. J. Gulliver, J. Turner, and W. Tyler.'

Shortly after and maybe as a direct result of the floodlit football event, working-class clubs were formed in the north Leicestershire town, including Loughborough Victoria, Loughborough Amateurs, Falcon Works, Loughborough Eagle, Loughborough Alliance and Loughburians. Enthusiasm for the game grew rapidly it seems, particularly in the Loughborough, Coalville and Sheepshed areas, judging from some comments by 'Beacon' in the *Loughborough Echo* on 2 March 1882, 'What a fashionable game football has become during the last few years, boys, young men, and women indulge in the pastime. However fashionable as it is and maybe, it will never out rival the national game of cricket, though wise persons may say to the contrary.'

Victoria and Loughburians, the two dominant teams in the town, merged to form Loughborough Football Club, nicknamed the 'Luffs'. The club was often incorrectly referred to as Loughborough Town at this time. George Upton was the chairman of the new club, and Mr Gibbs and Mr H. Jackson were appointed as treasurer and secretary, respectively. They played their first game against Derby Wanderers at the Hubbards Ground, located behind the Greyhound Hotel, Nottingham Road, Loughborough, on Saturday, 25 September 1886. Charles Gadsby had the honour of scoring Loughborough's first in a commendable 1-1 draw.

Mr Jackson had arranged a comprehensive fixture list for their inaugural season, including games against Castle Donington, Coalville, Sheepshed, Keyworth, and Melbourne Town. Twice they faced Long Eaton Athletic at home, losing the first match 5-1 and winning the second 2-1. They were clearly the best side in Loughborough, demolishing Loughborough Liberal Club 8-1 and Loughborough Olympic 7-1. The first Leicester-based club they faced were Leicester Town on 20 November 1886, in a game that ended 0-0.

Of that first match, the *Nottingham Daily Express* reported on 27 September 1886, 'The opening match of the Loughborough Town Football Club was played on Saturday, in splendid weather, at Loughborough. Derby having come a man short, a substitute was quickly found in a Mr H. Lockwood. The visitors won at the toss and decided to defend the south goal. The ball was put in motion a few minutes past three o'clock by C.H. Gadsby for Loughborough. Derby, having got the ball from the right wing man, a run was made towards the Loughborough goal, but, losing the ball, a shot was made at the Derby goal, but was returned. Try after try having been made at each goal, after 20 minutes play the substitute for the Wanderers placed the ball between the Loughborough posts. The ball again being put in motion, Loughborough tried to equalise matters and nearly succeeded, a corner being given. This however, was kicked away by Derby. At half-time Derby had scored one goal to Loughborough nil.

'The ball being again put in motion it was carried towards the home goal but was saved by the backs. Shot after shot was made at each goal, the goalkeepers, however, returned them in style. At last the ball was passed to Gadsby who made a shot at the Derby goal, the goalkeeper returned it but Gadsby again securing it a "maul" in goal took place, in which about 12 players were on the ground together. It was wriggled past the post, however, and a corner given, which resulted in nothing. The play now became fast and furious. After a slight run the ball was again passed to Gatsby, who, after avoiding the backs, brilliantly placed the leather between the Derby post two minutes before time. The next two minutes was played in good style, but neither side scored. At call of time the match resulted in a tie, one goal to one goal.

'Players: Loughborough Town: H. Collins (goal), F. Gibbs and Walter Cockain (captain) (backs), E. Onions, F. Stubbs and J. Smalley (half-backs), E. Coltman and L. Rodgers (right wing) C. H. Gadsby (centre), F.W. Simpson and W. Cockain (left wing).'

The Fosse entered into an engagement to play against the 'Old Loughburians' at Loughborough on 20 March 1886. When the Fosse team arrived at Loughborough on that day, they failed to find their opponents, or their secretary, or even the ground on which the match was to be played, and on presuming that the men of Loughborough had gone to the local races, the Fosse team did the same. The first encounter between the Fosse and the Luffs, a friendly, took place at the Athletic Grounds in Loughborough almost a year later on 5 February 1887. Leicester's team colours were switched at the start of the 1886/87 season to chocolate-and-blue halved shirts, while Loughborough played in black-and-white vertical stripes. Loughborough easily won the game 4-1.

The return game at Victoria Park, Leicester, six weeks later saw a reverse in fortunes as the Fosse won by three clear goals. Little is known about these matches apart from the local press reports. The difference in stature of the two clubs, however, can be gauged by comparing the venues for these first clashes. The Luffs were based at the Athletic Grounds, Leicestershire's first enclosed sporting arena, located behind the Greyhound Hotel on Nottingham Road in Loughborough, just five minutes from the Midland Railway station. The ground was originally for the sole use of cricket when it opened in 1862, but then, at different times, became known as either Hubbard's or Bromhead's Ground – each referring to the incumbent landlord at the Greyhound Hotel. In a particularly cold spell in the winter of 1871, the grounds were sprayed with water and used as an ice rink for several weeks! The name was finally changed to the 'Athletic Grounds', probably in 1878.

By the start of the 1888/89 season, the Athletic Grounds was one of the finest in the Midlands. Surrounded by a white hoarding, there was a refreshment bar and pavilion. With two balconies that overlooked the pitch, the 40ft by 30ft pavilion included a refreshment room, a dining room and two dressing rooms with hot and cold water, heating apparatus and a well-fitted bathroom. Two registering turnstiles were installed at the Nottingham Road entrance. Attached to the Greyhound Hotel was a fine sprint cinder path, on which some of the world's champion professional sprinters trained for Sheffield Handicaps and other big events. The popular annual Whitsuntide Sports regularly attracted crowds exceeding 10,000. Cycling events were also held regularly as well as more general attractions – a circus, Rayners Pavilion Theatre, brass band contests and a boar hunt, where the winner was the first competitor to keep hold of a greased pig released in the middle of the football pitch. This cruel event attracted the attention of the RSPCA and resulted in an unsuccessful prosecution of the hunt organisers.

In stark contrast, Leicester Fosse had a nomadic existence for the first seven years of their life, playing home games on several locations around Leicester, including Fosse Road, Victoria Park, Belgrave Cricket and Cycle Ground, Victoria Park (again) and Mill Lane before finally settling at Walnut Street (Filbert Street) in 1891.

Loughborough more than held their own in their inaugural season, winning seven, drawing seven and losing five of their 20 matches; it is thought that they played at least two other games, but the results of these matches are currently unknown. Financially, Loughborough ended their first season with an extremely healthy operating surplus of £8 9s 7d from a turnover of around £25. Leicester Fosse only lost four of their 20 fixtures, although the quality of some of the opposition was much weaker than the Luffs, including Wyggeston School Past and Present who they played twice at Victoria Park, thumping them 5-0 and 9-0. But Fosse's fixture list did include some teams from farther afield – Coalville, Barwell and even Nottingham. Club membership increased to 40 by the end of the 1886/87 season and a reserve team – Leicester Fosse Rovers – was formed. At the AGM the balance sheet indicated a healthy operating profit of £1 12s 9d.

1887/88

Leicester Fosse moved from Victoria Park to the Belgrave Road Cycle and Cricket Ground for the 1887/88 season. Opening in late May 1880, the ground was established thanks to the efforts of Mr Bilson, a rope merchant of Belgrave Gate, Mr Illsley, landlord of the Black Lion on Belgrave Gate, and M. Newton, also of Belgrave Road, who some months earlier had secured a 13-year lease on a large piece of land opposite the allotments. Shares were offered and speedily bought up, and shortly after that the ground was levelled and buildings erected. It was designed to be suitable for cricket and trotting contests, bicycle races, athletic sports, flower shows and all kinds of outdoor fetes. A 6ft brick wall surrounded the ground. There were two entrances, both from Belgrave Road, close to which the dressing rooms were located close by. These were 'fitted with every convenience for competitors'. The trotting track, measuring a third of a mile in length, was 25 feet wide. Inside this was the bicycle cinder track, 15 feet wide, with four laps to the mile. No expense had been spared and it was considered by all to be second to none in the world. At the top end on the Belgrave side, the two tracks joined, and continued together for some distance, with a rail fence separating them.

On the Ross Walk side there were two 'tradesman's entrances' through which paraphernalia belonging to travelling shows, etc., could enter the arena. There was a grandstand with a capacity of around 2,000, while a gymnasium and hotel also formed part of the initial plans for the site. More than 10,000 visitors attended each of the three-day opening sporting event, which included bicycle events for amateurs (£3 prize) and professionals (£50 prize), running events over a range of distances from 120 yards to five miles, trotting challenges and pony races.

Leicester Football Club (the 'Tigers') rented the Belgrave Ground in 1880. Formed in August 1880 at the George Hotel from the amalgamation of three clubs – Leicester Societies AFC, Leicester Amateur FC and Leicester Alert – the club played its first fixture, against Moseley, just 12 weeks later on 2 October. Kitted out in their original club colours of black with yellow stripes, they drew 0-0. The ground was enclosed, which allowed a gate to be taken. However, this harmed the ability to build a following, so the Tigers moved to Victoria Park in January 1881. The rugby club moved back to Belgrave for the 1882/83 season before reverting yet again to Victoria Park.

The attraction of Belgrave Road for the Fosse was the fact that it permitted the club to charge supporters an admission fee. The first game for which supporters were charged was against Burton Swifts on Bonfire Night 1887, which they lost 4-0. Fixtures against Wellingborough, Kettering, and Burton Swifts indicated the growing status of the club.

Loughborough strengthened their squad with the signing of Elijah Needham and J. Waring, from Sheepshed, H. Griffin and W. Kelham from Hathern and W. Cross from Hugglescote Robin Hoods. There was also an increase in club membership to 120 and this grew further in October 1887 when the club purchased the rights for the long-established Loughborough Athletic Club for £20. As a result, the club officially became Loughborough Athletic and Football Club, permitting its members to use the gymnasium in the Corn Exchange for a small fee. Most importantly it gained control of the financially lucrative annual Whit Tuesday Sports event, which would in subsequent seasons subsidise the activities of the football club as it strove to join England's footballing elite. Further ground improvements took place including the fencing of the football pitch with wire rope and the development of a members enclosure.

Leicestershire Football Association Cup

A meeting of gentlemen interested in the national winter pastime – football – was held at the George Hotel, Haymarket, Leicester on Saturday 24 September 1887, 'to take into consideration the desirability of forming an association in the county'. Clubs that sent representatives were Leicester Fosse, Leicester Town, Mill Hill House, St Matthews, Loughborough, Sheepshed, Market Harborough, Kegworth, St Andrews, Ravenstone, Castle Donington, Melton Rovers, St Saviour's, Coalville, and Hinckley Trinity.

Mr Gardner, secretary of Fosse FC, said the idea of forming an association had been talked of for several seasons. At the committee meeting of his club some time previously, he had been instructed to write to the clubs of Leicestershire to ascertain whether they were of the opinion that such a society would be beneficial. About 25 clubs were written to and of these 15 promised to support the association, two replied that they were unable to do so, while six did not answer at all. If an association was formed, they would be able to send out a representative team against other shires and enter cup competitions. Mr Upton (Loughborough) proposed, and Mr Ashmole (Fosse) seconded, that such an association should be formed. This was carried unanimously. It was decided that the title should be 'The Leicestershire Football Association'. In 1887, its first year, the Leicestershire FA had 17 affiliated teams. Four years later, the extent of playing and watching both rugby and soccer had grown so much that the *Leicester Daily Post* observed that in 'no other town in England, perhaps, has its rapid growth been better attested than that of recent years in Leicester. Why, it seems to me but yesterday that scarcely 500 people could be got together to see a good match "free, gratis and for nothing". Now what do we find? Why five or six thousand people on each of two football grounds on the same afternoon, freely paying admission money.' In an end-of-year survey of the social life of the town, the paper noted that: 'Only a few years ago [football] was nowhere as compared with cycling. Already, however, the once sensational contests on the cinder track have become a faded memory while association and rugby football has the field.'

The county's first association football competition, the Leicestershire Challenge Cup, was full of drama, incident, and controversy. The first-round draw was made in mid-October 1887:

Ravenstone Druids v Mill Hill House
Castle Donington v Hugglescote
Fosse v St Saviour's
Loughborough Town v Kegworth St Andrews
St Matthews v Hinckley Trinity
Coalville v Melton Rovers
Sheepshed v Market Harborough

The ties had to be played on or before 19 November 1887. The outcomes of no fewer than four games were disputed and investigated by the Leicestershire Football Association committee. Cup favourites Loughborough Town took the lead at the Athletic Grounds after 15 minutes when a Kegworth defender headed through his own goal. After dominating play they were three up at the end of the first 45 minutes. The second half began with the Luffs bombarding the Kegworth goalmouth, resulting in two quick goals from Rodgers. A good shot gave Kegworth some consolation, before Loughborough piled on the pressure and got their sixth and final goal in an emphatic 6-1 victory. Immediately after the final whistle blew, Kegworth lodged a protest with the referee alleging that Shannon, one of the Loughborough players, was not eligible to compete having taken part in other cup ties during the season. It was also alleged that a second member of the Loughborough XI was 'similarly situated'. Loughborough were subsequently disqualified from the competition after a brief hearing of the Leicestershire Football Association Committee prior to the draw for the second round.

This resulted in a squabble between Loughborough Town and the county association. Despite this, Leicestershire Football Association honoured the club by allowing it to stage its first fixture when a North Leicestershire XI captained by Luffs' Walter Cockain beat South Leicestershire 2-1 in a county trial fixture.

The *Leicester Daily Post* printed a letter from Loughborough Town's secretary, Charles Gadsby, outlining his view of the situation regarding the disqualification of Loughborough from the Leicestershire Challenge Cup competition for fielding an illegal player, Shannon, against Kegworth St John's. Shannon had played earlier in the season for Derby Junction in the FA Cup, Birmingham Cup and Derbyshire Cup, making him ineligible to play in the Leicestershire Challenge Cup, claimed Kegworth. This view was upheld by the association, without Loughborough being given the opportunity 'to prove to the satisfaction of the committee that the offence had not been committed'. Although Loughborough were represented at the meeting, Gadsby had been on refereeing duty at a cup tie in Leicester and went to the meeting unaware that a protest had been lodged, and thoroughly unprepared to offer any defence. Loughborough believed that the only rule that applied (unless the player is a professional) was the first in a summary of the rules for the cup ties supplied by the secretary to the various clubs, 'Competing teams shall number 11 players, bona fide members of their representative clubs. Players may be changed, but no member can play for more than one club.'

The Loughborough committee maintained the last word of this rule, 'club', referred to 'the respective clubs' who had 'competing teams' in the competition, and did not include clubs belonging to altogether separate associations, and that the meaning of the rule is the same as that of the corresponding rule of the National Competition, which read, 'No individual shall be allowed to play for more than one competing club, but members of each representative team may be changed during the series of matches, if thought necessary.'

The letter ended with the following statement and threat, 'It is evident that we are innocent. I know most of the representatives of the Leicestershire clubs on the committee were only too glad to get the chance to throw the club out of the competition, it being well-known that our chance of winning the cup was the rosiest of all, and that is why we were disqualified. Unless we can be offered a chance of defending ourselves we shall certainly withdraw from the association, but if permitted an impartial hearing, and we cannot then satisfy the committee as to our innocence, and are consequently disqualified, we hereby challenge the eventual winners of the cup to play a game on our ground, all profits of which shall be devoted to the association funds.'

Given what is stated in the letter, along with other decisions made by the same committee, as we shall see, justification for the disqualification of Loughborough was somewhat flimsy to say the least. There may well have been an element of self-interest in the other clubs voting for their expulsion.

Incidentally, Sheephed the first trophy holders did not accept Loughborough's invitation, although they did beat them 3-1 a week or so before the final.

Leicester Fosse's fixture against St Saviour's was also the subject of a protest. At Belgrave Cricket and Cycle Club Ground, Fosse went one down within the first few minutes and equalised before half-time through Hassell. A shot by Galloway for St Saviour's was saved, but he scored from the rebound, only for the Fosse to hit back immediately through Knight to even the score again. With the light fading rapidly and both sets of players struggling to see the ball, James and Bankart scored for the Fosse, to win the tie 4-2. St Saviour's protested that they lost the game due to bad light, and it was upheld by the association. The game was replayed at the Belgrave Road enclosure, the Fosse winning by five clear goals.

Sheepshed's biggest crowd of the season, around 600, witnessed their first-round encounter with Market Harborough. As with several other cup ties, the away team arrived late. Travel around the county in the late 19th century was torturous, relying on non-punctual trains that criss-crossed the county, often requiring several connections or horse-drawn carriages. So the journey of the Harborough team, based 12 miles to the south of Leicester, to Sheepshed, a similar distance north, must have taken several hours, with the return taking even longer. Kick-off was delayed until 3.30pm. Late November days are short, and the game ended after 82 minutes as the players could barely see each other let alone a muddy brown ball; the home team cruised through 7-2.

The Castle Donington and Hugglescote Robin Hoods tie, 'played under protest', was witnessed by a 'large number of spectators'. The visitors arrived extremely late and kick-off was delayed even further when the captain of the Robin Hoods objected that the field was not fit to play upon. Castle Donington scored on either side of half-time, but owing to the darkness the referee stopped the game 20 minutes before time. The association refused Hugglescote's request that the fixture should be replayed.

Coalville FC's home fixture against Melton Rovers at the Fox and Goose Hotel also kicked off well after 3.30pm, due to travel issues experienced by the visiting side. After half an hour of fast and furious play, the opening goal was registered, only for Melton to equalise two minutes later.

Johnson, the centre-forward, kicked an easy goal. Soon afterwards, the home team took the lead with a header, only for Melton to make the score 2-2 after rushing the ball through following a 'sharp skirmish'. Some idea of the pace of the game can be gauged from the fact that these four goals were scored in less than 15 minutes.

After half-time one of the visitors' forwards, following some neat passing movements, fired a shot that went through the goal, but the referee blew for offside. Poole, the Coalville goalkeeper, could have easily stopped the goal, but the visitors claimed the goal on the basis that the whistle was not heard until the ball had passed through the posts. After heated discussions, the Coalville captain resumed the game under protest. Home supporters decided to take matters into their own hands and occupied the goalmouth, which they refused to leave until appealed to by the Coalville umpire and the police. Shortly afterwards, the game was stopped by the referee, as it was too dark to continue. Coalville were furious and protested to the association because of the late arrival of Melton and the disputed goal. The game was ordered to be replayed at Melton, and the home side won 2-0.

The fixture between St Matthews and Hinckley was, by comparison with the other round-one games, rather dull, with the home team winning 5-0 in a one-sided encounter. In the remaining ties, St Matthews easily beat Hinckley Trinity 4-0 and Mill Hill House, a team of school teachers, thrashed Ravenstone 5-0, after the first game played at Victoria Park ended in a draw.

The draw for round two was as follows, with the ties to be played on or before New Year's Eve:

Mill Hill House v Barwell Villa
Leicester Wanderers v St Matthews
Castle Donington v Kegworth
Fosse v Sheepshed
Melton Rovers – bye

Sheepshed, playing in red, scored within a couple minutes after kicking off against Leicester Fosse on the Belgrave Road Grounds on Christmas Eve. Waldren made a high kick, the ball dropping into the goalmouth, where it was easily rushed through. A splendid run by Knight for the Fosse followed by a good shot equalised matters. Soon afterwards, Savage added another for the visitors and Thompson scored for the Fossils. The slippery conditions of the ground rendered accurate shooting difficult, and no more goals were scored before half-time. Soon after the change of ends, Savage added a third goal for the 'Reds' and Fosse yet again levelled the score. Play was fast and exciting, the tie ending in a 3-3 draw.

It was replayed at Sheepshed on 21 January 1888 in front of a highly excitable crowd exceeding 3,000. Fosse took the lead after 20 minutes, a feat that was greeted with great enthusiasm by the large contingent of Leicester supporters present. Just two minutes later Leicester doubled their lead. As matters started to look ominous for Sheepshed they began to take the upper hand, scoring just before half-time. The men in red equalised early in the second period. Although play was fast and furious neither side were able to take the initiative, the game ending in stalemate. The tie was finally decided in favour of the north Leicestershire club the following Saturday. Sheepshed pressed from the kick-off at the Athletic Grounds in Loughborough and scored the opening goal, causing great excitement among the several hundred Sheepshed spectators present. A few minutes later, another goal was recorded for the men in red. Fosse managed to pull one back in the second half through Knight.

A terribly strong wind blew across Victoria Park at the start of the tie between St Matthews and Leicester Wanderers. The Saints set the ball in motion and ten minutes from the start the first goal was scored by Wanderers' captain Taylor. After a period of even play in the centre of the field, the Wanderers worked the ball into the opponents' territory, Narroway, the right-wing forward, doubling the lead. In the second half the Wanderers continued to have the better of the play, long kicks being the order of the day. The wind made outcomes very uncertain, the ball being speedily transferred to all quarters. A third goal was scored by Johnson. Soon afterwards the referee stopped the game for bad light, the Saints losing 3-0.

Victoria Park was also the venue for Mill Hill House v Barwell, which attracted considerable interest. The game was a disappointing spectacle. Barwell were outclassed in a one-sided game, losing 5-0. Little is known about the last match, between Castle Donington and Kegworth, apart from the fact that the latter went through to the third round.

The third-round draw paired Sheepshed with Kegworth and Mill Hill House with Melton Rovers. Leicester Wanderers were granted a bye. There was a huge turnout for the tie between Sheepshed and Kegworth played on a bitterly cold Saturday in late February 1888, and the home side were three up by half-time. Just minutes into the second half, a heavy snowstorm visited the ground and players, and spectators alike were subjected to much discomfort. The referee stopped the game while the snowstorm lasted and the Sheepshed men were out on the pitch as soon as it was over. The visitors however were nowhere to be found. After waiting a considerable time, the referee made the following decision, 'Owing to the visitors failing to come out to the ground again, the match is awarded to Sheepshed, giving Kegworth the right to appeal to the committee of the association if they think well.'

Given that they were inferior in every way and that Sheepshed's goalkeeper and backs were impassable, Kegworth did not contest the decision. Kegworth protested against the result but as they had not paid their deposit to the association, the matter was not discussed. Since Leicester Wanderers had been granted a bye, the result of the only other round-three tie was Mill Hill House 3 Melton Rovers 0.

The semi-final draw was made by the association at a meeting of the committee on Saturday, 25 February 1888 at St George's Hotel in Leicester. Mill Hill House were granted a bye into the final, their opponents being the winners of the only semi-final, between Leicester Wanderers and Sheepshed. Incidentally, the association sent notice to all member clubs that players would be liable to suspension if they played in six-a-side games.

A large Leicester contingent saw the Wanderers get blown away 5-1 by Sheepshed at Loughborough on the first Saturday of March to face Mill Hill House in the first Leicester Senior Challenge Cup Final. The Fox and Goose Cricket Ground at Coalville staged the game, which ended in stalemate. The match report given below, taken from the *Leicester Chronicle* edition of 24 March 1888, is one of the most comprehensive published by Leicestershire press during this period and provides a fascinating insight into the game of association football played in the late 1880s.

'The final tie of this competition was played at Coalville before an enthusiastic crowd of spectators, many of whom journeyed from Leicester, Sheepshed, Whitwick, and surrounding villages, the contest from its commencement having been invested with a greater degree of interest in the outlying districts than in the town of Leicester itself. The visitors won the toss and decided to play with the wind. Danvers, for Sheepshed, started the ball at 3.40pm and the "reds" at once pressed, and McAlpin, to save, had to kick out, the result being a kick from goal.

'Dally now dribbled the ball well towards the Sheepshed goal, but in making his centre the leather was accidentally fouled by one of the "reds'" forwards who chased but failed to out-rival the House right wing. The free kick brought no immediate advantage, but from a scrimmage in the mouth of the Sheepshed goal another foul was claimed and allowed for the House; Pearce's kick was stayed by Needham, who, being passed by the visitors' forwards, had to kick out to save danger.

'The "reds" now began to "feel their feet" and continually attacked the House goal, which, by the aid of McAlpin and Pilsbury, was relieved. After getting behind the ball and dodging the whole of the right-wing of the "reds" made a centre, which was a grand one, but badly missed by Thornton. Again, the Sheepshed forwards rushed and Bennett in shooting, narrowly missed a goal. Pearce took the kick from goal, and "feeding" Atter nicely, the latter made another brilliant run up the left wing, aided by Rippon, but was knocked off his feet in attempting to centre, and the play was carried into the centre of the ground, where continual scrimmages were kept up among both sets of forwards, until ultimately Bennett got behind the ball and never left it until he made his shot, which proved of little advantage to Sheepshed, as the leather was taken by some magnificent passing among the visiting forwards very closely to the Sheepshed goal, where, to save, a corner kick was allowed the House, but Rippon, in taking the ball from the corner, fouled, and now gave the "reds" an opening. From the free kick the ball was taken quickly to the House goal, where a scrimmage of long duration occurred, but by the capital defence of McAlpin, Pearce, and Pilsbury relief was at last obtained, and play was more even for the next few minutes.

'The "reds" now collared the ball again, and made a most determined rush, and amid this greatest excitement and deafening cheering Waring put the ball through the House uprights. Rippon without delay, restarted, but in attempting to feed Atter the ball fell short, and dropped nicely for Bennett, who, with Smith, managed to get the leather near enough to the House uprights to shoot, but Bennett's shot, which was fairly judged, did not call upon Brice, the ball going behind the goal line. From the kick from goal the House left wing showed some flair passing, Atter and Rippon going quickly up the field, but the former missed his centre, giving a goal kick to Sheepshed. From the kick-out Dalley and Exton were favoured and caused Bennett to concede a corner to save, and Exton, who stood wide had exceedingly hard luck in not scoring, as his shot was quick and straight, but rebounded from one of the Sheepshed backs. However, the ball was kept in a close scrimmage round the Sheepshed goal, and during the "hustle" Thornton equalised.

'From now up to half-time the game was pretty equal, both teams playing on the defensive, the Sheepshed appearing to be a little overworked, the game up to the present being amazingly fast. After ten minutes stay at half-time Rippon restarted, and passing to Dalley, gained the "reds'" territory, when Dalley centred to Rippon, who had hard lines in not scoring, Cotton repulsing the shot beautifully. The "reds" now attacked the House goal in earnest, and carried on a continued scrimmage near their uprights, and had it not been for the superb defence of McAlpin (who was frequently cheered from all parts of the ground), Pearce and Pilsbury, not to mention the goalkeeper (Brice), who handled once or twice, the "reds" would have secured a well-deserved goal. By combination among the House forwards, they again took the ball into the mouth of the Sheepshed fortress, and the leather was centred splendidly by Atter to Thornton, who missed an easy chance of scoring. Up to call of time both teams now played their hardest to decide the victory, but neither gained much advantage, the ball being carried from one end of the ground to other in quick succession. Result: One goal each.

'Players; – Mill Hill House: A.E. Brice, goal; D. McAlpin and K.H. Pearce, backs; S. Stretton, H. Wing, and H. Pilsbury, half-backs; J, Atter and A. Thornton, left wing; J. Rippon, centre; T. Exon and A. Dalley, right wing. Sheepshed: J. Newbold, goal; E. Needham (captain) and J. Cotton, backs; W. Johnson, W. Waldron, and A. Kidger, half-backs; E. Savage and J. Waring, left wing; J. Bennett and A. Smith, right win; W. Danvers, centre.'

The final was replayed at Kegworth in front of a 'large number' of spectators two weeks later, with Sheepshed beating the Leicester side 8-1.

The *Leicester Chronicle* on 7 April 1888 reported, 'Notwithstanding the recent rainfall, the ground was in fine condition for play, and the weather taking a favourable turn, the game was witnessed by many spectators. Rippin kicked off, and after some pretty play by Whitworth, Atter, and Exton, which caused Newbold to handle, the House missed an easy chance of scoring. From this point up to half-time Sheepshed hotly pressed and scored three goals from the feet of Bennett, Savage, and Waring, the latter also having kicked an offside goal.

'In the second half the Leicester men tried hard to avert farther disaster, bat utterly failed, as the Sheepshed score was increased to eight goals, the last five being obtained by Waring, Savage, Johnson, and Danvers (2) while Mill House failed to notch a single point.

'Players: – Mill Hill House: A.E. Brice, goal; D. McAlpin and F. Wright, backs; F. Whitworth (captain), H. Pilsbury, and S. Bretton, half-backs; J. Atter and J. Rippin, left wing; T. Exton, centre; H. Brain and A. Dailey, right wing. Referee, Mr. R.J. Smith (now secretary Derbyshire Association). Sheepshed. J. Newbold, goal; E. Needham (captain) and J. Cotton, backs; W. Johnson, W. Waldron, and A Kidger, half-backs; E. Savage and J. Waring, left wing; W. Danvers, centre; J. Bennett and A. Smith, right wing forwards.'

It is presumed that the J. Rippon listed in Mill Hill House's team for the first match is the same person as J. Rippin who is listed for the replay.

More than 50 people sat down to a public dinner on Saturday 14 April at the Charnwood Forest Railway Hotel in honour of Sheepshed, the first winners of the Leicestershire Association Challenge Cup. Influential inhabitants of the town celebrated in full force, namely members of the Local Board, the Guardians, the Burial Board, the postmaster, and other officials. After the 'Queen and the Royal family' had been duly toasted, the club vice-chair, Mr Bosworth, a local solicitor, gave the toast 'Success to the Sheepshed Football Club' and remarked how proud and pleased he was to be present to share in the honour of the first winners of the cup. However, due to a lack of funds and some 'collateral mismanagement with the association', the cup was conspicuous by its absence.

Three days later, on 17 April, the Football League was formally created and named in Manchester, with 12 member clubs from the Midlands and north of England: Accrington, Aston Villa, Blackburn Rovers, Bolton Wanderers, Burnley, Derby County, Everton, Notts County, Preston North End, Stoke, West Bromwich Albion and Wolverhampton Wanderers. Each club would play each other twice, once at home and once away. The original league rules stated that teams' positions should be calculated 'from wins, draws, and losses', without further detail. It was not until two months into the inaugural season that a points system was decided upon, with teams being awarded two points for a win and one point for a draw. Goal average was used to separate teams who were level on points.

However, it would be several years before a Leicestershire club would join the ranks of the elite in the Football League.

By the end of April 1888, Leicester Fosse were homeless, having been outbid for the use of the Belgrave Cricket and Cycle Ground by Leicester Football Club (rugby union). The Tigers would remain at Belgrave Grounds until they moved to Welford Road, their current home ground. Leicester Fosse had little option but to return to Victoria Park, a severe blow for the ambitious club. Membership increased by the end of the season to 72. Although the expenses of the club had been very heavy due in part to the move to Belgrave Road, the Fosse ended the season with a balance on the right side. The expenses amounted to £32 14s 9.5d, receipts were £35 8s 1.5d, (including £8 4s 0d gate money), giving a surplus of £2 13s 4d.

At a meeting in May at St George's Hotel, Leicester, Fosse's secretary Mr Gardner remarked that the club had opposed much stronger teams than in former seasons and taking this into account he congratulated the club on the results of those matches. The first team played 20 matches during the season; of these they won seven, lost nine, and four were drawn; 35 goals were scored and 51 conceded. He remarked that there was every prospect of an even more successful season before them, and if the club worked together as in the past then that success was assured. They had had a good fight for the Leicestershire Cup, having had to meet the winners three times, and then they lost by the narrow majority of one goal. Next season he trusted they would be more fortunate. Press coverage had significantly increased, with the *Daily Post* sports correspondent coining the club's first nicknames 'Fossils' and 'Ancients'.

1888/89

To demonstrate their ambition, despite being 'homeless', to become the premier side not only of Leicester but also of the county, Leicester Fosse signed their first professional – Harry Webb, from Stafford Rangers in October 1888. He was paid 2s 6d per week plus travel expenses. Now based back at Victoria Park, Leicester Fosse entertained several teams from out of the county, including Burton Swifts, Notts County Reserves, Bulwell United, Wellingborough and Kettering as well as the best sides in Leicestershire.

Meanwhile the Luffs' home, the Athletic Grounds, was one of the finest in the region. At the end of the previous season, the Midland Brewery Company signed a seven-year lease of both the ground and the Greyhound Hotel and embarked on a substantial programme of ground improvements that were completed for the start of the 1888/89 season.

Fosse and had Luffs played two friendlies in 1888/89, the first at the end of September and the second several weeks later in mid-November. Loughborough won both games comfortably and since the Fosse were playing home matches on an open public park, for financial reasons, the Luffs hosted both encounters. In the first clash, the Luffs fielded a strong side that included new signings McKay (Heart of Midlothian), Albert Peters and George Spiby (Notts County), Smith and William Lowe (Long Eaton Rangers). Despite being the underdogs, the Fosse pressed the home side, but weak shooting let them down. Lowe opened the scoring for Loughborough from a pass by Bailey. Just before half-time, Loughborough went down to ten men after McKay severely sprained his ankle. After the restart, another of the Luffs' new signings, Smith, doubled the lead from a header. Just minutes later Smith got his second and the Luffs' third from a low shot. Outstanding goalkeeping by De Ville between the Ancients' posts kept the score down, although Cross claimed a fourth for the home side with just minutes to go.

The second match was hastily arranged, inflicting Fosse's first defeat since their first encounter. Both sides were weakened, Loughborough by the absence of Bailey, Peters, and Smith, while the Fosse were without Gardner, Glover and Ashmole. The match kicked off in heavy rain. Rodgers scored after ten minutes for Loughborough. Fosse appealed for offside, but this was rejected. Webb equalised after sustained pressure, then Gibson gave Loughborough the lead with a splendid shot. Both sides made combined runs, resulting in shots that required the goalkeepers to punch out to save. Just on the call of time a scrimmage in front of the Fosse goal resulted in the ball being rushed through, Loughborough winning 3-1.

Loughborough were clearly impressed by the performance of Tom De Ville as they signed him along with Fosse's captain, Ashmole, after the second game. Their departure was no doubt linked to the fact that the Luffs, who were at the time the best side in the county, had a private enclosed ground. De Ville, however, would return to the Fosse for their first Midland League season.

Leicestershire fans of the 'kicking game' reached new levels of interest and excitement as the Fosse and Loughborough were drawn to face each other for a place in the semi-finals of the Leicestershire Association Challenge Cup. Earlier on, however, the draw for the first round of the second running of the competition took place in September, pairing the following teams:

Market Harborough v Kegworth
Leicester Fosse v Syston Wreake Valley
Leicester St Matthews v Melton Rovers
Sheepshed v Belgrave
Leicester Park Rovers v Hathern Liberal Club
South Wigston v Coalville Town
Mill Hill House v Hugglescote
Leicester Teachers v Leicester Wanderers

All matches had to be played on the ground of the first named and be completed by 10 November 1888. As with the inaugural cup competition, there was much drama and controversy. Mill Hill House's first-round tie against Hugglescote Robin Hoods did not kick off until 3.55pm due to the late arrival of the visitors. The home side were three up by half-time. Hugglescote adopted a 'rough' style of play encouraged by shouts of support from their noisy travelling support. Within minutes of the second half commencing, an appeal was made to the referee that the ball had gone into touch on the Hugglescote left wing within 14 yards of their goal line, but it was not given. The ball was centred from the wing, and shot through the visitors' uprights, the goal being allowed by the referee. Some of the visitors objected on the ground that the ball had been out of play, but the referee refused to change his mind, and after further wrangling blew for 'onside' on account of the bad light. Several Hugglescote men refused to continue the game, which was duly awarded to Mill Hill House.

At a Special Committee meeting of the association, Mr Ashmole read a letter which he had received from Mr S. Briers, captain of the Hugglescote Robin Hoods, who expressed the opinion that the match should not be awarded to Mill Hill, their principal grounds for complaint being that they were unfairly dealt with by the referee. Having heard statements from independent and totally 'disinterested persons', the committee passed a resolution unanimously awarding the match to Mill Hill, against whom there was really no definite appeal.

Leicester Teachers, down to nine men due to injuries by half-time, lost 2-0 to Leicester Wanderers at Victoria Park. Just a few yards away on an adjacent pitch, Melton Mowbray Rovers beat St Mathews 4-3 in an exciting end-to-end encounter. The arrival of the Melton team on the 7pm train was greeted with 'much gratification'. In another entertaining game, Kegworth got a quick goal and secured victory at Market Harborough, while Coalville slaughtered South Wigston 6-0 away from home. Hathern Liberal Club overcame Leicester Park Rovers 4-1 at the Old Pastures (St Margarets). Holders and firm favourites Sheepshed, in front of an 'immense crowd', demolished Belgrave 8-0 at home. In the remaining tie, Leicester Fosse managed to outscore their arch-rivals in their humiliation of Syston Wreake Valley 12-1 (still a club record), Webb scoring six times.

You may have noticed that Loughborough were not part of the first-round draw. During a protracted meeting of Leicestershire Football Association meeting on 19 November 1888, there was much discussion about the membership status of Loughborough Athletic and Football Club and whether they were entitled to take part in the cup competition. At the end of the previous season, Loughborough announced they would leave the association. However, no formal resolution was passed by Loughborough to this effect, and no record appeared in the minutes of the association. The last date for sending in entries for the 1888/89 cup competition was 15 September, and upon this day a letter was received in Leicester to enter the Loughborough club in the association, but as it was sent to the business place of the secretary it did not get into his hands until after the draw for the first round of matches had taken place on the evening of the same day. The committee decided that the Loughborough club had been members as from 15 September, with Mr Upton of Loughborough FC stating that he had been instructed to offer the free use of the Loughborough ground to the association for inter-county contests. The committee, perhaps not surprisingly, readily availed themselves of this generosity and Loughborough were awarded a belated first-round bye.

The draw for the second round in the competition, for matches which had to be played on or before 29 December, resulted as follows, the first-named team in each instance having the choice of ground:

Loughborough v Leicester Wanderers
Kegworth St Andrews v Mill Hill House
Sheepshed v Hathern Liberal Club,
Coalville v Melton Rovers
Bye: Fosse

After beating Leicester Wanderers 8-2, Loughborough, drew Leicester Fosse in round three, a tie which caused intense excitement in both towns. Mill Hill House were granted a bye, while Sheepshed were drawn at home to Coalville in the only other third-round game.

More than 800 spectators watched the first competitive encounter between the Fosse and Loughborough, played at Loughborough on 23 February 1889. The teams were evenly matched, with each side having a strong body of support within the crowd. Kick-off was 15 minutes later than advertised. The Fosse started fast and furious. Gibbs was hurt which necessitated a change in the Loughborough formation, with Gadsby taking over at left-wing forward, Ashmole going back and Gibbs going in goal. Fosse defended well and as the game progressed, they began to take control, pressing almost continuously. Leicester's first professional, Webb, sent a screamer just over the bar and Gibbs had to repel a series of difficult shots.

The visitors continued to press but wasted several clear-cut opportunities. 'Jammer' Radford in the Fosse goal had to fist out a screw shot just before the interval. On resuming, the Luffs rushed the ball across the ground, but it was quickly returned, and Gibbs was called upon to save. After a corner on each side and a fist-out by Radford, play became more even. The Loughborough right-wing forwards neatly centred and by a clever move Smith scored the opening goal of the game, amidst considerable cheering. Fosse pressed but bad shooting let them down. Loughborough doubled their lead with just five minutes remaining after a smart centre from Gadsby was kicked through the goal by Gibson. The Fosse were unfortunate, particularly in the first half. Loughborough play lacked combination at times, but unlike their opponents they were clinical in front of goal.

The peculiar rules of the competition proved lucky for the Luffs, as just three teams went into the semi-final draw, with Loughborough gaining a bye, their second of the competition, into the final. Holders Sheepshed met Mill Hill House at Loughborough on Saturday, 9 March 1889 to decide Loughborough's opponents. The weather was exceptionally fine, and a crowd of 1,500 passed through the turnstiles. In a closely fought, even game, both sides played some outstanding combination football, the tie ending in a 2-2 draw with Mill House equalising in the last ten minutes after taking the lead midway through the first half. A short consultation took place as to whether another half an hour should be played, but Mill Hill House declined.

The replay the following week, also at Loughborough, generated such controversy that it caused a rift between Sheepshed and Loughborough clubs that took years to heal and almost destroyed the young association. Sheepshed objected to the appointment of Mr Ashmole as an umpire on the grounds that he was a 'Leicester man'. Since they refused to play with him officiating, Mr Ashmole withdrew. Mr Cooper, the second umpire, feeling that Sheepshed should abide by the decision of the association, refused to enter the field. The referee selected Mr Burton of Coalville and Mr Mellors of Kegworth to replace them.

In an exciting encounter played in front of 'fully 1,000 spectators', the Leicester team took the lead. Adopting a 'rough' stye of play, the 'reds' of Sheepshed equalised and scored a second almost immediately following the restart following a corner. While defending the Mill Hill House goal, McAlpin, in attempting to stop the 'reds' forwards rushing the leather through the posts, stopped the ball on his back and it rolled through into the back of the net for their third goal. Playing with the wind in the second half, the Leicester side pressed and were encamped in the Sheepshed goalmouth. They were eventually rewarded with a goal just five minutes from the end and even then were unlucky not to equalise, before the whistle for full-time sounded. The winners were loudly cheered as they moved to the pavilion, leaving the Leicester team tired and demoralised on the field.

Mill Hill House protested against the outcome on the grounds that the umpires selected by the association were objected to, and that Sheepshed refused to play if they stood as umpires. The Leicestershire Association committee met on the evening of Saturday, 23 March 1889 at the Victoria Hotel in Leicester to discuss the appeal.

Although conceding that the tie was not played under protest and that it was completed to avoid disappointing the spectators and to ensure the association did not lose their gate, the Sheepshed representative, Mr Foston, stated that both captains had agreed to play with the new umpires and that no objections were raised by Mill Hill House until they lost. After considerable deliberation, the chairman proposed, and Mr Smith (Melton) seconded, that the match be replayed at Coalville on Wednesday, 27 March. Mr Foston said that the Sheepshed men would not play after having won fairly and without a protest being lodged. He was not surprised that Loughborough were so anxious to meet the weakest team of the two. Sheepshed's committee agreed unanimously not to play the match.

Much interest was expressed by Sheepshed residents on hearing the outcome of the proceedings and a huge number attended an 'indignation' meeting held in the town's Bull Ring a couple of days later. Mr Foston, who received a cordial reception from the excitable crowd, proceeded to give his account of what had taken place at the meeting. He said that no protest had been lodged by Mill Hill House, and no fee had been paid (association rules for a protest to be considered), and on behalf of Sheepshed he objected to the matter being discussed. He thought they would agree with him that it was a question of right against wrong, but to his surprise and anger he was overruled by the majority at the meeting.

The Sheepshed players were prepared to meet Loughborough, as arranged, in the final, and he had no doubt that Loughborough were afraid of meeting them, or they would not have 'raised the bother'. Sheepshed were not informed of the business for which the association was called together, although they were perhaps the most interested parties, and no time was given to them to prepare their defence. The Sheepshed committee decided not to meet Mill Hill House on the Wednesday, but to play Loughborough as arranged on Saturday. Mr W. Hollis then moved the following resolution, 'That this meeting expressed its indignation at the unfair manner in which the majority of the Leicestershire association have acted towards Sheepshed football players, and their total disregard of the rules governing the association and records its approval of the action of the Sheepshed football committee in refusing to replay the match with Mill Hill on Wednesday next, and their determination to meet Loughborough in the final as arranged.'

The following letter was sent to Mr Ashmole by J. Waring, on behalf of the Sheepshed committee, on 25 March 1889, 'In reply to yours this morning, I am directed by our committee to state that they decline to meet Mill Hill House FC on Wednesday. The match of the 16th last was fairly contested without any protest from the Mill Hill captain, and, in fact the match was not played under any protest whatsoever. What object, therefore, the majority of the association can have in ordering the match to be replayed is not plain. It is quite certain their action is unfair and against all the rules of the Football Association. If a protest had been lodged with the usual fee, at the proper time we should have been prepared to abide by the decision of the association. I may add that we shall go to Coalville as arranged to play Loughborough in the final. Our brake is engaged and all our arrangements are complete, and we have no intention of making any alternative.'

The local newspaper reporter, 'Observer', neatly summed up the thoughts of most football spectators, 'It is greatly to be regretted that these cup competitions cannot progress without the spirit which should characterise them being spoilt by so many petty squabbles,' while the *Leicester Daily Post* football correspondent wrote, 'The Leicestershire Football Association Challenge Cup is about full to the brim – with bitterness. From its birth, "Double, double toil and trouble" has sadly retarded its growth into a healthy sport-promoting institution, until it is today a byword and a reproach among right-thinking people. I wonder how many of those gentlemen who subscribed their half-guineas to the very handsome cup would not have stayed their hands had they possessed only half an idea of the squabbling the trophy would create.'

The final was marred by the unseemly behaviour of a small section of the crowd from Sheepshed, who were aggrieved at the disqualification of their team. Mr Ashmole, secretary to the association, who was playing for Loughborough, came in for some 'rough usage' and had to be escorted from the ground by the police at the end of the game. Mill Hill House were outclassed by the men in black and white, the Luffs winning the coveted trophy 3-0, witnessed by 1,800 spectators at Coalville. Loughborough FC could rightly call themselves the champions of Leicestershire.

Controversy surrounding the cup competition resurfaced at the first annual dinner of the Leicestershire Football Association at the Victoria Hotel in April 1889. It was stated that 17 clubs were affiliated, and the funds were 'flourishing'. It was acknowledged that the challenge cup competition had not progressed too smoothly, and a discussion was held as to whether cup competitions produced a healthy or fractious rivalry leading to 'play of a rough or brutal character'. Referring to the 'unfortunate dispute' which had arisen in the semi-final in March, chairman Mr Wright acknowledged that errors had been made by all parties and that 'in the future the association should be most careful not to leave itself open to the merest shadow of unfairness towards its component parts'.

The gate money of the match between Sheepshed and Mill Hill was handed over to the association. Since the association refused to acknowledge the match owing to the action of Sheepshed, the latter through their delegate Mr

Foston at the June meeting requested that that the money should be divided between Sheepshed and Mill Hill House. Mr Thompson (Loughborough) moved an amendment that the money should remain in the hands of the association, which was carried by seven votes to four. A letter was read out from Mr Johnson, the treasurer, stating that he had received shabby treatment from members and he had lost all interest in the association.

Sheepshed's Foston reminded members that in 1888 prior to the annual meeting the Loughborough club had joined the association, and then withdrawn, and publicly expressed through their secretary their intention not to have anything further to do with the association. Since no formal withdrawal had been received, a levy of five shilling was requested by the association from each affiliated club; Loughborough were asked to contribute. They did not do so, whereupon the delegate at the last annual meeting he moved that they should not be admitted into the association. This appeared on the minutes as a suggestion – by alteration of this minute the meeting considered that Loughborough were not eligible to compete for the cup. The amended minutes having been passed, Mr Foston moved that Loughborough were therefore were not eligible to compete, and that they should return the cup immediately. Mr Thomson submitted an amendment that it should not be recalled. He said such an action would place the association in a ridiculous position. Besides, Loughborough had re-joined the association at the start of the 1888/89 season and were not members at the time of the levy. The original motion was carried by six votes to five and the Loughborough club were instructed by letter to give the cup back. Loughborough's representative also announced their intention to enter the FA Cup for the following season.

At the AGM of Loughborough FC in July 1889, their 1888/89 season was neatly summarised in the report and balance sheet presented by club's honorary secretary, Mr J. Cooper. Out of the 27 matches played, 19 had been won, with 92 goals scored and 49 against. Every match was played to a definite conclusion with no draws, and to cap it all they had won the Leicestershire Challenge Cup – a record of which any club would be proud.

However, bringing first-class football to the town of Loughborough had come at a cost. Unlike the Fosse, Loughborough FC were part of an athletics and sports club. This meant that not only did they have first-class facilities at the Athletic Grounds, the best in the county, but could use other activities of the club, such as the lucrative Whit Tuesday sports day, to subsidise football. Although attendances were not what might be expected considering the quality of the teams playing at the ground, they were better than any other place in the county. The balance sheet showed that in September 1888 there was a balance in hand of £8 2s 6d: subscriptions amounted to £19 7s; honourable members' event, £15 2s 6d; bicycle club subscriptions, £5 10s; football matches, £125 16s 11d; sports, £152 18s 2d; smoking concert, £1 16s; balance from hall, £10 8s – these with other items bought up the receipts to £330 16s 5d. Payments included: For players, railway expenses, other teams, etc., £128 4s 7d; petty cash, £10 9s 10d; printing and stationary, £13 7s 9d; rent of ground, £8; footballs, £5 4s 0d; subscriptions for the football association, £1 19s;

old accounts, £27 17s 4d; Whitsuntide sports, £123 10s 4d; total £323 15s 3d; balance in hand, £8 0s 9d. The club assets were valued at £32 0s 9d.

The Fosse also had a good season. During 1888/89 they played 45 games, winning 25, drawing five, and losing 15. It was also reported, 'The ball was sent under the bar 109 times with success, the opposing forces totalling 61.' The Fosse had beaten every club they had met in town and county, with the exception of Loughborough. A nice little balance was held by the treasurer.

1889/90

Just a superficial glance at the fixture list of the 1889/90 season, which included games against Notts County Reserves, Long Eaton Rangers, Grantham Rovers, Wellingborough and Bulwell, shows there can be no doubt that the Fosse were the best side in Leicester. Although football was played in Leicester before the formation of the club just five years earlier, the Fossils practically pioneered the game in the town. They devoted great energy towards increasing the popularity of the 'kicking game' in Leicester and 'all signs are not wanting that the gallant wearers of the "chocolate and blue" will ere long reap a right reward for their labours'.

Key to this was the acquisition of a private enclosure, off Mill Lane, for the 1889/90 season. The Mill Lane Ground was developed on a field owned by Leicester Borough Council, situated between a tree-lined branch of the Grand Union Canal and Outram Street. The only entrance was on Mill Lane, so called because it led to Swan's Flour Mill adjacent to the canal. It had a capacity of around 2,500. Poorly drained, the pitch easily become waterlogged and looked more like a ploughed field than a sports arena. Nevertheless, it was the Fosse's first true home, and allowed the club to turn professional. The Fosse squad was considerably strengthened by the arrival of several new players, the most notable acquisition being William Davies, a full-back, from Nantwich FC, along with half-back Albert Vickers from the same club. The mantle of club captain, after the retirement of G.A. Knight, fell upon the shoulders of James 'Jimmy' Johnson.

The season began on a sour note for Leicestershire's top club, Loughborough, who were expelled from the Leicestershire Football Association and were told to hand back the Leicestershire Challenge Cup for the non-payment of a levy of five shillings. Following a personal hearing, the member clubs voted 13-5 in favour of Loughborough and against association officers, who had no alternative but to reinstate the Luffs.

Loughborough became members of the English Football Association and consequently entered the FA Cup. They were awarded a bye into the second qualifying round. On Saturday, 26 October 1889; Loughborough became the first Leicestershire side to play in the famous competition when they faced Derby St Luke's at the Athletic Grounds. Loughborough won 2-1, with goals from Coltman and Simpson. The St Luke's captain raised an objection over the outcome, on the grounds that G. Bosworth, Loughborough's goalkeeper, had played in a six-a-side contest three months earlier during the close season, contrary to the rules of the Football Association. The protest was sustained, and the game was replayed at Derby St Luke's Peet Street Ground on 9 November. After yet another long struggle; the game went into extra time where Derby scored in both periods to go through 2-0 to the next round.

Anticipation and excitement were high as the Luffs had arranged for the famous Everton to play them at the Athletic Grounds on Fairs Saturday just nine days later. However, only nine second-XI Everton players arrived, with the home side winning 7-0.

At least Loughborough had the opportunity to defend the Leicestershire Challenge Cup (now known as the Senior Cup). Loughborough were again granted a first-round bye in 1889/90. Round-two opponents Leicester Wanderers failed to turn up for their tie on 23 December 1889 and Loughborough went through to the semi-finals, to face their arch-rivals Leicester Fosse without even kicking a ball. Leicester had also been granted a bye in round one and disposed of Leicester Teachers 2-0 at Mill Lane on 14 December 1889.

Loughborough, as Leicestershire's premier club and cup holders, were the firm favourites in the semi-final. Fosse played Samuel Rowson and James Eggleston in place of James Atter and Ernest Nuttall, who were ineligible, while Loughborough also had two of their regular men away. Both teams took a good number of enthusiastic supporters to the Sports Ground in Coalville and their ranks were considerably swelled by local fans of the 'kicking game'.

Fosse started against the strong wind that blew sleet and snow straight down the field and had to act on the defensive for the majority of the first half, their back division playing superbly. Loughborough's shooting was rather wild, but Charles Walker, the Fosse goalkeeper, had to make several outstanding saves to keep them out. In spite of determined efforts, the Luffs could not score. At the other end Fosse created several chances, Spiby defending well, and from a centre from the left wing, Webb scored first for Fosse. During the second period the Fosse had the best of the play, and soon added a second. Wilders, the Loughborough 'custodian', totally missed an effort from Webb after a goalmouth scrimmage, the ball rolling slowly between the posts and doubling Leicester's lead. Wilders, despite his error, saved several times in good style. Kelham and Cross worked hard for Loughborough but could not get past the Fosse defence.

Corner kicks were rather erratic owing to the wind, but Murdoch calculated very carefully and at last dropped the ball into the middle of the goal but 'with a barleycorn or two to spare', Johnson scored a third. Gibson, the Loughborough centre, had to leave the field after dislocating his knee cap. Unable to cope with the conditions and down to ten men, Loughborough struggled. Fosse notched a fourth not long before the whistle blew for time, when Murdoch sent in a long-range shot. A convincing win for Fosse. The Luffs protested over the eligibility of Rowson and Eggleston. The Fosse were accused of illegally approaching Eggleston, an amateur player after he appeared for Hinckley against Fosse Rovers, and paying him excessive travelling expenses, as well as providing him with tea. No substantive evidence was provided to the adjudicating cup committee asked to investigate the issue. Rowson was eligible, but the Fosse were requested to prove the 'bona fide membership' of Eggleston. However, Eggleston had left to work down south by the time of the hearing. Fosse were reprimanded for being unable to provide receipts but allowed to face Coalville in the final.

Fosse played in their first cup final on a glorious spring afternoon in late March at Loughborough, in front of 1,500 (some reports suggest 3,000) spectators. Leicester took the lead when 'Webb, fed from the left wing, followed up the ball and just as Coalville returned the ball, he headed it past and rushed it through the goal in fine style,' according to press reports. The applause that followed was silenced by cheers from the Coalville spectators a minute later when a 'combined rush' resulted in an equaliser. Play was fast and furious and often 'too wild to be scientific, little attention being paid to passing'.

Fosse half-back Perry received a nasty kick, which stopped play for a full five minutes, 'A huge cheer announcing the player was not "hor de combat" [hurt]'. Fellow Fosse half-back Bentley had to leave the field after a severe kick to the head. Just before half-time Fosse were within an ace of scoring, but the ball rebounded over off the crossbar. Perry had to retire just ten minutes after the restart, Fosse playing the remainder of the game with just nine men. Despite this, Leicester possibly had the best chances, but their weakness in front of goal was their undoing. Another shot rebounded off the crossbar, this time from Webb, while Murdoch shot a foot wide when it seemed easier to hit the target. As the players tired, play became monotonous towards the end, resulting in a 1-1 draw.

Loughborough staged the replayed final on 12 April. In a one-sided encounter, Fosse took the lead just after half-time with a high shot that 'nonplussed' Coalville's goalkeeper Compton as it passed through just under the upright. A second followed from Frank Gardner who kicked the ball into the back of the net while lying on his back in the goalmouth. Two more goals came in the last 15 minutes, one by Thompson and the other from a long kick by Murdoch from the halfway line. Coalville scarcely had a look-in during the second half as Fosse won their first silverware. As soon as the final whistle went, Fosse's Jimmy Johnson secured the ball, which was one of his most treasured possessions for many years after his playing days were over.

Overall, the season which had started with so much promise for the Luffs ended in disappointment as they were knocked out of the FA Cup despite beating their opponents, losing to their arch enemies in the Leicestershire Senior Cup and failing to win any of their last five games of the season against mediocre opposition.

The highlight of the first part of the season was a 8-2 demolition of their north Leicestershire revivals, Sheepshed. Despite a decrease in gate receipts as the standard of play declined, the balance sheet at the end of the season showed an overall surplus of £13 3s 1d. A local newspaper reporter, 'Jacko', commented, 'The committee of the Loughborough Club have failed to catch the public sympathy, and now at the close of the season they are unable to look back upon one match that has not been played at a pecuniary loss. With such a record, coupled with defeats, no wonder that the committee are not popular now. Players instead of advancing with the season have either remained stationary or declined.'

Alderman T. Wright JP, during his speech at the annual dinner of Leicester Fosse in May 1890, stated that Fosse, during the season, 'Played a distinctly flair and honourable game at football and especially eschewing the rough tactics pursued, he was afraid, by too many others, they had fought their way to the top of the tree in Leicestershire, and now had a fitting reward in the possession of the County Challenge Cup.'

The amount of money which passed through the treasurer's hands was a considerable increase on the previous season, being £93 7s 7½ d, against £34 2s 2½d from the year before. The receipts included £26 19s from subscriptions, £11 concert, £42 18s 5d match receipts. There is, however, a balance due to the treasurer of £6 7s 10d. This, it was stated, was accounted for by the alterations to the club ground, and several home matches falling through. Medals were presented to the victorious cup team and a handsome travel bag to Mr Gardner in recognition of his 'arduous and invaluable services as secretary'. Mr Gardner announced that a very attractive list of matches would be arranged for the ensuing season, in addition to which the club would compete for the FA Cup, the Leicestershire Cup, and the Kettering Charity Cup. The Fosse committee decided not to join the newly formed Leicestershire Football League 'as at present constituted'.

1890/91

By the start of the 1890/91 season the Fosse were recognised as the premier side of Leicester and Loughborough were top of the pile in the county. The Fosse changed team colours to white shirts, with deep-blue trousers, while Loughborough maintained their black-and-white-striped shirts and black trousers.

During the close-season, Loughborough had agreed to join the newly established Leicestershire Football Senior League, but just as the ink was drying they resigned and instead accepted an offer to join the newly formed Midland Alliance League. The lure of top-class opposition such as Doncaster Rovers, Rotherham Swifts, Sheffield FC, and Notts County clearly swayed them, although the decision no doubt annoyed many in the Leicestershire association.

The Luffs committee knew that to both attract supporters and to stand any chance of being successful, they had to strengthen their squad. They signed William Freestone (Notts Mapperley), John Plackett (Long Eaton) and Valentine Smith (Notts Swifts).

At 3.10pm on 21 September 1890 Loughborough became the first Leicestershire club to play in a league when they faced Doncaster Rovers away at the Intake Ground. Originally it was called the 'Deaf and Dumb Ground' as it was located in a field rented from the Yorkshire Institute for the Deaf and Dumb. There were no dressing rooms and the players changed at a nearby hostelry, either the Rockingham Arms or the Doncaster Arms. So, although they were moving up a class in opposition, the same cannot be said for the quality of the amenities.

Luffs, playing with the strong wind that blew diagonally across the field, failed to score in the first period. In the second half Doncaster made the most of the weather conditions, netting four times, although the final score of 4-0 rather flattered the Yorkshiremen. Another away defeat the following weekend, this time in Sheffield, was followed by the Luffs' first victory, at Notts Jardine. The Luffs drew their first home league game, 3-3 against Heanor on 18

October, with William Lowe having the honour of scoring the club's first home goal in the Midland League. November yielded just 3 points from four games, which made what followed remarkable. Due to awful weather, the Black and Whites' first game in December did not take place until five days before Christmas when they slaughtered Sheffield FC 7-2. This result sparked a run of six consecutive wins that sent them to the top of the league for the entire month of January. The run ended at home to the eventual champions, Notts County Reserves, on Valentine's Day. Sadly, they lost two of their remaining three games to finish in third place, on 18 points after winning seven, losing five and drawing two of their 14 league games. Nevertheless, it was a more than satisfactory first season.

FA Cup

Leicester Fosse and Loughborough FC both entered the English Challenge [FA] Cup in 1890. The draw for the first qualifying round was made in September, and the ties involving Midland League teams were as follows:

> Gainsborough Trinity v Lincoln City
> Loughborough v Derby Midland
> Derby Junction v Sheffield United
> Leicester Fosse v Burton Wanderers
> Matlock v Derby Leys
> Derby St Luke's v Belper
> Byes: Leeds Albion and Burton Swifts

Fosse's first FA Cup tie was something of a reality check when they had their first taste of top-class opposition in a competitive game, played on Saturday, 4 October at the Mill Lane Ground. In front of a large crowd that generated record gate receipts of £15, Burton Wanderers took the lead within a few minutes of kick-off. Brown, the scorer, doubled the lead midway through the half. Wanderers were faster and better organised and at times ran the home side ragged. Dickens scored a third and a fourth was added just before the full-time whistle blew.

Meanwhile Loughborough overcame another Derby club, Derby Midland, 3-2 in one of the best matches ever witnessed at the Athletic Grounds. Luffs took the lead after 30 minutes when Smith kicked into an unprotected goal after the Derby keeper was still on the floor after saving an earlier attempt. After prolonged applause for the whole Loughborough team from excited spectators, as the Luffs players appeared to be taking things easy, Wood equalised with a low lightning shot. Rose clawed a goal back for the Midlands after rushing the ball into the net when Harris, the Luffs keeper, fisted out. Two goals, one from each side, quickly followed. Just as extra time seemed inevitable, Cross pounced on a shot from Smith that rebounded off the post to snatch a 3-2 victory for the Luffs.

Loughborough were drawn against Burton Wanderers at home in the second qualifying round three weeks after the first-round tie, on 25 October 1890. Burton were without three of their influential players, while the Luffs were at full strength. The game was marked throughout by neat passing and 'first class combination' by the Loughborough forwards, who scored no fewer than eight goals, conceding just one. Their away game to Belper Town in the third qualifying round was switched to the Athletic Grounds following a cash inducement. The gate was around 1,500, and the excitement was equal to that of two years earlier, when they won the Leicestershire Challenge Cup. Whether sufficient money was collected to recoup the 'consideration' paid to Belper is debatable. But given the superiority of the Luffs at home and the prospect of a potentially lucrative fourth qualifying round draw, it was clearly worthwhile. Belper did not field a first-class XI and were outplayed. This was particularly noticeable in the second half, when had not the visitors' goalkeeper showed excellent form and their backs put up a good defence, the Loughborough goal tally would have been much heavier than their eventual 5-2 win.

Loughborough faced Sheffield United in the final qualifying round. Having the privilege of selecting the ground, the Luffs choose to play away from home at Bramall Lane on a conditional payment of £30 by the United committee. A special train run by the Midland Railway took 96 supporters to the Yorkshire town, but though the train started at Leicester no more than a dozen had booked from that station. Sheffield fielded their strongest side, which included two Scottish 'imports' – Calder and Robertson – while Loughborough were without their inspirational half-back Ernest Coltman.

Within the first ten minutes, Loughborough hit the crossbar and pressed well. Much to the surprise of the excited spectators, William Harris in the Loughborough goal allowed a straightforward shot to pass through into the goal without making an attempt to stop it. This did not deter the Luffs, who were unlucky not to score after United made a goal-line clearance; minutes later yet another shot sailed just over the bar and Carnelley, just back from injury, missed a sitter. Loughborough deservedly equalised from a header by Smith, but just before half-time Sheffield took the lead. On resuming, however, it was soon evident that the heavy nature of the ground told upon the visitors, who were more accustomed to the lighter soil of the Athletic Grounds. As the Luffs tired, United proved smarter and quicker on the ball. Sheffield scored two goals in quick succession as the Luffs collapsed. As the home team 'out-distanced' their opponents both in speed and combination, they scored another two before the final whistle sounded, with the ultimate score Sheffield United 6 Loughborough 1. United were in all phases of play superior to Loughborough, a quickness in seizing the ball, fine combinations and fleetness of foot giving them a decided advantage. But had Loughborough been able to maintain their first-half form, they might even have won the game.

Loughborough's committee gave their players a complimentary dinner to thank them for 'creditably representing the club in the preliminary rounds of the English Challenge Cup' in January 1891. After Major Alderman Bampus proposed a toast to 'the health of the team and the prosperity of the club', he congratulated Loughborough on their achievements to date: 'It did not seem more than five or six years since it was a matter of astonishment to hear of two or three thousand people attending a football match in the winter.' He hoped that the enormous increase that had accrued in the public interest arose in the main from the fact that the game had very much changed, and added, 'That it was not now as it once was, a brutal contest, in which sheer violence won the day, but had become what might be described as a scientific contest. It is because football had so changed and raised its character that the public took such an interest in it.'

Leicestershire Challenge Cup
The first-round draw took place in September 1890 and produced these ties:

Leicester Fosse v Melton Rovers
South Wigston v Leicester Teachers
Hugglescote Robin Hoods v Syston Wreake Valley
Gresley Rovers or Coalville v Loughborough Athletic

Owing to the ongoing dispute, Shepshed FC (renamed from Sheepshed in 1888) entered the Kettering Charity Cup instead of the Leicestershire Challenge Cup in 1889 and for the following few seasons. To the surprise of many, Loughborough withdrew from their Leicestershire Challenge Cup tie against Gresley Rovers in January 1891, a week before it was scheduled to take place, to concentrate on the Midland League. This action must have been deeply disappointing to Rovers, but Loughborough felt that they had little choice.

The primary principle of the Midland League was to play the best possible team in all matches, and in order to maintain their firm adherence to an organisation that had done nothing but good for the Loughborough club, they found it impossible to raise a side for Gresley without poaching from the Alliance team. The executive body of the Leicestershire Football Association awarded the tie to Gresley, while Loughborough were required to pay the club five shillings as well as a small indemnity for breaking the fixture. Other business before the meeting included a protest against the validity of the Fosse v Melton Rovers tie, in which Fosse walked home to the tune of 10-0, and one by South Wigston against the bona fide membership of Teddy Thompson, who had assisted the Teachers to beat South Wigston. Neither of the appeals was entertained, and the draw for the semi-finals set up Fosse v Teachers and Gresley Rovers v Hugglescote Robin Hoods.

In foggy weather before a fair number of spectators at Coalville, Fosse beat Leicester Teachers in an exciting encounter, to reach the Leicestershire Challenge Cup Final for the second consecutive year. Their opponents were Gresley Rovers, who had dismissed Hugglescote Robin Hoods in the other semi-final. Fosse supporters were outnumbered by Gresley's in a lacklustre final played at Loughborough's Athletic Grounds on Saturday 21 March 1891. Spectators were scarce and 'they were by no means enthusiastic'. Little was known about Gresley Rovers, even by the football reporters of local newspapers, and it was said they 'played poor football, relying almost entirely on long and strong kicking, with no combined play worth mentioning'. Playing with the wind in the first half, Fosse scored twice, while both sides wasted several chances, with Gresley's shooting being especially wild and uncertain. In the second half the play was even worse; no goals were scored, and Leicester retained the trophy.

The Derby Games

The first derby of the 1889/90 season was held ten days before Christmas. Leicester Fosse's rugby rivals, the Tigers, postponed their game at the Belgrave, sending many people to visit the Mill Lane Ground for the first time in the hope of seeing the best association football game that Leicestershire could muster. Both teams fielded their strongest sides. Press reports suggest that around 3,000 spectators were crammed into the enclosure, which only had a capacity of just 2,500, paying record gate receipts of £23 3s 0d. Unfortunately, however, their time proved to be ill spent as a dense fog enveloped the field of play and only occasional glimpses could be obtained of the ball or a player or two.

As far as Loughborough players were concerned, 'It would have been better for their reputation if they had never been seen at all.' Deliberate fouling and tripping was extensively practised by some Luffs players. During one smart dribble down the wing, James Atter was tripped three times, and as he succeeded in keeping going upon each occasion an opponent as a last resort rugby-tackled him. The Leicester press were not impressed by the Loughborough side, who were riding high in the Midland League, reporting, 'If that is a specimen of the much vaunted Loughborough style of football, then the "new borough" is hardly to be complimented upon the possession of those who are responsible for its introduction. Of course, there is the law, giving a free kick for such infringements, but what a poor penalty for an infringement which might under the conditions prevailing on Saturday, easily have caused a lifelong injury. I cannot myself imagine more unsportsmanlike conduct.'

The game ended 1-1. Fosse took the lead in the first period from an error by the Luffs keeper, Harris, who in stopping a long-range shot from Murdoch accidentally carried the ball into the goal. The crowd went wild with excitement, taunting Harris throughout the rest of the match. Loughborough equalised from a corner when Kelham's shot rebounded off the Fosse goalkeeper, Charlie Walker, and William Cross kicked the ball into the back of the net. According to legend, Walker was left standing between his goal posts at the end of the game and only discovered missing from the dressing room 20 minutes later. When found, he was reportedly still under the impression that the game was still in progress and that the Fosse were attacking the other end.

Because this game ended in an unsatisfactory fashion, the *Leicester Post* newspaper suggested through its football columns that the clubs should play a holiday match during the Christmas period, the proceeds going to the 'Suffering Humanity' fund.

With both clubs showing willingness, the affair was taken in hand by Mr A.T. Porter, who managed to organise and promote the game in such a short time frame. Snow had been cleared off the Belgrave Road pitch and more than 3,000 spectators braved the bitterly cold weather on 29 December 1890. Players demonstrated exceptional skill considering the state of the playing surface. Spills were frequent, with high incidences of foul play by both sides. On the whole the contest was evenly matched, the Fosse, if anything, having perhaps slightly the best of the exchanges, but not sufficient to establish any superiority. If one side pressed for five minutes, the other would do so in turn, while each side had about an equal number of chances. The result was a 1-1 draw.

Fosse's goal was probably unfair, Flint appearing to have crossed the goal line with the ball prior to centring into the goalmouth for Lomas to rush it through. The evenness of the game was further illustrated by the fact that Loughborough's goal was also apparently scored from illegal play, Lowe being offside when he received the ball. As the game was played for a charity, it could have come to no better ending. After paying expenses, a sum of about £30 was handed over.

Some indication of the rapid rise in popularity of association football in the town of Leicester is that one of the most popular attractions of Christmas 1890 was the game between Leicester Fosse and London Casuals. The Casuals, who included the legendary C.B. Fry in their team, were an amateur club based in London, formed in 1883. They merged with Corinthian in 1939 to form Corinthian-Casuals, a club that still exists. In the snow, the 'forward five' of the Casuals, though weak in front of goal, gave an exhibition of scientific play. 'Passing back when tackled formed a remarkably pretty and effective feature of their play, and so as a very, very little of this is seen in Leicestershire football the opportunity may be taken of commending it to the serious consideration of home players,' read one report. The only goal of the game was scored by W. Johnson midway through the second half.

The return derby at Loughborough on 7 February 1891 was played on a pitch suitable for fast play in dull weather in front of a record crowd of 2,500 spectators, who paid a total of £23 to watch the eagerly awaited encounter between the two best sides in the county. The home supporters mustered in rare force, and a special train from Leicester conveyed at least 1,500 Fosse followers. Loughborough played their regular team, with the exception that A. Smith filled the place of E. Coltman at right half-back, while the Fosse side had one change, F. Handford, signed from Leicester Teachers, playing left forward instead of E. Johnson, whose absence was caused by a family bereavement.

Left-winger Atter almost scored with a fine screw shot, Harris in the Loughborough goal got thoroughly mixed up and Murdoch, through over-anxiety, missed the goal, and Loughborough got off with a goal kick – an incredibly lucky escape. As the Fosse pressed, loud chants of 'Play up, Loughborough' echoed around the enclosure. This encouraged Luffs' pack of forwards. Within the space of a few minutes, the Fosse defence stopped Cross in his steps, Freestone missed an easy opportunity and following a free kick for hands in a dangerous position Cross sent a shot just over the bar. Atter was floored as the Fosse continued to have the best of the play. From a counter attack following a Leicester corner, Cross received the ball when having only the goalkeeper to beat, and despite the fact that the whistle had been blown for offside, he shot past Fosse's goalkeeper, Walker, who made no attempt to stop the ball. The goal was disallowed.

After a prolonged period of pressing, Harris repelled a moderate shot from Webb, the Leicester players swarmed round the goal, and during a 'bully' in which six or seven players took part, the ball was scrimmaged through into the goal. The Luffs appealed, but to the delight of the Fosse faithful, the referee immediately allowed the goal. This woke up Loughborough and, attacking down the wing, Lowe seemed certain to score, but Walker cleared with a grand throw.

It was clear as the second period began that Loughborough had evidently made up their minds to spare no effort in turning the tide and adopted a rough style of play. Plackett, when 'floored' as a result of one of his own charges, deliberately pulled down Atter with his hands. Lowe clearly evaded Nuttall and shot straight at Walker, who, in clearing, gave the ball back to Lowe, whose return shot went between the posts. Minutes later, Loughborough went into the lead when Freestone scored with a fast low shot from a splendid cross. The Luffs were now firmly in charge, with Lowe, on the right wing, being the provider for Val Smith to score their third, Cross charging Walker out of the way. Fosse broke away once or twice on the counter, with Flint striking the upright. The final whistle was greeted by a wild outburst from the home supporters as Loughborough won 3-1. Twelve miles south, Loughborough Reserves beat Fosse Reserves 2-1. Also played in thick fog, the game ended in controversy as the referee disallowed a late Fosse equaliser.

At the Loughborough Annual General Meeting in August 1891, secretary Mr Cockain stated that the past season's results had been of a 'most satisfactory character'. They played 36 matches, won 22, drew five, and lost nine, scoring 107 against 59 with just one home defeat. The balance in hand was £5 13 s 5d compared with a £58 11s 1d loss the previous year. With a balance of £30 14s 10d from the sports section of the club, Loughborough began the 1891/92 season with £36 8s 3d in hand. The balance sheet showed that the players' wages and refreshments amounted to £113 7d 11d, travelling expenses £40 16s

10d, and guarantees to visiting teams £48 10s 9d. On the credit side were gate money and a guaranteed £238 13s 5d, subscriptions £15 5s, membership fee £11 3s.

Much to the regret of their supporters, admittance to the Midland League, and an improved list of fixtures, meant the annual match between the Luffs and the London Casuals was allowed to lapse.

The forward line was materially strengthened by the signing of Albert Carnelley from Notts County. Carnelley ended the season as the club's top scorer with 19 goals – 14 in the Midland League and five in the Challenge Cup. This included four on his home debut in an 11-2 slaughter of Doncaster Rovers, a hat-trick against the Fosse and five in the 7-0 destruction of Hereford Association in the FA Cup. Mr R. Barker, who played at the back for London Casuals, assisted the defence for the first part of the season.

Meanwhile, more than 50 attended the annual dinner of Leicester Fosse held at the end of April 1891 at the Victoria Hotel. From humble beginnings, the club had made remarkable progress during their seven years of existence.

Although the fixture list comprised much stronger opposition than they had previously played, they won 23 of their 37 matches, losing nine and drawing five, with 113 goals for and only 57 against. The Fosse committee also took the opportunity to announce their intention to apply for admission into the Midland League. The club's second team, under the name Fosse Reserves, would play in the Leicestershire Football League and a full fixture list would be organised for a third team.

3

The Midland League Years

AT THE annual dinner of Leicester Fosse, held at the
Victoria Hotel in late May 1891, honorary secretary Mr.
F Gardener gave an upbeat speech. He stated that so far
from being against the rugby club, there was plenty of room
in Leicester for two great football organisations and that,
encouraged by their past success, the club had applied for
admission into the Midland League.

The Midland League was founded in 1889, just one year
after the Football League. In its inaugural season 11 clubs
participated – Burton Wanderers, Derby Junction, Derby
Midland, Gainsborough Trinity, Leek, Lincoln City, Notts
Rangers, Sheffield, Staveley FC, and Warwick County –
from six counties. Sheffield, Notts Rangers and Leek did
not complete the season. Lincoln City, the first champions,
and four others would go on to play in the Football League.
During the early days, the champions were elected to the
Football League and in return those Football League clubs
who failed to be re-elected were welcomed into the Midland
League. Both Doncaster and Lincoln had spells oscillating

between the Football League and Midland League. As the elite clubs became bigger and stronger, they applied to send their reserve sides into the Midland League and in less than a decade those teams accounted for more than half of the competition.

The Luffs had also applied to be admitted to the Midland League. All applications were considered at the league's annual general meeting held in May 1891 at the Maypole Hotel in Nottingham. It was unanimously resolved that each club becoming a member should pay £5 in addition to the usual subscription, the money to be handed over at the same time as the subscription and be forfeited in the event of any club not fulfilling entire its fixture list and to be refunded to those who did complete their matches. Staveley and Derby Junction were re-elected, and in addition to the Fosse and Loughborough there were applications for membership from Doncaster Rovers, Grantham Rovers, Sheffield Attercliffe and Wednesbury Old Athletic. The election of both Leicestershire clubs, along with Wednesbury Athletic – to fill the vacancies caused by the retirement of Lincoln City, Kidderminster, and Warwick County – was widely celebrated by the county's association football fans, who would get the opportunity to watch the likes of Rotherham Town, Burton Wanderers, Derby Junction and of course Luffs v Fosse clashes in a prestigious league competition.

Leicester Fosse were given notice by Leicester Corporation to leave their Mill Lane enclosure after just two years, as the land was required for building. Homeless, the club gratefully accepted an offer from Leicestershire County Cricket Club to rent the Aylestone Road (Grace

Road) cricket ground for £25 on a temporary basis. Grace
Road had opened as a cricket ground 13 years earlier.
Covering eight acres, the ground also had a bicycle/athletics
track of about half a mile in circumference encircling the
cricket pitch. It must be remembered that cycling was an
immensely popular sport attracting thousands of spectators.
There was also a hotel, stabling and room for lawn tennis
and quoits. Fosse's arrival was not a popular move, with
much criticism in the local press from cricket-lovers, who
were worried about the impact of playing football on
the turf.

Fosse played just eight games at Grace Road: five
friendlies (Football League teams Derby County and
Notts County were visitors), an FA Cup game against Small
Heath (who later became Birmingham City), and Midland
League fixtures against Derby Junction and Grantham
Rovers between September and October 1891. Due to its
out-of-town location, lack of public transport – there was
one-horse drawn trams – and the popularity of Leicester
Football Club (Tigers) who were playing at Fosse's old
Belgrave Cycle and Cricket Ground, attendances at Grace
Road were poor, never exceeding 300.

Leicester's first Midland League game was played on
Saturday, 12 September 1891 at home to Derby Junction, in
front of just a few hundred spectators. Derby Junction were
founded as an old boys' team for Junction Street School in
the early 1880s and were renamed Derby Junction Street
in 1885. At some point the Street was dropped from the
club's name. They played at Derby Arboretum, a park in
the town centre. Most notably they were one of the founders
of the Midland League and FA Cup semi-finalists in the

1888, in a run that included a 2-1 victory over the holders, Blackburn Rovers, before they lost to eventual winners West Bromwich Albion. The following season they were defeated in the first round by local rivals Derby County, and folded in 1895 as professionalism began to spread into the game.

The encounter between Fosse and Derby Junction was played under a burning autumn sun. Derby, resplendent in their green shirts with a gold sash, white knickers, and green socks, played the first half with the sun in their faces. Leicester had the worst of luck, with 'several shots only failing by going over a trifle too high'. George Old in goal was in sparkling form for the Fosse. In the second half, both teams played a 'fine game'. Jimmy Atter broke the deadlock with a 'fine shot', scoring Leicester's first goal in the Midland League, to secure the two points.

The Luffs made an unfortunate start to their 1891-92 Midland League campaign in front of 1,500 spectators at Cobridge stadium against Burslem Port Vale. Tomlinson (goalkeeper), Spiby (back), Plackett (half-back), Lowe, Needham, Carnelley and Cross reached Burslem, but the remaining four players missed the connection at Derby, and were left behind. Mr Kingscott, the referee, allowed the Luffs to play four local men as substitutes. Although they did their best, they were 'useless'. Considering the circumstances, perhaps it wasn't a surprise that Burslem scored seven goals, three of them before half-time. Late in the game a beautiful pass by Lowe was converted into a goal by one of the substitutes playing in the centre. Walter Cockain, Loughborough's secretary, had to write to the press explaining that the team's poor performance was not the norm and that the team was the strongest it had been. They proved this in their next game with an 11-2 destruction of Doncaster Rovers at the Athletic Grounds.

Billed as the 'Championship of Leicestershire', the eagerly anticipated first Midland League Leicestershire derby took place at the Athletic Grounds on 14 November 1891. The Fosse went into the game as the team in form since they had won two of their opening three Midland League encounters, compared to just one in five for the Luffs. However, Fosse were severely weakened by the loss of their influential captain Ernest Nuttall with a knee injury and Harry Bailey with a heavy cold. Their places were filled by Albert Vickers at left-half-back and William Davis at right-back. In addition to these two players, who formed half the backbone of the side, Fosse were also minus Arthur Bennett and according to the local newspaper reporter, 'All that could be hoped from a Leicester viewpoint was to give Loughborough a good game.'

To date little has been mentioned about the players who represented the Fosse and the Luffs on the field of play. Not much is known about many of the early teams, but historians have collated biographical information of those who played in the Midland League and Football League. So, the first competitive league encounter seems an ideal opportunity to learn about those who took the field that autumnal Saturday afternoon. The Luffs side contained no fewer than five Williams – Harris, Lowe, Kelham, Cross and Freestone. There was a strong Nottingham connection, with six being born in the county – George Spiby, Albert Peters, William Freestone, and Valentine (Val) Smith – and three Leicestershire players: Harry Griffin, William Kelham and William Cross. William Lowe, at 5ft 10in, was the tallest player on the pitch. Spiby, who joined the Luffs from Notts County, as had Freestone and Peters, was the club's first professional. Val Smith would become the only Luffs player to have played in the Midland Alliance and all four Midland League campaigns for the Luffs and was an ever-present in at least two of those seasons. John Plackett went on to play a total of at least 95 known games for the Luffs and would become the club's trainer during their Football League years.

In terms of scoring, William Freestone averaged more than a goal every two games during his time with Loughborough, and William Cross was the only Luffs player to score a hat-trick in their only Midland Alliance campaign. Lowe was the youngest Luffs player aged 21 years, with Peters being the oldest at 27. Almost all the players are thought to have worked in addition to playing. Known trades undertaken by the Luff players who participated in the first Leicestershire derby league encounter include an iron founder, framework knitter, tailor's cutter, and labourer.

By comparison, the Leicester Fosse side, who had a slightly lower average age, were less experienced in playing first-class football. Four players – Samuel Hufton, Ernest Mouel, James Atter and Henry 'Harry' Webb – were 21 years of age or younger, with only George Old over the age of 30. Nearly half of the Fosse team that day had joined the club in 1891 – Jabez (Jack) Lord from Derby Junction, Hufton from Ilkeston Town, George Vickers from Nantwich, Robert Herrod from Doncaster Rovers, Ernest Mouel from Cambridge, and Lord from Derby Junction – four of whom spent only one season with the club. The exception was Lord, an ever-present in the first Midland League season who stayed with the club for six seasons, which included three playing in the Second Division. The appropriately named George Old was the oldest player on the pitch, aged 31. A bricklayer, he started Leicester's first Midland League campaign in goal, making just seven appearances before he was replaced by Tom De Ville. Samuel Rowson had played for the Fosse in both Leicestershire Challenge Cup finals, while James Atter, the only Leicester-born player and the youngest man on the pitch at 20, appeared in the first two Leicestershire Challenge Cup finals for Mill Hill House. Fosse's first professional, Harry Webb, who would go on to claim first Leicester's first FA Cup hat-trick along with Billy Dorrell in the 7-0 win over Rushden in October 1892, led the forward pack. Outside football, the Leicester players were mainly shoemakers, one of whom went on to form his own shoe manufacturing company (E A Johnson & Co. of Ash Street, Leicester), along with a trainee solicitor, labourer, and a coal miner.

More than 3,000 spectators crammed into the Athletic Grounds, the match being one of the leading attractions of Loughborough's annual Fair Week. Two football special trains bought a large contingent of Fosse supporters, who made themselves heard with renditions of their well-known 'Play up, Fosse' chant. In a fast, end-to-end first half played on heavy ground, William Freestone missed an open goal for the Luffs and the Fosse had two goals disallowed within minutes of each other, both for offside, before Leicester took the lead thanks to a blistering shot from Mouel. George Old kept out several hard shots before Albert Carnelley dribbled through a host of players, and equalised for Loughborough with a low shot. The Fosse broke away after a period of intense pressure from the Luffs before Mouel centred accurately, enabling Atter to score. This stimulated the Fosse, and Tomlinson was called on to make a specular save. Loughborough retaliated, with Shelton heading the ball past Old, making the score 2-2 at half-time.

But in the words of the press, 'Oh dear and oh dear! – what a Fosse falling off there was in the second half.' The Luffs penned the Fosse in their own half for much of the time. Lowe scored after a smart sprint down the right wing and the Luffs extended their advantage with a lightning shot from Carnelley. Fosse heads dropped and almost every man adopted rough tactics. Carnelley now dominant tore Fosse's defence apart, scoring his third and the Luffs' fifth. The best goal of the day, however, was the final one by Freestone, who scored after a centre from Lowe, the goalkeeper having no chance. Although Loughborough were clearly the better side, numerous allegations were made against the decisions of the referee. But for this unfortunate shortcoming, the Leicester press reported that the defeat would have been 'less pronounced' and that the 'man behind the whistle is more to be pitied than blamed – that he erred in ignorance rather than intent'. The result was 6-2 in favour of the north Leicestershire side. It was the only match played in the Midland League that day, and put the Luffs and the Fosse on the same points.

The reverse fixture, two weeks later, was an incredibly special one in the history of Leicester Fosse, as it was the inaugural Midland League game staged at their new Walnut Street ground. According to legend, Joseph Johnson, a local businessman and a senior Fosse committee member, was strolling along the river with his niece, Miss

Westland, when she noticed an area of land bordered by Grasmere Street and Filbert Street on the edge of borough of Leicester and thought it would make an ideal location for a football pitch. Leicester Corporation leased the three-and-a-quarter-acre site to Leicester Fosse for their new home, with Mr Johnson personally guaranteeing the rent. Considerable work had to be undertaken to enclose and develop the land fit for Midland League football. Since Filbert Street was a very minor thoroughfare, as can be seen from the 1902 map, the ground was initially known as Walnut Street, as it was felt that few fans would know how to find it. The first game was against Notts Forest's reserve side on 7 November which ended in a 1-1 draw, although Fosse reserves had beaten Melton Swifts 3-2 on the new pitch three weeks earlier (17 October).

Initially, the Walnut Street ground consisted of simple earth banks, with a small stand on the west side. In 1900 the simple wooden terracing behind the south end was replaced by some earthwork banking to create the Spion Kop. It was named after a battle in the Second Boer War – in Afrikaans 'spion' means 'spy' or 'look-out', and kop means 'hill' or 'outcrop'. The Battle of Spion Kop, a British defeat, was fresh in the memory having taken place in late January 1900. In 1908, Leicester Fosse's first promotion to the First Division was marked by a roof being built over the Spion Kop terrace. It was not until 1921 that a much larger main stand was constructed. In 1927, the double-decker south stand of brick and concrete and steel was built. The roof, which had covered that end of the enclosure, was moved to the north side. The first phase of ground development concluded with the covering of the east, or 'popular', side in 1939.

Excitement for the Leicestershire derby was intense. The Luffs' John Tomlinson, a local boot and shoemaker, missed the train and Loughborough had to start the game without a recognised goalkeeper. Luckily for the Luffs, William Ward, their giant 6ft 2in reserve custodian, who was watching the game as a spectator, went between the sticks. Playing with the wind, Loughborough were chiefly on the attack throughout the first half. The stubborn defence of Old and Rowson together with the bad state of the pitch for shooting kept the scoring down, although Loughborough went into half-time up by two goals, from Freestone and Carnelley. Just a few minutes into the second half, Leicester scored their only goal. Mouel sent in a long shot, and Ward, moving with great difficulty in his ordinary boots through the mud, failed to reach the ball. To protect their vulnerable keeper, the Luffs switched to playing four backs and outclassed the Fosse to the end, winning the game 2-1. Although the Fosse had strengthened their team, they hardly showed any improvement in form since their 6-2 drubbing at the hands of the Luffs and the forwards had fewer shots on goal. Considering the circumstances, Ward performed well, but had nothing like as much to do as his counterpart in the Fosse goal. The Luffs played the best they had all season and produced some 'pretty combination' football. Plackett, Luffs' specialist left-half, broke his nose after heading the ball simultaneously with an opponent.

A fine set of results, including a 5-0 victory over league leaders Wednesbury Old Athletic, saw the Luffs rise to second in the table by mid-February. Sadly, they could not maintain the momentum and just one point from their last four games saw them slide down the table to finish the season in eighth place. Nevertheless, it was a creditable first league campaign for Loughborough. Albert Carnelley was the Luffs' leading scorer in the Midland League with 14, followed by William Freestone with ten, and the team averaging two goals per game.

Leicester had to wait until 9 January 1892 to win a league game at their new ground for the first time, when they beat soon-to-be-crowned Midland League champions Rotherham Town 4-1. This proved to be the highlight of Leicester's season. The Yorkshire side got their revenge in the reverse fixture in April 1893, when they humiliated ten-man Fosse 11-0 – the club's record Midland League defeat. The missing player was Amos Atkins, who has an unusual and rather short Fosse senior record of 'played one, missed one'. Apart from a 1-0 home victory against Wednesbury Old Athletic, Fosse failed to win another game in their first Midland League campaign. They ended the season bottom of the league, sharing the wooden spoon alongside Derby Junction, with 13 points from 20 games. Both clubs had to seek re-election. Fosse scored just 21 goals in 20 games, with Jimmy Atter leading the way on six and Ernest Mouel adding five. Jack Lord was the only ever-present, with over 30 players used throughout the season.

There were also two 'friendly' derby games held in 1891/92. The first, at Walnut Street in front of 1,500 spectators, saw the Luffs win 4-1 in January 1892. It proved much less interesting than was usual. The Fosse never settled to good football, their play being of a 'weak character', apart from Bailey and Nuttall who both played 'plucky' games. Loughborough's forwards shone as a unit, with goals from Jackson, Smith, and a brace from Carnelley. The rest of the Luffs side did 'what was required of them'.

The second friendly and fourth Leicestershire derby of the season was staged at Walnut Street in April 1892, before a good crowd. Both clubs fielded strong sides. Fosse started strongly and struck the bar twice before conceding a soft goal. William Freestone fired in a long shot that Fosse keeper De Ville left to one of the backs to clear, and between them the ball went through untouched. In the second half, a shot by Carnelley was grandly saved by De Ville, but Lowe rushed through and bundled the ball into the net. Fosse pressed hard and were rewarded with a consolation goal by Mouel. The game ended Fosse 1 Loughborough 2. There could be no doubt that, having beaten Leicester Fosse four times during 1891/92, Loughborough were the champions of Leicestershire.

Leicester had failed to win any of their last eight games, conceding 22 and scoring just one goal. A public meeting took place at the Co-operative Hall to 'consider the question of raising the standard of Association in Leicester', and the best means of helping Fosse Football to attain this end. A fundraising committee was elected and raised £200. The club's general meeting was held a few week later on a Monday evening in late May at the Victoria Hotel. The secretary's report showed that the first team had played 43 matches, of which they had won just 12, lost 23, and drawn eight, 70 goals having been scored for them and 104 against. Fosse's balance sheet provides a fascinating insight into the finances of a late-Victorian-era football club. Treasurer Mr Cooper, in his annual report, showed a balance in hand on 29 May 1891 of £15 17s 7.5d; gate money, including reserve enclosure, £471 6s 11d; guarantee from club, £15 9s; members' subscriptions £46 4s 6d; sales of season tickets £21 6s, the total being £582 9s 7.5d. The chief items on the expenditure side were railway fares for the three teams (first team, Fosse Rovers and the third team) of £148 10s 4d; wages to professional players of £157 4s 0.5d; guarantees to clubs of £85 17s 11d; rent of the Walnut Street ground at £15; insurance at £9 15s; Midland League expenses of £7 5s; bill posting and associated costs at £43 7s; advertising at £16 0s 11d; printing costs of £33 43s; playing materials at £22 11s 4d; the total being £599 1s 11d, and the balance on the year's play £16 12s 3.5d. Interestingly, a motion in favour of withdrawing from the Leicestershire Football Association was referred to the committee for discussion.

At Loughborough's annual meeting, held at the Pavilion on their Athletic Grounds, a speech was made by club secretary Mr Cockain. He stated that during the 1891/92 season Loughborough had played 35 matches, won 17, lost 16, drawn two and scored 90 goals against 70. Having defeated the Fosse four times, they were entitled to regard themselves as the champions of Leicestershire, a comment that generated applause from attendees. They also defeated Rotherham Town, the champions of the Midland League, and runners-up Gainsborough Trinity away, which was Gainsborough's first home defeat. Loughborough reported a loss of £45 6s 9d in 1891/92. This deficit was offset by a 'guarantee fund' (established by prominent gentlemen of the town) and £45 raised from the thousands who attended the annual Whit Tuesday Sports held at the Athletic Grounds. Concern was expressed at the poor attendances, which were on average less than 1,000. Only fixtures against the Fosse and the top teams attracted the number of spectators the club needed to bring top-class football to Loughborough.

1892/93

Both Leicester Fosse and Derby Junction were readmitted into the Midland League in May 1892. Burslem Port Vale had left after being invited to become founder members of the Football League Second Division and the number of teams in the league was increased from 11 to 12. As a result of these changes, there were two vacancies, taken up by Kettering and Mansfield.

During the close-season Fosse significantly strengthened their squad with the acquisition of goalkeeper Jimmy Thraves from Notts County and winger William 'Billy' Dorrell from Singers. Thraves played for County in the 1891 FA Cup Final, losing 3-1 to Blackburn Rovers in front of 23,000 spectators at the Kensington Oval, and also against the Fosse in the final game staged at Mill Lane. Dorrell was scouted by Leicester Fosse playing for Singers in Coventry, and replaced Jimmy Atter, Fosse's leading scorer in 1891/92, on the left wing. A firm favourite with the fans, Dorrell's dribbling and 'trickery' attracted the attention of Aston Villa, who he joined for £250 in May 1894. He scored five goals in 11 First Division appearances for Villa and was allowed to move back to the Fosse in March 1896. During his second spell with the Fosse, he scored 24 goals in 63 appearances.

Loughborough also made several 'star' signings: William Sharpe from Ardwick, John Start from Long Eaton Rangers, Charles Butterworth of Derby County, Jack Kent of Everton and Thomas Culley from Birmingham St Georges.

The outside-left for two of Luffs' Midland League seasons, Sharpe scored six goals before being transferred to serve Football League Second Division side Woolwich Arsenal. Start joined his brother, striker Frank, for just one season at the Athletic Grounds, netting an impressive 11 goals in his 20 Midland League games for the club. Opera-singing outside-left Charles Butterworth also spent just one season at the Luffs where he was one short of being ever-present. Unfortunately Kent's time in Leicestershire was not a happy one, twice breaking his leg, the latter – against the Fosse – so severe that it ended his playing career. The final signing, Culley, although scoring in Loughborough's opening two wins of the season, made little impact after that.

Both clubs started the season full of hope and enthusiasm. For perhaps the first time in the Fosse's history they had a place they could call home, allowing them to concentrate on building a top-class team. Fosse started the season with defeats at Mansfield (4-1) and Rotherham (6-1), before drubbing Newark 7-1 at Walnut Street, with Slack scoring a hat-trick. Jimmy Thraves missed his train connection and turned up 35 minutes late for his debut against Mansfield Town, so his place in goal was taken by William 'Kiddy' Lowe, who conceded three times while waiting for the arrival of a very embarrassed Thraves. Lowe scored Fosse's consolation goal. Thraves made amends with 148 consecutive appearances for the Fosse and in the process became a club legend.

Two 4-0 wins away at Kettering and at home to Derby Junction led up to the first championship-of-Leicestershire game of the season. Loughborough's form leading up to the derby was patchy, winning two, losing two and drawing two. The highlight was a 6-0 slaughter of Mansfield Town the week before the eagerly awaited clash with Leicester on 12 November 1893. Fosse supporters turned up in their hundreds to Loughborough. In addition to the crowds who came by train, numerous horse-drawn, four-wheeled carriages conveyed Leicester people in the hope of seeing their team win.

Rain fell in the morning, making the ground very slippy. Although previous encounters between the Fosse and the Luffs had been 'rough-charging, bullying battles', this encounter was a display of scientific football, and so was as much in contrast to the old-time days as one can conceive. Sadly for the Fosse faithful the outcome was the same and they lost 2-1 to their arch rivals. Early exchanges were even until William Freestone scored for Loughborough. Slack should have equalised almost immediately but shot wide. Carnelley scored a second for the Luffs with a great strike. Fosse's shooting was poor, but just before the whistle sounded for half-time Slack pulled a goal back from a Dorrell cross. Play was fast and furious and end-to end, Loughborough having the best of the play and forcing Thraves into several outstanding saves. However, there was no doubt that Loughborough were the better team on the day – and hence still the champions of Leicestershire. For energy, individual skill, combination, and strategy they were more than one goal superior to the Fosse. Perhaps the Fosse were a little below par. But as with most games there were always lots of 'ifs' and 'buts'. 'If' Webb had only shot straight for goal as he should have done; 'if' the referee had ruled Loughborough's first goal offside, as many spectators thought, then the Fosse could have won the game. 'But' if any other Midland League goalkeeper but Traves had been in goal, Loughborough would surely have scored a bucketload.

Loughborough's season was dominated by their exploits in the FA Cup. They dispatched Riddings 8-1 at home in the first qualifying round in October, followed by a 3-1 home win over Heanor Town and then Kettering 2-1 away to reach the final qualifying round for the first time. Drawn away from home in front of 1,500 spectators, they demolished Buxton 6-0 in December 1892, played on a pitch covered in deep snow. The joy of Loughborough's fans reached new heights with the prospects of a Football League side appearing at the Athletic Grounds in the first round proper. Buxton won an appeal against the result due to the state of their own pitch. The game was replayed on New Year's Eve, the Luffs winning 3-0 the second time around.

By then Loughborough knew that their opponents would be Northwich Victoria of the Second Division. The first-round tie was a great spectacle on and off the pitch for the town of Loughborough. Although they lost 2-1, gate receipts were £94, and the 5,000 spectators were well looked after. Straw was placed along the touchline to keep feet dry and those lucky enough to be in the stand, which was opened for their first cup match of the season, had hot water bottles to keep them warm. Butterworth hit the bar for Loughborough after five minutes, then Northwich had a goal disallowed for offside, before Carnelley ran through and scored for the Luffs. The lead lasted just ten minutes, with Bradshaw equalising for Northwich with a soft shot. Bogged down by heavy ground, the second half was disappointing, with Drinkwater winning the tie for the Cheshire side.

Fosse's FA Cup run was unspectacular by comparison. Having beaten Rushden 7-0 and Notts Olympic 7-0 after a replay, they succumbed 2-1 to Buxton, who Loughborough demolished to reach the first round, at Walnut Street.

Fosse entertained their arch rivals in the reverse Midland League fixture in March 1892, in what local newspaper reporters described as 'one of the best games ever played in the Midland League'. The weather was bright but there was a keen wind. Loughborough had the best of an even game, Start scoring past Thraves in the first half. The Fosse made desperate efforts to equalise before losing the advantage of the wind, but Slack threw away their only real chance. Restarting, the Luffs had both the wind and sun in their favour, and for the first five minutes they attacked almost continuously. In a rare excursion, Start was given the ball and after a fast run he centred beautifully, Dorrell missed the ball, but Hardy with a crisp shot scored a magnificent goal. The Fosse fans went wild, cheering frantically, and thus encouraged, the Fosse made further onslaughts on their opponents' goal. Loughborough replied vigorously with Carnelley almost scoring with a low shot. The game became fast and wonderfully even. After a couple of unproductive corners in succession, their attack gradually weakened and the recently introduced strict training regime of the Fosse team began to tell. Playing with great dash and flair, Fosse's forwards kept the Luffs' defence actively employed, and they were more than up to the task. Urged on by their respective fans, both teams pressed hard but to no avail, the game ending 1-1.

The 1892/93 season ended with two further friendly derbies. The first, on 5 April 1893, was in front of 5,000 spectators at Loughborough. Playing with a strong sun in their faces, Loughborough made a gallant opening with Carnelley running through Fosse's backs and passing to Freestone who scored. The lead was doubled after 20 minutes when the Fosse backs bungled, allowing Carnelley to score a simple goal, and a second error by Smith within minutes enabled Freestone to add a third goal with a 'capital' shot. A foul against the Fosse near the Luffs' goal resulted in the ball travelling up the home left wing, Sharp centring, and Thraves clearing weakly to Farmer who shot home. Dorrell scored at the beginning of the second half. The Fosse, playing much better, pressed hard but repeatedly shot wide. The game ended with Loughborough winning 4-1.

An estimated 13,000 fans crammed into Walnut Street three weeks later in the final game of the season. Both teams suffered from absentees, Loughborough being without Kent and Culley, and Fosse were minus Atter as well as their captain Nuttall. A trial was given to J. Paton of Bolton Wanderers, but he had few chances to impress. The Luffs started as usual at a hot pace and played some pretty football. After Start hit a lightning shot just over the Loughborough crossbar, Sharpe and Freestone got down the field rapidly by good passing and Farmer scored with a high shot for the Luffs. Fosse drew level and before the interval gained the lead after splendid play from Henrys, Dorrell, and Slack. Both teams went at it like 'Trojans', after the interval, with the Fossils gradually wearing down their opponents and scoring twice more, including one from Paton, amid frantic cheering. Lowe sustained a nasty twist

THE MIDLAND LEAGUE YEARS

to one of his ankles and had to retire. Although down to ten men, Fosse more than held their own and after a period of high-quality combination football scored their fifth and final goal of a 5-1 victory.

The season was a great success for Loughborough. Not only did they become the first Leicestershire club to reach the first round of the FA Cup but they suffered just three defeats in the 24-game league campaign, two of which were against the champions Rotherham Town and runners-up Burton Wanderers, scoring 64 and conceding 30. The Fosse also had their best season to date, finishing five points and one place behind the Luffs in fourth place.

Buoyed by their growing reputation, Loughborough applied to join the Football League. Unfortunately, their application was rejected, with Liverpool and Woolwich Arsenal being successful instead. However, success had come at a cost. Loughborough's wage bill was £574 4s 7, with an overall loss of £138, which was not covered by the £119 profit from the lucrative Whit Tuesday Sports event. By comparison, the Fosse's balance sheet looked healthy. Total receipts had been £383 3s 11d, and the expenditure, including a two-guinea donation to the Infirmary Sports fund, amounted to £277 18s 7d, leaving a balance of £105 5s 4d, while they also had in hand for future use '£10 worth of fixtures, &c [an abbreviation for etc., commonly used at the time]'.

1893/94

During a Fosse executive meeting held at the Co-operative Hall, High Street, Leicester in September, to discuss football matters in general and Fosse's prospects before the commencement of the 1893/94 season, club president Mr Ashwell announced that they had been offered a place in the Second Division of the Football League. He said that he hoped to be in the Second Division next season, though they could not enter it for the forthcoming season, as they were committed to playing in the Midland League.

Significant improvements to the Walnut Street ground took place during the close-season. A new members' stand, with a frontage of 72 feet, open stands (two-tier) behind each goal, and a long slope bank along the full length of the '4d side' (east side), and 20 feet deep, rising at the back about five feet, and estimated to be able to accommodate 4,000 people. New exit gates were placed at the corner of Walnut Street, and a new thoroughfare for the public was constructed by the filling in of a hollow at the end of Filbert Street. During the summer, the ground was drained, but owing to the exceptionally dry season, the committee struggled to improve the quality of turf.

Loughborough strengthened their team with the acquisition of Harry Storer, reputedly the best goalkeeper in the Midland League, from Gainsborough Trinity, along with Walter 'Dolly' Rose and Samuel Mills from Derby County. Storer spent one year at Loughborough, missing just one game, having joined with club with his older brother William. He left in May 1894 to join Second Division side Woolwich Arsenal, before helping Liverpool to promotion in 1896 and to the First Division runners-up position in 1899, when he retired. Rose was a stalwart of the Luffs side that finished third and fourth in the Midland League and an ever-present in the club's first season in the Football League. Winger Mills, who had scored seven goals in 45

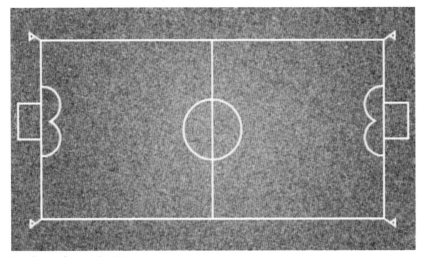

Pitch markings of 1891

Venue of Leicester Fosse's first-ever game, Fosse Road, Leicester. OS Map 1884.
Reproduced with the permission of the National Library of Scotland

Victoria Park, Leicester. OS Map 1884. Reproduced with the permission of the National Library of Scotland

Victoria Park (Racecourse) Pavilion

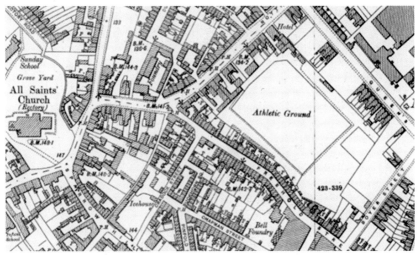

Athletic Grounds, Loughborough, 1888. Reproduced with the permission of the National Library of Scotland

Loughborough FC. One of the earliest known photos of a Leicestershire football team, taken in the mid-1870s. Reading from left to right: Hickling; Pickering; G. Bromhead; T. Mills; H. Perkins; W. Cockain; W. Wright; Jas. Cartwright; J. Tyler. Front row: T.B. Cartwright; A. Mounteney; H. North. It was probably taken to the rear of the Greyhound on the ground then known as 'Bromhead's' before a match. Note George Bromhead, third left, son of the owner John. Reproduced with the kind permission of Barry Wilford and Panda Eyes

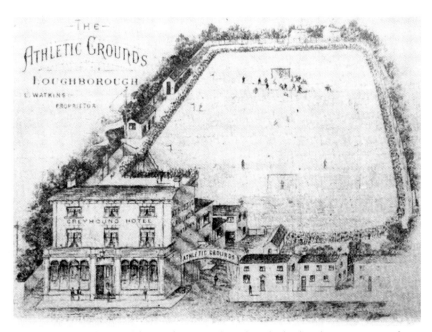

Athletic Grounds, Loughborough. Reproduced with the kind permission of Barry Wilford and Panda Eyes

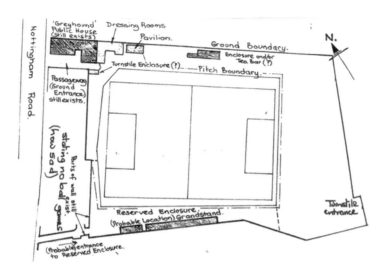

Plan of the Athletic Grounds drawn by Barry Wilford: 'The Athletic Grounds of Loughborough'. Reproduced with the kind permission of Barry Wilford and Panda Eyes

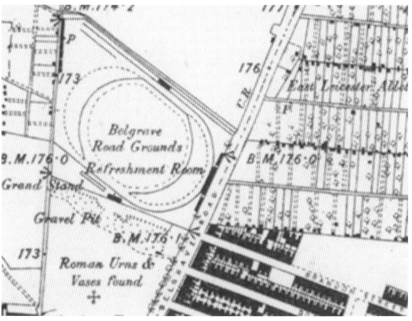

1880s map of Belgrave Road Cycle & Cricket Ground

Sheepshed Leicestershire Association Challenge Cup winning team 1888. Joe Bennett is on the left, second row, the man on his own in the middle is Kidger. Reproduced with the kind permission of John Bennett and family, Shepshed.

Loughborough Town Football Club,
winners of the Leicestershire Senior Cup, 1888-89.

Standing: J. Cooper (Hon. Sec.), G. Spiby, W. Coltman, W. Cockain (captain), W. Kellam, J. Smith
Seated: H. Griffin, C. H. Gadsby, L. Rodgers, F. Gibbs, F. W. Simpson, W. Gibson

Reproduced with the kind permission of Barry Wilford and Panda Eyes

*1893/94 Back row: Walter Cockain (Hon. Sec.), Stokes, Mills, Carnelley,
Weightman, Sharpe, Will. Cockain (Trainer). Middle row: O. Farmer, J. Plackett,
W. Storer, H. Storer. Front row: W. Ross, V. Smith.* Reproduced with the kind
permission of Barry Wilford and Panda

In Loving Remembrance of the

Loughbro' Town F.C.

Played to death on Walnut-st. Ground by Leicester Fosse,

On Saturday, March the 28th, 1893,

INTERRED IN LEICESTER CEMETERY.

Good-bye Poor Loughbro' for this year!
In next year's League you shall again appear;
You have strove your utmost the Fosse to expel,
But they have beat you quite easy, you know, very well.

Football Funeral Card: This card belonged to Sam Bailey who played for the Fosse and lived in Loughborough. He had altered the match date on the card from the original '18' to '28' for some unknown reason. The sale of funeral cards commemorating the demise of an opponent became a major trend at football matches throughout much of the 1890s. Reproduced with the kind permission of Malcolm Bailey, Sam's grandson

WALNUT ST. GROUND.

ENGLISH CUP TIE. COMPETITION PROPER.

SATURDAY, JAN. 27th, at 2.30 p.m.,

FOSSE v. SOUTH SHORE.

Admission 6d. Enclosure 6d. extra. Members' Stand 1/6.

The Wyvern, 26 January 1894. Reproduced with the kind permission of Barry Wilford and Panda Eyes

Loughborough v Woolwich Arsenal. Reproduced with the kind permission of Barry Wilford and Panda Eyes

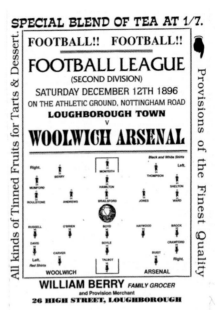

Loughborough Athletic & Football Club Football League Division Two 1897/98 Top row: L-R: H. Dunn (Secretary), Clifford, Hardy, Mumford, F. Stenson (Committee), F Bailey, G Mee (Trainer). Middle row: L-R: W. Johnson (Committee), J. W. Clarke (Committee), Parry, Hodgkinson, Roulstone, S. Elliott (Committee), F. Fearn (Committee). Bottom row: L-R: Parker, Pegg, Keech, Culley and Pike. Reproduced with the kind permission of Barry Wilford and Panda Eyes league games with Derby, had a reputation for charging goalkeepers, which was either reckless or brave behaviour.

Fosse players commenced pre-season practice every Tuesday and Thursday evening from 6pm at the Walnut Street ground from 19 August. Two practice matches took place, while Fosse were granted a bye in the preliminary round of the FA Cup and arranged to meet Northwich Victoria, conquerors of Loughborough, on the date of the bye. The committee were confident of a 'prosperous' season and believed that the current side was 'far ahead of any they had placed on the football field'.

Local lovers of football were very enthusiastic as evidenced by the several hundred fans who turned out on 24 August to watch Loughborough's first team take on the second team in a practice match at the Athletic Grounds ending 7-2 to the first team.

The first derby of the season was staged at the Athletic Grounds on 7 October 1893. Both sides were in good form. Loughborough, playing in their new strip of black-and-white shirts and blue shorts, started the 1893/94 season on 2 September at Mansfield with a creditable 3-3 draw, with Carnelley scoring a brace. The Luffs then drew two and won one of their next three games before the eagerly anticipated clash. The Fosse, having lost their season's opener 2-1 at home to Burton Wanderers, beat Long Eaton Rangers, also at home, and drew away at Gainsborough Trinity before travelling to the Athletics Ground.

Both sides left no stone unturned to put their men on the field in the peak of condition for the meeting of Leicestershire's footballing giants. Fosse's training had been significantly enhanced, with long walks and runs being the order for the week leading up to the game. Worrall was doubtful for the Fosse due to an ankle injury sustained at Notts County, while Dorrell was not in the best of health. The Fosse executive were not entirely satisfied with the forwards, transferring Seymour from half-back to partner Dorrell to give greater weight and power up front. Harry Taylor, who had performed so well the previous season, filled the vacancy alongside Arthur Henrys.

The Luffs' defence was weakened by Coulton's leg injury sustained at Long Eaton the previous week. His place was taken by George Spiby, who had played in all the matches against the Fosse the previous year. A new stand at the Athletic Grounds, accommodating nearly 1,000 spectators, was completed especially for the game. The admission charge to the new stand was a whopping 2s 6d!

Heavily packed excursions ran from Leicester, and when the game commenced, the Athletic Grounds presented a most animated appearance. Right up to the time when the players entered the field of play, people swarmed into the ground. When the game finally kicked off, nearly 30 minutes late due to the delayed arrival of the 'Fosse special', there were at least 9,000 fans present, and this number greatly increased later on. Although there is no accurate data, the crowd is thought to have exceeded 10,000, and was certainly the highest ever for a Loughborough home game.

The weather was fine, with the autumnal sun shining directly across the ground from the town side. Fosse chose to defend the Nottingham Road end after winning the toss. Farmer, appearing for the first time as captain of Loughborough, kicked off and immediately Mills scored a goal, but it was ruled offside. After a period of intense pressing by the Fosse, Loughborough broke away down the left and forced a corner. The flag kick resulted in a 'bully' in front of goal, from which a judicious pass to Mills, who was clearly offside, led to him scoring with a lovely shot off the underside of the crossbar. The referee disallowed the goal.

Unfortunately for the Fosse, they essentially went down to ten men midway through the first half as Worrall, scarcely in a fit condition to play, was limping badly. A round of passing between the Fosse attacking division left Seymour in possession close in on goal. He sent in a stinging shot at Harry Storer, who with one hand saved in a manner nothing short of marvellous. Both goalkeepers were called upon to make save after save in a fine display of end-to-end football.

In the second half play was fast and furious, with the game full of exciting incidents and the old rivals displaying all the energy they could muster. For many minutes both goals appeared certain to be broken, as each defence took it in turns to escape, invariably by long kicking.

Luffs' star player William Storer, brother of goalkeeper Harry, opened the scoring 25 minutes into the second half with an excellent 'dropping shot', giving Thraves no chance. The home fans went wild with excitement with wave after wave of deafening cheering and applause. In their endeavour to equalise, Fosse did not appear to care as to the means employed, for a wholly unnecessary bout of 'vigour' was imported into the play, which was penalised by the referee. Loughborough bought William Storer back to strengthen the defence as the Fosse probed and pressed. The final whistle was greeted with a huge cheer as the

Luffs fans excitedly made their way home. News of the result was anxiously awaited in Leicester by large groups assembling where telegrams were expected and as one of the local newspapers reported, 'It is safe to state that at no time in the history of pastime has a match caused so much excitement in the district or commanded such attention.'

This would be the last time Fosse fans would suffer disappointment at the hands of their arch rivals, apart from in an essentially meaningless friendly. The championship of Leicestershire would reside at Walnut Street from now onwards. However, we are getting ahead of ourselves; that is all waiting for us in the future. This victory launched Loughborough on a great run of results, including a 6-0 thrashing of Long Eaton Rangers, that saw them go top of the Midland League by the middle of December. Fans flocked to the Athletic Grounds with 3,000 for the league game against Burton Wanderers and over 10,000 for a friendly against Middlesbrough Ironopolis of the Football League Second Division (gate receipts £170). But the Fosse ended their title aspirations on 6 January 1894, just two weeks after knocking the Luffs out of the FA Cup (see Chapter 4 for further details). For several days, the game was in doubt due to the severe weather. Although more fit for 'snowballs than football', the referee deemed the ground playable, after the snow had been cleared off the pitch on the morning of the game.

Fosse fielded their full-strength side, but the Luffs were in a parlous state. The back line in particular was weak with the long-term absences of Coulton and Kent, who had sustained a broken leg in an earlier cup encounter with the Fosse. Val Smith was called from half-back to fill Kent's place, and Culley was parachuted in from the reserves into the half-back line, while the forward line was shuffled.

Notwithstanding the extremely cold weather, every part of the ground was fully occupied, and there could be no doubt as to the intense interest taken in the match. Special trains bought an enthusiastic travelling support for the Luffs and excitement among the immense crowd ran high from start to finish. The players were repeatedly cheered by the 8,000 spectators as they ran on to the field of play. There was a slight wind blowing from the town end, which Loughborough had the advantage of in the first half. Although players from both sides struggled to control their movements given the conditions, Dorrell and Hill ran the show up front for the Fosse, with Brown shooting just wide. The Luffs went on their first sustained attack and Mills, up the right wing, was so far offside in scoring that Thraves made no serious attempt to stop the ball. Mills raised a cheer among the Luffs faithful at this feat, but their tune was altered when the referee gave a free kick.

On 15 minutes the little right-winger Hill dribbled beautifully down the centre of the field, and well into Loughborough territory he passed to Dorrell, who tricked his way past all of the backs before running in on goal and banging the ball into the back of the net. The enthusiasm of the crowd knew no bounds with round after round of 'tremendous' applause greeting the goal. Hill went on to score an 'easy' goal and Brown netted from a Dorrell cross before half-time.

Exchanges in the second half were even for a little time but Fosse further extended their lead when Lord followed the ball into the mouth of the goal, and with a soft shot sent the ball straight through the hands Harry Storer. This calamity provoked great shouts of 'Pile it on, Fosse!' from various parts of the ground. The quick, short passing and ready understanding of each other's play gave the Fosse halves and forwards an immense advantage and being backed up by a defence of the safest type, they simply outplayed the Luffs in all aspects of the game.

In the earlier stages, Loughborough did well considering their depleted forces, for although it was noticeable from the outset that Val Smith made a poor substitute for the injured Kent, the others played so well to begin with that hopes were high for a closely contested game. However, discouraged by a palpable offside and Fosse's first goal, the Loughborough feel to pieces. Spasmodic efforts were made by individual players but there was an entire absence of that concerted action which had been such a prominent feature of Luffs teams in previous Leicestershire derby day matches.

Buoyed by their victory over their north Leicestershire rivals, Leicester finished runners-up in the Midland League, three points behind champions, Burton Wanderers and two points ahead of the Luffs in third place.

Matches between the Fosse and the Luffs lingered on in the memories of supporters decades later, as evidenced by a letter from F.G. Hartshorn of Hinckley in the *Leicester Mail* on 20 December 1947:

'Noel Tarbotton's history, "From Fosse to City", recalls reminiscences of one's boyhood days. Last Thursday's article brought recollections of travelling across Leicester with my brothers from Berners Street to the then Walnut Street ground to see the Fosse play. I remember the keen rivalry when Loughborough Town came to Leicester, as following the game there generally came a parody of a popular song of the day. One went something like this:

Strolling round the ground. when Fosse played
Loughborough Town.
Oh the game it was a treat, the Loughborough chaps were
fairly beat.
Four goals were scored by Dorrell, Miller and Brown,
Wasn't that a pasting for the poor old
Loughborough Town?

'Another one comes partly to mind:

After the ball was started, attar the whistle blew.
After the ball was passed to Mill, Dorrell banged
it through.
Many a sigh was uttered, by the Loughborough men.
Many a heart seemed to vanish after the ball.

'Thanking you for taking us back to the early days of the Fosse.'

Loughborough, meanwhile, achieved an almost legendary feat of football prowess by beating Aston Villa in the Birmingham Cup on 10 March 1894 at the Athletic Grounds. That season Loughborough had entered for the FA Cup, the Bass Charity Cup and the Birmingham Cup competitions, much of the success in securing their entry to the latter being due to the efforts of Walter Cockain, licensee of The Stag and Pheasant. Famous teams taking part included Small Heath, Aston Villa and West Bromwich Albion.

At this time, the Villains were leaders of the First Division and over 6,000 spectators thronged to the enclosure. The report in the *Loughborough Echo* read, 'As Aston Villa trotted into the gaze of the spectators there seemed to be about them an air of victory, an easy carriage that never dreamt of defeat, a condescension, in fact, that they, the champions of England, should come to show their form in thrashing a village team.'

With one goal each at the interval, the second half provided no additional scoring, and with ten minutes to go in the extra half hour, Carnelley 'bags the ball into the net at a terrific speed'. The report added, 'Carnelley, who was an international player, always played in his cap. It is known and recorded that when Carnelley, who was the hero of the hour, removed his cap, a goal was a certainty, and that is what happened!'

Villa went on to win the First Division championship for 1893/94. This result was hailed as a famous victory and the public houses of the town that night, with beer at 3d and 2.5d per pint, were full to over-flowing. The report concludes, 'I won't say that the better team won, but I can truthfully say that the losing team were downright beaten after trying all they knew to win and exerting every effort to make a draw.'

There is a story told about this match to the effect that Aston Villa were so confident of beating Loughborough that when they were passing through Trent Junction on the train, one of the players poked his head out of the carriage window and shouted to a porter, 'Hey, where's Loughborough?' On the return of the team through Trent Junction, the same porter was on duty and, noticing the players sitting rather disconsolately in their carriage, he shouted, 'Hey, you know where Loughborough is now, don't you!'

Loughborough went on to lose 6-1 to West Bromwich Albion in the semi-final, and towards the end of the season they had a dispute with the Football League that would prove to be costly. The conflict rose after the Luffs had signed several Football League players to take the places of their star players poached by Football League clubs. Goalkeeper Harry Storer and star striker Albert Carnelley were taken from the Luffs by Woolwich Arsenal and Nottingham Forest respectively, without the club's permission or payment. This was not illegal. Football League rulings at the time stated that clubs were not obliged to pay a transfer fee to non-league clubs, although Midland League clubs wishing to acquire a Football League player had to pay a fee. The Loughborough committee decided to take revenge against the ruling by signing Walter C. Rose, George Swift and Robert Edge from Wolverhampton, John Berry from Burton Swifts and Charles Booth from Woolwich Arsenal, without paying a fee.

After applying a second time for permission to join the Second Division, the Loughborough committee decided to boost their chances by sending out a circular to Football League clubs outlining the composition of their team and asking for their support. The Wolverhampton Wanderers' secretary replied, complaining that Loughborough had engaged four of their players and stating that it would be in Loughborough's best interest to meet him in Manchester on a particular day. Mr Thompson, a Loughborough committee member, met him at the stated place only to find that he was accompanied by several other officials from

Football League clubs. The Wolverhampton official asked, 'What are you to pay for these men you have taken from us?' to which Mr Thompson replied, 'Not a copper.'

Another official challenged the right of Loughborough for the engagement of 'Dolly' Rose, who had played all season. Questions were fired so fast that the Loughborough man asked for them to take turns. The secretary of Wolverhampton Wanderers, since he had the most serious complaint, went first and Mr Thompson asked at once what he wanted. To that, the Wolverhampton man replied, 'You won't get into the league if you don't pay for these men.' After a bit of beating about the bush, he demanded a certain sum for the players Loughborough had signed from Wolverhampton, but Mr Thompson would not concede a single inch.

Loughborough, in light of these threats, communicated with both the chairman and secretary of the Football League, but neither responded. Subsequently Wolverhampton wrote asking for a delegation from Loughborough to meet the Football League in conference, but after extensive discussions the Luffs committee replied that unless they stated in writing what they definitely wanted they could not see their way to meeting them. No reply came. Refusal to pay Wolverhampton cost Loughborough heavily and maybe marked the beginning of the end for the north Leicestershire club.

Accrington, Blackpool, Bury, Burton Wanderers, Manchester City and Rotherham sought election to the Second Division along with Leicester Fosse and Loughborough. The delegates of each team were called into the meeting room. Accrington stated that Sunderland knocked them out of the FA Cup, and Bolton Wanderers out of the Lancashire Cup; they had got a new ground, and were taking in new players in place of those who had played roughly in the past. Bury pointed out that they had a good ground, had won the championship of the Lancashire Palatine League and had held their own against Football League clubs they had met. Blackpool highlighted that they had been runners-up twice and won the Lancashire Palatine League championship once. Burton Wanderers declared that they were an old team – 22 years – and had not lost a match in the Midland League, and were knocked out of the FA Cup by the ultimate winners.

Leicester Fosse, meanwhile, communicated their good record, and good gates, the Derby County cup tie for example bringing in over £430. Loughborough were not represented, but their application pointed out that they were centrally located, had outstanding facilities, a good team, and had recently beaten Aston Villa in the Birmingham Cup. Manchester City reported that they were a new company; shares worth £600 had been taken up, and a further £1,200 would be taken up if they were admitted to the Football League. They had taken over the Ardwick football ground and stands, and had advertised for players, and if elected they would do their best to keep up the prestige of the competition.

Rotherham Town lamented the bad luck they had suffered during the season. Rossendale, through their representation, thought that if elected they would be able to account for most of the Second Division teams.

Voting was then taken without any comment on the individual applications, and the result was as follows:

Manchester City 20 votes; Leicester Fosse 20; Bury 17; Burton Wanderers 17. Loughborough, not surprisingly, were not successful, although they received more votes (13) than many expected. Leicester Fosse and Manchester City were duly elected, while the Loughborough committee were devastated.

To rub salt into the wound, all Football League clubs were forbidden to arrange fixtures with Loughborough until the 'dispute' had been dealt with. This meant that the lucrative fixture with the Fosse arranged for Fairs Saturday could not take place, disappointing not just both clubs' committees but also the thousands of fans in both towns for whom derby day matches meant so much. Luckily for both sets of fans, the clubs would be drawn together in the FA Cup in what would turn out to be an epic encounter.

Luffs were lucky not to be thrown out of the Midland League. At its AGM held on 28 May 1894 in Derby, Burton Wanderers and Leicester Fosse tendered their resignations after gaining admission to the Football League, which were formally accepted. Newark, Mansfield, Gainsborough were re-elected members after retiring (in accordance with the rules) after finishing in the bottom four places in the competition. Applications to fill the vacancies were received from Heanor, Derby Town, Ilkeston, Matlock and Rushden, and all five were elected, with the result that the membership was raised to 13 clubs. At the end of the meeting a lengthly discussion took place regarding Loughborough's conduct, as they were alleged to have been playing 'fast and loose' with the Midland League. Proof was given that they had applied for admission to the 'Senior League' on two occasions, and once the doors were closed to them, Loughborough had fallen back on the Midland League. Although this conduct made them liable to expulsion, they were let off on this occasion with a vote of censure.

Although the 1893/94 season had been the best in the Loughborough's history, it had come at a cost, with a financial loss of £258 4s 7d (compared with £110 the previous year), even though gate receipts almost doubled, and subscriptions had significantly increased. Expenditure amounted to £1,691 9s 2d, which included a deficit at the commencement of the year of £137 6s 7d; players' wages were £832 18s; travelling expenses came to £105 10s 11d; dinners and refreshments were £35 9s 11d, and guarantees to visiting clubs reached £321 19s 9d.

The Fosse were in a much better financial state and clearly ready for life in the Football League. Their income for the season was £2,907 11s 2d, of which the vast majority came from gate receipts, which realised £2,669 7s 1d – the principal sums included £436 4s for the Derby County friendly, £286 1s 6d against South Shore and £117 1s 6d for the Midland League encounter with the Luffs. Players' wages were £964 2s 2d. After taking into account ground expenses, transfers, and policing, there was a surplus of £185 15s 2d, which was accounted for by the construction of the new stands and the acquisition of plant. The fixed assets of the club were valued at £629 13s 10d.

4

Football League Encounters

THE FOOTBALL LEAGUE was the brainchild of William McGregor. The draper moved to Birmingham from Scotland in 1870 after completing his apprenticeship, and became involved with local club Aston Villa, who played at Aston Park, close to his business premises. His interest in Villa stemmed from the large Scottish contingent playing for the club, their exciting playing style and the club's link to a Methodist chapel. During his long association with Villa, the devout Christian helped secure their finances and was instrumental in establishing them as one of the leading clubs in England. In 1888, frustrated by the regular cancellation of Villa's matches, McGregor sent the following letter to four other clubs on 2 March 1888, which led to the formation of the world's first league football competition:

> 'Every year it is becoming more and more difficult for football clubs of any standing to meet their friendly engagements and even arrange friendly matches. The consequence is that at the last

moment, through cup-tie interference, clubs are compelled to take on teams who will not attract the public.

I beg to tender the following suggestion as a means of getting over the difficulty: that ten or 12 of the most prominent clubs in England combine to arrange home and away fixtures each season, the said fixtures to be arranged at a friendly conference about the same time as the International Conference.

This combination might be known as the Association Football Union and could be managed by representatives from each club. Of course, this is in no way to interfere with the National Association; even the suggested matches might be played under cup-tie rules. However, this is a detail.

My object in writing to you at present is merely to draw your attention to the subject, and to suggest a friendly conference to discuss the matter more fully. I would take it as a favour if you would kindly think the matter over and make whatever suggestions you deem necessary. I am only writing to the following – Blackburn Rovers, Bolton Wanderers, Preston North End, West Bromwich Albion, and Aston Villa, and would like to hear what other clubs you would suggest.'

McGregor went on to suggest Friday, 23 March 1888 as the date for the conference, which was to take place at Anderton's Hotel in London. That date was deliberately chosen as it was the day before the FA Cup Final between

West Bromwich Albion and Preston North End. The name 'The Football League' was agreed at a further meeting on 17 April at Manchester's Royal Hotel, and the inaugural season kicked off on 8 September 1888 with 12 member clubs – six from the Midlands and six from the north of England: Accrington, Aston Villa, Blackburn, Bolton, Burnley, Derby County, Everton, Notts County, Preston North End, Stoke, West Bromwich Albion and Wolverhampton Wanderers.

The Football League was limited to 12 clubs, mainly because of the number of available Saturdays for fixtures without encroaching too much on summer sports. It was not until mid-November, with the season well under way, that a system of two points for a win and one for a draw was adopted. An alternative approach considered was simply to award one point for a win.

Interestingly, out of the five games played on the opening day, only one kicked off at 3pm. Although teams often arrived late, and incorrect scores were recorded, the first season was an incredible success, with Preston North End – the 'Invincibles' – winning both the FA Cup and the inaugural Football League championship. They won 18, drew four, and lost none out of their 22 matches. A second tier was formed in 1892/93 by absorbing the rival competition, the Football Alliance. The original members were Ardwick (now Manchester City), Bootle, Burton Swifts, Crewe Alexandra, Darwen, Grimsby Town, Lincoln City, Northwich Victoria, Port Vale, Sheffield United, Small Heath (now Birmingham City), and Walsall. Relegation and promotion between the two divisions were determined by end-of-season Test Matches. Similar to the current play-off system, they involved the top sides of the Second

Division against the bottom sides of the First Division. Football League rules also allowed direct election of clubs into the First Division. The last club to benefit from this were Arsenal in March 1919.

1894/95

Fosse's preparations for life in the Football League began before the news of their successful election to the Second Division was formally announced. The Walnut Street ground was further developed by increasing the standing capacity by 5,000. Some 1,000 tonnes of soil had been banked up along the Aylestone Road side and the new area afforded great convenience for spectators when the covered stand was crowded. Admission for Football League fixtures varied from 6d on the banked-up side to 1s 6d in the main stand. The minimum admission was reduced in March 1895 to 4d in support of the town's boot and shoe workers, who had been 'locked out'. The turf was also in the best condition it had ever been thanks to Leicester's groundsman and goalkeeper, Jimmy Thraves. Several hundred yards of new turf had been laid. Taking a lesson from the dry weather of the previous season, a well was sunk, and piping was purchased to ensure there was sufficient water for the whole ground.

The greatest alteration from the previous year's XI was in the forward ranks, and the quintet were according to the Fosse committee, 'The heaviest and trickiest lot that ever donned the Fosse colours.' Club vice-president J.J. Curtis, at the half-yearly meeting of the Fosse committee, also made the following plea to fans, 'Not to cross the pitch, and thereby show some regard to the condition of the ground,' and added, 'If they found the team was not as successful as they anticipated or wished them to be, not to discourage or jeer the players, but continue their support of a team playing a sportsmanlike and gentlemanly game and keeping up the character of the 11 on and off the field, and, by placing the utmost confidence in the men, helping the club to attain a prominent place in the second division chart.'

Excitement was high within the town, with pre-season practice matches attracting several thousand spectators. Leicester Fosse played in white shirts, with dark blue knickers and socks for their inaugural season in the Football League, the same strip that they had worn since 1892. They were also required by the Football League to register reserve colours – black-and-white quarters, 'after the same pattern, not the colours as other clubs in the Football League'.

The mayor of Grimsby kicked off Fosse's first Football League fixture, at Grimsby Town's Abbey Park ground, on 1 September 1894, in front of 4,000 spectators. Fosse's side that day included four Scots in Jimmy Brown, Jack Hill, Willie McArthur and David Skea, four former Middlesbrough Ironopolis players in Archie Hughes, McArthur, Seymour and Hill, and Leicestershire-born duo Harry Bailey and James Priestman. Hughes and Skea were making their Fosse debuts.

Goalkeeper Thraves, signed in 1892 from Notts County, was an ever-present in Leicester's inaugural Football League campaign. He went on to play 148 games for the club. Hard-hitting Leicestershire County Cricket club player Harry Bailey made over 100 appearances for the Fosse, before running several public houses, including the Belgravia Hotel on Spinney Hill, and the Crown and

Anchor on Belgrave Gate. Jimmy Brown, aged 25, was the club captain. Tom Seymour and Nottingham-born Arthur Henrys were Leicester's oldest players at the age of 28. Henrys had two spells at Newton Heath (now Manchester United) before moving to the Fosse and was a member of Gainsborough Trinity's Midland League championship side as an outside-left, but also played at left-back throughout Fosse's first campaign in the Second Division. Later he became club captain and towards the end of his time with the Fosse he was suspended several times for 'alcohol-related' offences, before finishing his playing career with Notts County.

Fosse's playmaker was Hughes, who played in an FA Cup Final with Bolton Wanderers. However, Hughes's stay in Leicester was cut short due to poor discipline after he had twice been suspended by the club. Signed from Bury in 1894, 23-year-old David Skea played in Fosse's first two seasons in the Football League, scoring an impressive 37 goals in 52 games before leaving to join Swindon. The star striker went into the record books as the scorer of Fosse's first Football League goal, hit a hat-trick in Fosse's first Football League home game against Rotherham and ended the season as the top scorer with 23 Second Division goals (31 from 35 games in all competitions). Skea also scored in his first four Football League games for Leicester, which remains a club record.

Willie McArthur, Skea's main strike partner, finished the season as Fosse's second-top scorer with 16 Football League goals (22 from 25 games in all competitions). Before leaving to join Dundee, McArthur would score 36 Football League goals in 65 games. Versatile reserve striker James

Priestman played 15 games in total, eight of which were in the Football League, and scored five goals.

Having gone behind after just seven minutes to Grimsby, the Fosse eventually lost the game 4-3, with Skea (two) and McArthur scoring their goals. Press coverage, which was extensive, was generally favourable. Several hundred Fosse fans had made the trip to the Lincolnshire coast.

Fosse's first victory in the Football League came the following week at home, David Skea scoring a hat-trick in the 4-2 defeat of Rotherham. Four consecutive defeats followed and then in the first qualifying round of the FA Cup the Fosse humiliated Notts Olympic 13-0, still a club-record score. William Miller, acquired from Bolton in 1893, and McArthur both scored four and Skea claimed his second hat-trick. The following week at home to Newcastle, Leicester staged a remarkable recovery, coming back from 4-0 down to claim a point. If Miller had not missed Leicester's first penalty awarded in the Football League, then they would have claimed both points. Inspired, the Fosse went on a five-match unbeaten run, which included a 5-1 win over local rivals Notts County at Walnut Street. More than 6,000 spectators witnessed the game and the club's first successful penalty by Skea, in yet another hat-trick performance.

Much to the annoyance of the Football League, Loughborough, still banned from playing teams from the top two tiers of English football, were drawn against Leicester Fosse in the final qualifying round of the FA Cup. Contested over three epic clashes in December, Fosse eventually emerged as victors, only to be knocked out of the competition after a 4-1 defeat to Bury in the next round. Christmas was ruined when Bury beat Fosse by that same scoreline, but that was quickly forgotten when the new year started with a bang, thanks to a a 9-1 home destruction of Walsall Town Swifts – Skea only managing to hit the back of the net twice.

Two weeks later the Fosse found themselves on the wrong end of an eight-goal drubbing at the hands of Darwen at Barley Bank in a farcical encounter. Originally the home of Darwen Cricket Club, football was played on a pitch in the north-west corner of the Barley Bank ground. Spectator facilities included a covered 1,200-seat stand on the western touchline, with an embankment running the remainder of the length of the pitch on that side. During the football season, a temporary stand was erected on the eastern side of the pitch, with tents in the south-east corner of the ground used for dressing rooms. The first fixture with Darwen on 30 December was abandoned after just two minutes when the referee declared it impossible to play a league match after the goal posts had been blown down by a raging gale. Darwen won a 50-minute friendly 'that amused' the 1,000 or so spectators 6-0. The rearranged game took place on a Tuesday, Darwen's weekly half-day holiday. The Fosse left Leicester railway station at 7.22am. On arrival in Darwen, they found that the pitch was in an awful condition, being covered with half-melted ice, sand, snow, and slush. One end of the field was totally unfit for play, and the usual pitch was under water, so the goal posts were erected on the cricket ground and a pitch was hurriedly marked out. The referee, for some inexplicable reason, deemed it fit for a league game. To add to the discomfort of players and spectators alike, a persistent drizzle commenced as soon as the teams arrived on the field of play.

Fewer than 1,000 spectators braved the inhospitable weather. Fosse won the toss and decided to defend the 'dirty' end first. Darwen quickly acclimatised to the treacherous conditions, adopting a long ball game and through the use of swathes of felt wrapped around their boots were able to cope much better with the mud, sand and puddles than the Fosse players, who struggled to keep upright. By half-time, Fosse had conceded seven, and even the ever-reliable Thraves could not deal with the slippery conditions. In the second half, Fosse abandoned their short passing game and started to hoof the ball as far forward as possible. When the game ended, much to the relief of everyone concerned, the score was Darwen 8 Fosse 2. Apart from this blip, the Fosse coped well with life in the Football League and were unbeaten in their last 13 games of the season, finishing the season in a very creditable fourth place with 38 points from 30 games. They had the same points as, but an inferior goal average to, Newton Heath, who qualified for the end-of-season Test Matches. Walnut Street staged the final Test, between Second Division runners-up Notts County, and Derby County, who had finished bottom of the First Division. Derby won 2-1 to maintain their place in the top flight of English football.

The Leicestershire clubs also met in the semi-final of the Kettering Challenge Cup, on 11 March 1895. At Kettering Town's North Street ground, the Fosse won 3-1 in front of 2,000 spectators. Seven minutes after the start Brown scored for the Fosse from a free kick, but just two minutes later Owen equalised. In the second half, both sides wasted opportunities in an end-to-end encounter, and Leicester scored two goals just on the call of time to win 3-1 and go on to face Burton Wanderers in the final. The kick-off was arranged for 4.30pm and the Fosse team and supporters left Leicester on the 2.25pm train. In dazzling sunshine, Burton took the lead just less than a minute before half-time following a combined rush by the Wanderers' forwards ending in a grand shot by Arthur Capes. In a hard-fought encounter, endeavours by the Fosse to get on even terms were effectively frustrated by Burton's compact and well-organised defence and in the end the Leicester men suffered defeat by the smallest possible margin. Burton Wanderers were also Fosse's opponents in yet another final, the Bass Vase, which sadly the Leicester side also lost.

Admission to the Football League had come at a financial cost as Fosse recorded a £200 loss for the season. Gate receipts were £2,587 9s, while wages had increased almost 50 per cent on the previous season to £434 9s 10d.

The Loughborough committee felt they had no option but to spend, spend, spend to achieve Football League status. The appointment of a full-time trainer, John Jackson, and the acquisition of a new squad of players paid immediate dividends as Loughborough won the Midland League title in 1895 in style, finishing seven points clear of runners-up Stoke Swifts. They only lost three games, the first in April after going 17 unbeaten, and the other two came in the last two matches of the season after clinching the championship.

Loughborough scored 84 goals, which included eight against Newark, seven against Matlock, Rushden, and Ilkeston, and six in consecutive games against Rushden away and Doncaster Rovers at home. Robert Edge, one of the infamous 'Wolverhampton four', was Luffs' top scorer with a near goal-a-game record, before returning to Molineux ahead of the end of the season.

Gaining 18 votes, Loughborough Town were duly elected to the Football League, where they replaced Walsall Town Swifts. Leicestershire 'derby days' from now on would be in the Second Division. Loughborough were formally crowned Midland League champions at the 28th annual sports day, held on 2 June 1895 at the Athletic Grounds, before a large gathering. There was a huge cheer as club president Mr J.E. Johnson-Ferguson, MP for the Loughborough division, unfurled the flag after it was ceremonially presented to him by Mr A. Kingscott, of Derby, secretary of the Midland League. Success, however, came at a cost as the Fosse had also discovered. Unfortunately Loughborough's deficit was huge and would eventually strangle the club to a premature death.

Loughborough made a loss of £258 4s 4d in 1893/94, against £110 the previous season. Unfortunate injuries to Kent and Coulton, and several other players, resulted in an additional expenditure of nearly £100. Players' wages and travel expenses had increased by £294 to £938 1s 16s, mainly as a direct result of having to sign fresh players to take the place of those injured, and a large proportion of the players not residing in Loughborough.

FA Cup Encounters

While friendlies and league encounters were exciting, FA Cup battles between the Leicestershire clubs were the games that fired passion in both sets of supporters. Loughborough became the first Leicestershire side to compete in the FA Cup when they played Derby St Luke's at the Athletic Grounds on 26 October 1889, in the second qualifying round, after being granted a bye at the first stage.

Loughborough won 2-1 thanks to goals by Coltman and Simpson. However, the 'Saints' lodged a protest against the Loughborough goalkeeper, Bosonworth, who they stated was ineligible. The Football Association upheld the protest and ordered the game to be replayed two weeks later. St Luke's beat the Luffs, minus Bosonworth, 2-0.

The Fosse, meanwhile, made their first FA Cup appearance against Burton Wanderers a year later, losing 4-0 to the Derbyshire side at Mill Lane on 4 October 1890. On the same day, the Luffs recorded their first FA Cup victory, beating Derby Midland 3-2 at home. That season they thrashed Burton Wanderers, Fosse's conquerors, 8-1 and beat Belper Town 5-2 to set up a tie against the mighty Sheffield United. This match was drawn to be played at the Athletic Grounds, but was switched to Bramall Lane after a cash inducement was offered to the Luffs. Belper, having been drawn at home in the previous round, also agreed to play at the Athletic Grounds for cash. The Blades outclassed the Luffs and beat them 6-1 in a one-sided encounter.

The following season, the Luffs played their reserve side in the third qualifying round against Brierley Hill Alliance as the tie clashed with the Midland League game against the Fosse. The Luffs were slaughtered 7-0, while the Fosse, playing at Aylestone Road, were knocked out 6-2 by Small Heath. In the 1892/93 season, Loughborough reached the first round, where they lost 2-1 at home to Northwich Victoria in front of 5,000 fans. That same season, Fosse disposed of Rushden and Notts Olympic, the latter after a replay, before being knocked out at home by Buxton in the third qualifying round.

A large crowd congregated outside the Fosse headquarters on the Aylestone Road on Thursday 7 December 1893 to await news of the draw for the final qualifying round. Leicester had beaten two Mansfield sides, 'Town' and 'Greenlaugh' (named after a cotton mill). When the telegram from Mr T.S. Ashmole was posted up announcing that the Fosse were drawn to play at Loughborough, who had beaten Kettering, Newark, and Rushden, all at the Athletic Grounds, the local press reported that the draw generated genuine disappointment. Presumably, the Leicester committee were hoping for an easier passage into the next round.

Both teams put in extra training for the match. Loughborough players had undergone a week of 'thorough training' for the 'great fight'. The club committee offered a £1 per player win bonus. All the players apart from Mills and Rose, who were unable to leave their employment, were in residence at the Stag and Pheasant, the house of the trainer William Cockain, who was 'unremitting in his attention to his men'. On the Monday before the game, Harry Storer, Kent, Spiby, Plackett, Smith, Sharpe, Carnelley, Farmer, William Storer and Culley had a good run around the outskirts of Loughborough accompanied by their trainer. They ran as far as Rempstone, a distance of about six miles. On the Tuesday, the players started soon after nine o'clock for Nanpantan, but the men were not out exceptionally long due to the heavy rain and spent the rest of the day indoors. Training was not neglected as gymnastic exercises were entered into at the trainer's residence. On Wednesday afternoon, a large number assembled at the Athletic Grounds to witness a half-hour's practice with the ball. A 'boisterous' wind, however, prevented accurate kicking.

As the big day approached, excitement reached fever pitch. The prize for the winning team was a big one, a place in the FA Cup 'proper' rounds and a potentially lucrative payday against one of England's leading clubs.

Midland Railway ran football specials to Loughborough, taking at least 1,000 Fosse fans to the game. The gates opened at one o'clock on a sunny afternoon, just nine days before Christmas. Admission prices were 4d to 2s 6d as between 8,000 and 15,000 crammed into the Athletic Grounds, occupying every vantage point. Given that the population of Loughborough at the time was around 25,000, the attendance was one of the largest for a sporting event in the county.

The tie was not a spectacle of fine, flowing combination football, however. It was 'rough' even by Victorian standards and ill-tempered. The boisterous crowd reacted noisily reacting to every twist, turn and episode of foul play. So violent was the game that the referee had to administer a general caution to players who indulged in blatant kicking and barging of their opponents. One Loughborough paper criticised the Luffs for 'disgraceful tactics', stating, 'Why men have been given months of hard labour without option for assaults far less brutal than at least one we saw committed on the Loughborough playing field.' Leicester won by a single goal, scored by Fosse fans' favourite forward William 'Billy' Dorrell after just eight minutes. Dorrell was also involved in the incident that marred the encounter and ended the career of Luff full-back Jack Kent. Shortly after the start of the second half, Kent charged Dorrell but slipped and unfortunately broke his leg in two places, the bone protruding from the skin. He had fractured the same leg eight months earlier, while playing at Leicester for a Midland League team against Rotherham. This only made the incident even sadder, given that after his last injury he had suffered a lengthy illness, and had only sufficiently recovered to take his place in the Loughborough team at the start of the season. There was a delay of between 20 and 35 minutes as he was stretchered off to hospital. Some newspapers reported that a local doctor who had been watching the game reset the leg at the side of the pitch before Kent was taken to hospital. Given that anaesthetics and pain management were in their infancy, the agony must have been excruciating.

The spectators were not slow to recognise the value of Kent's services, and the considerable financial loss likely to be entailed by another illness, for they readily responded to an appeal for assistance. A collection was taken at the ground and a 'most substantial' sum was realised. Doctors A.E. Lyster of Long Eaton, and A. Eddowes and W. Yorke from Loughborough, attended the patient as he was taken to Loughborough Hospital, followed by a large crowd. It subsequently was announced that the collection amounted to £20 10s 6d. Although the remaining game was much more exciting, with end-to-end football, an atmosphere of gloom hung over the ground, but Fosse's victory was roundly cheered by their substantial travelling support.

The day after the game, several members of the Loughborough committee, together with some of his companions and sympathisers, visited Kent in the hospital. The patient passed a bad night on Saturday, but became easier during the course of Sunday, and was quite chatty. He disavowed any further idea of playing football, even should his recovery permit him to do so. Kent passed a good night on the Sunday after the game and on the Monday was reported to be doing well. In consequence of the large number of inquiries on Sunday, a notice was posted on the hospital door to the effect that the patient was doing well. The club chairman visited Kent the following Saturday and was informed as to how the accident happened. Kent and Dorrell raced together for the ball, and as the Leicester man tried to trap it, Kent kicked at it right under Dorrell's foot with all his might. The result was that Kent's foot was trapped and his leg snapped. Numerous visits were made to the hospital by newspaper reporters during the following week and they wrote that the patient was progressing satisfactorily. Mr Hall, the referee, gave ten shillings to the fund and Mr Tooth, the Conservative parliamentary candidate, who was present at the match, contributed £1 1s.

On Wednesday, 20 December 1893, the draw for the first round of the FA Cup took place and saw Fosse drawn at home to South Shore.

Both teams went into a strict training regime the week before the tie. South Shore, who would later amalgamate with their neighbours Blackpool, travelled to Leicester the day before the game and made the White Hart Hotel on Belgrave Gate their base. Excited fans crammed into the Walnut Street ground. South Shore played a rough game, subjecting the Fosse forwards, in particular Dorrell, to some brutal treatment on a day with winds reaching almost gale force. Fosse, having won the toss, chose to play with the wind, and thanks to Hill and Brown, they managed to take

WALNUT ST. GROUND.

ENGLISH CUP TIE. COMPETITION PROPER.

SATURDAY, JAN. 27th, at 2.30 p.m.,

FOSSE v. SOUTH SHORE.

Admission 6d.   Enclosure 6d. extra.   Members' Stand 1/6.

The Wyvern, 26 January 1894

a 2-1 lead by half-time. Fosse spent much of the second half defending against both pretty combination play by South Shore's forwards and the wind. Tension mounted as time edged slowly towards the 90-minute mark, several of the crowd were unable to control themselves, and a man even threw his umbrella on the field of play. Thanks to a spirited defence and outstanding saves by Jimmy Thraves, the Fosse prevailed.

In the second round, the mighty Derby County, flying high at the time in the First Division, were Leicester's opponents. On 10 February 1894, just three days after the draw was made, a record 13,000 excited spectators crammed into the Walnut Street ground came close to witnessing a giant killing. More than 2,000 fans travelled from Derby on two football special trains. A goalless draw resulted after extra time, with the Fosse attacking and defending splendidly throughout. England international and Derby's record goalscorer Steve Bloomer broke his collar bone after a collision with Fosse half-back Peggy Lord after 22 minutes. The anthem 'Steve Bloomer's Watchin'' is played at every Derby home game and there is a bust of him at Pride Park Stadium. He is also listed in the Football League 100 Legends and is a member of the English Football Hall of Fame. A few minutes after Bloomer left the field of play, Leicester's Lord made a grand shot from a free kick that dropped just over the heads of those in the goalmouth, before hitting the back of the net, which was greeted by 'tremendous cheering' when the referee awarded a goal. But after an appeal, the referee, Mr Fox had a 'talk' with several players and after consulting one of the linesmen, Mr Adams, the goal was disallowed. No reason was given.

Derby adopted rough tactics as both sides shot from all distances and angles in an attempt to settle the tie, but extra time failed to separate the sides. Derby's captain, Archie Goodall, was fined £5 and costs for assaulting Fosse fan Frank Main, a clerk from Market Harborough, at the end of the game. On leaving the ground, groups of spectators who were mostly Leicester people, threw mud and pieces of orange peel at Goodall and the rest of the Derby players as they walked the 100 yards to the 'wagonette' dressing room. Main went up to Goodall and said, 'You are the dirtiest **** player on the field.' Goodall turned round to him and said, 'What do you say? If you say that again I will hit you.' Main repeated the accusation and Goodall hit him, causing a 'contused wound on the right eye, with great ecchymosis', and there was also a small superficial wound beneath it. He also lost his hat which he never recovered. Two other Derby players then took hold of Goodall and led him away. Main did not report the incident to the police for some days.

Leicester Fosse and Loughborough Town were drawn together for the second and final time in the FA Cup in 1894. It took three games to separate the teams, with the Fosse eventually overcoming their local rivals to move into the first round proper where they lost away at Bury. Enthusiasm does not adequately describe the depth of feeling and passion surrounding the tie, at Leicester's Walnut Street ground on 15 December 1894. It was bordering 'on the mild, if entirely harmless form of madness'. For both Fosse and Luffs fans, it was the event of the season. Supporters discussed the excellence of the Fosse team and the utter weakness of Loughborough, and, of course, vice versa, until the neutral onlooker almost believed that the match was over and duly recorded in the county archives.

The excitement surrounding the encounter caused the *Leicester Daily Post* football correspondent to analyse the popularity of football, 'Truly the attractions of a football game are extraordinary. That thousands of people should willingly, nay eagerly, put themselves to much personal inconvenience, to say nothing of the expense and risk of injury to health, to see some men careering about after a ball, is a problem fit for discussion at a conference of the sages. However, meanwhile the reason of the phenomenon remains untold.

'To those who take but a passing interest in the game, and who remember vividly the stern battles of a few short months ago, it may seem a matter of wonderment that the thing does not become stale and pall upon the appetite. Therein lies the great attraction of the game as played in these ultra-professional days – a game played not for the good done to the players, with whom it is a matter merely to put money into the pockets of the shareholders of a club company. Leicestershire has not escaped the fever. There is a great demand for high-class football, and as that commodity could not be readily manufactured, it had to be imported – under free trade principles, of course. Players were bought and sold just as in the ordinary way of trade, and both clubs with which we are now dealing were run on strict commercial lines.

'Suffice it to say that the men now employed by the clubs are undoubtedly entitled to benefit by their ability on the field, and though cynics may carp at a team of Scotchmen posing as Leicester Fosse, or Wolverhampton men as Loughburians, what does it matter so long as the crowd are pleased? Football is a game *ad captandum*.'

The Luffs were in excellent form, having won 13 of their 16 games and losing just once, a friendly early in the season, scoring 55 goals and conceding just 12. Their Midland League form in particular was impressive with eight wins and two draws from the opening ten games. Fosse had begun the season indifferently. The department that was regarded as the weak spot became the strongest – the forward line. McArthur's return to form and the introduction of Gordon had worked miracles. In the 20 matches played, Fosse had won 11, lost six and had drawn two, scoring 66 and conceding 41. Both sets of supporters were confident of winning, in perhaps the most evenly contested encounter between Leicestershire's footballing giants to date. Given the importance of the encounter, it hardly needs saying that every effort was made to get the players into the best of form. Loughborough made the Greyhound Hotel, adjacent to their home ground, their place of abode, the players indulging in long walks with their trainer. On recent displays the Fosse side needed little special training, and the decision was made to continue the old course of quiet practice to prevent staleness.

Unfortunately, two of the three games required to settle the cup tie were spoilt, one by mud and the other by wind; the third was so even that neither side could claim superiority. The starting line-ups for the first match, announced well in advance, revealed the loss of a valuable player by each side. Fosse were without Arthur Henrys, who although recovered from his injury was not deemed fit enough to take part. Charles Booth, the Loughborough left-winger, had a freak career-ending accident on a train during the week leading up to the match, when a falling light fitting badly cut his knee.

Saturday, 15 December 1894 broke mild and dry. The gates of the ground opened at one o'clock, and from then until quarter past two – kick-off time – there was a continual stream of expectant fans, until there was an assemblage 'crowded in a space that left scarce room for motion or exercise'. Both teams were greeted on arrival on the field with rapturous applause. The game began in bright sunshine, with a strong breeze blowing from the river at the town end diagonally across the ground. A great deal of rain had fallen during the night, making the turf heavy and preventing good play. There was nothing in it at first, but then the Luffs were put under pressure and after 30 minutes Jacky Hill scored for the Fosse. Four minutes later, Sammy Mills whipped in a cross, and Robert Edge equalised for the Luffs, then thanks in part to William Rose's excellent goalkeeping, there was no further scoring. Loughborough's backs were equal to, if not better than, the Fosse defence. Fosse forwards passed in fair combination, but were woeful at shooting, while the forward line of Loughborough scarcely showed any combination at all. The short passing by the Fosse resulted in several chances that were squandered and on one occasion the ball hit the back of the Loughborough net, but the referee gave a foul. Gate receipts amounted to £368 17s 8d, and the number of people present was just under 10,000.

Rain fell almost constantly between the first game and the replay four days later and the 'battlefield' became 'another fine opportunity for mud-larking'. In the hope that their players might pull themselves together and settle the 'pretensions' of the Luffs 'once and for all', the Fosse committee sent them to train at Narborough until the replay, but as they found on arrival that they could not be comfortably accommodated, a change to Bradgate Park was agreed upon. At the foot of Old John, as the Fosse team prepared themselves for the re-fight, there was an altercation between the centre-forward Bob Gordon and the left-back Archie Hughes. At the weekly Fosse committee meeting two days later, Hughes was suspended for a week and Gordon for a month, for 'breaches of training rules'. This was a distinct blow to the Fosse, though the best efforts were made to secure capable substitutes, Miller and Lord of Fosse Rovers, to fill the positions vacated by the two players.

With the replay taking place on the Wednesday half-day holiday in Loughborough, and several of the factories also closing, the attendance of 3,000 was flattering to the teams considering the state of the weather, though significantly less than the Leicester gate. Almost 1,000 spectators travelled up from Leicester by train.

Plan of the field:

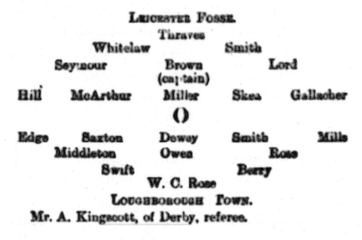

The visitors won the toss and elected to play with the wind from the Nottingham Road goal. Mr W.G. Jones was on the line for the Fosse and Walter Cockain for Loughborough, and the game kicked off on time at 2.15pm. An evenly fought first half saw Loughborough take the lead on 42 minutes. Luffs half-back Billy Owen dropped the ball beautifully among the pack of strikers from a free kick. It was knocked back to Robert Edge, who, in the neatest possible manner, lifted the ball into the net, but Fosse equalised within 30 seconds of the restart. The ball was passed on from the kick-off to Miller, who passed up to McArthur who ran a short distance before transferring to Skea. With a lightning kick Skea banged the ball in at the corner of the goal, the poor Luffs goalkeeper having no chance whatsoever of stopping it.

With 15 minutes remaining, Miller, Leicester's centre-forward who was in irresistible form, ran with the ball and slid a pass to Gallacher on the left, whose shot careered off Rose and over the goal line, Hill rushing in and banging it into the net. The Luffs attacked immediately and, within two minutes, Edge equalised with a high shot after receiving a pass back from one of his forwards. Extra time should have been played. The players however had quite had enough for one day and referee Mr Kingscott, after consulting with officials from both clubs and the secretary of the Football League, who had had stayed in Leicester overnight, agreed that an additional 30 minutes of play was out of the question. The president of the Football Association was telegraphed for instructions on how to proceed as the fans had already left the stadium in their droves, believing that the match would have to be replayed on neutral ground. The gate amounted to £92.

At a special meeting of the Divisional Emergency Committee of the Football Association, held at the Wellington Hotel in Nottingham on Friday, 22 December, it was decided that the replay should kick off at 2pm, and if necessary extra time should be played. This decision was made less than 24 hours before the replay was due to commence. Furthermore, should the two clubs then be unable to arrive at a definite conclusion, and failing mutual arrangements, the Emergency Committee ordered any further match to be played at Bramall Lane, Sheffield, no later than Monday, 31 December.

Mud had spoilt the first game and to a lesser extent the rematch and it seemed that the second replay would be threatened from another source. Throughout the Friday night, the wind blew half a gale, and it was still as bad the next morning. Accurate combination football was out of the question as the local reporter wrote, 'The so-called match simply degenerated into a question of which 11 could stay the longer and have the good luck to land the ball in the net.' The Walnut Street ground had also suffered from the violence of the weather. Some of the advertisement boards surrounding the enclosure had been blown down, and such was the force of the wind that even one of the stout goal posts had been blown over. Just to add further discomfort to the players and spectators alike, a sharp shower of rain fell as the players entered the playing arena. The attendance was miserably low, not surprising perhaps given the circumstances.

Loughborough named the same team as in the first two matches, while the Fosse strengthened their side with the inclusion of Arthur Henrys who had sufficiently recovered from an injury sustained the previous week. The closeness of the teams on the field followed them when it cam to tossing to decide ends, for twice the coin was thrown up only for it to stick in the mud, but at the third attempt Fosse's captain Brown was successful and chose to play from the town end, gaining the advantage from the elements with the wind blowing across the ground, but slightly towards the gasworks end. In such an overpowering hurricane, the number of mis-kicks was not a surprise and forward play was as challenging as defending. Forwards could not kick straight, while the kicks of the backs were often weak and feeble. Fosse were unable to take advantage of the elements as the Loughborough men played heroically, and looked odds on to win the game. Fosse, however, put on a brilliant show in the second half. Facing the town end, Fosse appeared to have their work cut out to prevent Loughborough from piling on a substantial score, but for some reason the Loughborough men went to pieces. Everything seemed to be in their favour and just when they had the game in their own hands, players were unable to make the most of the conditions and they became more and more demoralised. Two goals for the Fosse quickly followed, sucking all the life out of Loughborough while instilling confidence in the Leicester team.

The first goal resulted from an exciting scrimmage that took place in the Loughborough goalmouth. With Fosse fans shouting orders to shoot, Gallacher forced an opening while standing close in and scored. The crowd went wild with delight, and the lead was doubled three minutes later as Gallacher fought his way through the wind and passed infield to Skea, who, undeterred by an appeal for offside, dribbled coolly and steadily up to the goalmouth before shooting. His shot hit the upright and Hill rushed the rebound into the net. The Luffs fought back, striking the bar from a free kick, and Thraves had to work hard in the Leicester goal.

Hill was carried off the field with a leg injury after an almighty collision with an opponent and, after reappearing, was targeted by the Luffs and subjected to much rough play. Leicester were then awarded a penalty much to the amusement of the crowd after full-back Berry, acting as a temporary goalkeeper, caught a shot from Miller and threw it away. Skea took the penalty and shot hard. Rose saved, but the referee, for some inexplicable reason, ordered the kick to be retaken, and second time around Skea scored. Loughborough played like a thoroughly beaten team and allowed the Fosse to do what they pleased until the full-time whistle blew. In retrospect it seems such a pity that the cup tie was ultimately decided by the weather.

Despite a valiant effort, Fosse were knocked out by fellow Second Division side Bury at their Gigg Lane ground in the first round proper. Fosse travelled up on Friday on the 6.10pm express train to Manchester, where they had been booked into the Assize Court Hotel. The Woolwich Arsenal team were also on the same train to fulfil their game with Bolton Wanderers. Leicester's party comprised the 11 players with a reserve man, three committee members and the trainer. Gigg Lane had been completely cleared of snow and had also been sanded, but it was littered with deep pools of surface water. Fosse, playing in an all-white strip, struggled and were two down by half-time. They conceded another brace in the second period, with McArthur claiming a consolation goal. Bury were knocked out in the following round by Bolton Wanderers.

1895/96

The 1895/96 season was full of 'firsts' for the Luffs. Loughborough strengthened their squad for their first Football League campaign by recruiting goalkeeper Hugh Monteith from Glasgow Celtic and Charles Dickson, a prolific striker with 12 goals from 22 appearances, from Newcastle United. Dickson was reputedly earning £2 per week plus a £5 per game win bonus with the Magpies.

Dickson did not live up to his reputation and was offloaded the following year to Jarrow after scoring just five goals for the Luffs. Monteith, on the other hand, proved to be a great signing, an ever-present in 1895/96 and only missing two games in the following season, before Luffs were forced to transfer him along with two other players to Bristol City to help alleviate the club's financial crisis.

Preparations were significantly disrupted when Luffs trainer Jackson left the club to join Liverpool. Over 200 applications were received for Jackson's position after the committee placed an advert in the national press. There was one outstanding candidate, Richard Prince, who had trained Preston North Ends 'Invincibles' when they won the Football League and FA Cup 'Double' in 1888/89.

Taking a lesson from the unprepared condition of some players at the beginning of the previous season, Leicester Fosse's committee decided that training should commence one month before the first fixture of the campaign. New players for the season included Harry Davy from Blackpool, David Manson from Rotherham Town, Strachan and John Baird from Aston Villa, Richard Davies of Hanley Town, Harry Trainer of West Bromwich Albion, James Atherton of Blackpool and Jack Walker from Manchester City, all of whom were in residence in the town by August. The previous season's stalwarts, Jimmy Brown, Jimmy Thraves, Arthur Henrys, Willie McArthur and David Skea, were ready again to take up their positions. Missing were Harry Bailey, who was fulfilling his professional cricket engagement in Scotland, Hugh Gallacher, and Hogan, who was playing in a baseball tournament in London. Training began under the stewardship of Joe Newton with a brisk walk.

The Luffs' first Football League game was in Newcastle on 7 September 1895, at St James' Park in front of 6,000 supporters. They lined up with Monteith in goal, Swift and Berry as the backs, Hamilton, Middleton and Rose as the half-backs, and a forward division of Ball, W. Ward, Cotterill, Clarke and A. Ward. Four players made their Loughborough debut – Hugh Monteith, Joseph Clarke and the Ward brothers, Walter and Arthur. Monteith was an ever-present in the Luffs' inaugural Football League season, along with John Hamilton, and Dolly Rose and only missed two games the following season. In 1903 Monteith won the FA Cup while playing for Bury, beating Derby County 6-0 in the final in front of over 63,000 spectators at Crystal Palace. Left-back George Swift, who joined the Luffs from Wolverhampton Wanderers in 1891, signed for Leicester Fosse before the start of the following season, which caused yet another rift between the two clubs. Three of the Luffs side were Scottish – Monteith, Hamilton and Clarke. Henry Middleton, signed from Derby Junction in 1892, became trainer at Derby County on retirement and was one of the founders of Derby Baseball Club. There was not a single Leicestershire-born player present on the pitch.

Loughborough's first taste of the Football League ended in a 3-0 defeat and came at what was described by the local press as 'wretchedly contrived misnamed St James' Park'. Outplayed and outclassed by the Magpies, Loughborough were lucky to keep the score down to just three. Newton Heath were Loughborough's first Football League opponents at the Athletic Grounds the following Saturday. More than 2,500 watched the team in black and white draw 3-3, with Thomas Cotterill scoring the Luffs' first League goal with a spectacular volley.

The first Leicestershire derby in the Football League took place at Walnut Street on 5 October 1895. There was as ever an immense amount of local interest in the game. The previous Saturday, both Leicestershire clubs had faced opposition from Burton. The Luffs had beaten Burton Swifts – their first scalp in the Football League – at their fourth attempt, while the Fossils were surprisingly beaten at home by Burton Wanderers. As a result, it was hard to tell who would win. A large contingent from Loughborough added to the excitable atmosphere of the 8,000 spectators.

The Fossils had a cordial reception when they stepped on the field a couple of minutes before 3.30pm, but the visitors, who immediately followed, received a rapturous ovation from their very vocal travelling support. Swift won the toss for the Luffs and the Fosse kicked off in the direction of the gasworks goal, against a fairly strong wind. The first half provided a very entertaining spectacle, but the longer the game went on, the more dominating Leicester's forward line became. Inside-left Skea, in particular, was outstanding. Towards the end of the half he got the ball and after eluding several Luff's players he came across to the right where he centred, Brown scoring to the delight of the Fosse faithful with a brilliant volley. As the rain began to fall, Skea darted past Berry and netted with a stinging low shot, doubling Leicester's advantage. Loughborough, who went into the break two down, were shellshocked.

As the second half proceeded, the Fosse's dominance increased. Loughborough lost their shape and when opportunities did arise, they shot badly. On the other hand, the Fosse's forwards worked wonderfully as a coherent unit, and went on the offensive to improve their goal average. McArthur and Gallacher each in turn beat Monteith, then shortly before the end Skea collided with the goalkeeper and left the field without returning. Fosse's fifth and final goal was an own goal after a hard low cross by Gallacher glanced off the Luffs back, Berry, into the back of the net.

The final outcome, 5-0, was much more one-sided than anticipated, the Fosse claiming their record winning margin against their arch rivals in a competitive game. The 'powerful purgative' which a Loughborough writer asserted was being prepared by Luffs against the Fosse misfired and the cocksureness which the Luffs supporters openly paraded before the game came to nothing. The result came as a complete surprise to even the most ardent Leicester supporter. It was a complete performance by the Fosse. Seldom, as the local press reported, 'has the Fosse defence been so conspicuously successful. Thraves gave one of his best exhibitions of goalkeeping – sufficient testimony to a sterling display – and Baird earned high praise for his cool and scrupulously fair style, while Bailey rendered efficient service. Then when Fosse commenced to score, Loughborough's light went out and as promising as it had been their commencement, the finale was most ignominious.'

Some Loughborough supporters blamed the rain, while others were unhappy at Monteith's habit of kicking the ball when he ought to handle – 'always a dangerous system, especially with a wet ball'. As the *Leicester Post* football commentator stated at the end of his report on the game, 'It may be that the powerful purgative spoken of before the game was administered to them [Loughborough] by mistake.'

The reverse fixture at the Athletic Grounds took place six weeks later, on Saturday, 16 November 1895 in front of around 4,000 spectators. Yet again the weather would play an important role in determining the outcome of a Leicestershire derby. A brass band provided entertainment before the players appeared on the field of play, several minutes after the advertised 2.30pm kick-off time. Both teams were not in the best of form, winning just one game each in the period between the two derby meetings. Harry Trainer fell sick at the last minute for Leicester, and Richard Davies was called up from the reserves to complete an already weakened side. Fortunately for the Fosse the mainstay of the team, their half-backs, were intact. Loughborough played the same side that had drawn 1-1 with Burton Swifts the day before. That result raised Loughborough above the Fosse in the league table, which presumably gave the Leicester team extra impetus to beat their rivals and reverse this humiliating situation.

The Luffs were clearly disadvantaged after their exertions just 24 hours earlier and it showed during the first half as they had to compete against both the Fosse and the wind. Players had the utmost difficulty in commanding the ball, turning the game into a lottery. Leicester pinned the Luffs into their own half for most of the first 20 minutes. Bishop opened the scoring for the Fosse after seven minutes and Fosse were simply too strong for Loughborough. Lynes, having won possession, passed to Davies, who doubled the lead with a strong shot. A third goal on 40 minutes resulted from the first corner of the game with a low powerful strike by Davies as the ball rane free. All of Loughborough's attempts were thwarted by the strong wind blowing against them.

A change of ends saw a dramatic improvement, perhaps not surprisingly, given the inclement weather, in Loughborough's form. Luck, however, was not on their side. A combined rush gave McArthur an opportunity that he did not waste, scoring with a low shot to claim Leicester's fourth. Although four down, Loughborough refused to lie down. From a throw-in Loughborough scored, the ball going directly through into the net after a mis-kick by Leicester's Davy five minutes from the close, although the final result was a 4-1 win for Fosse.

Loughborough endured a dreadful sequence of results following the Fosse encounter, not winning a Football League game until leap year day, when they beat Woolwich Arsenal 2-1 at home. They managed just two points in 11 games and were firmly rooted to the bottom of the table. Attendances dropped dramatically to less than half of that of the opening fixtures but running costs remained high, exacerbated by the debt carried over from the previous season meant the financial situation was dire. The *Loughborough Monitor* football reporter commented, 'I have wondered how the club manage to live at all under its heaviness. The expenditure is continuous, whether the gate receipts are much or little, and it has had a hand to mouth existence for some time.'

The only way out for the club was to offload some players, but having reduced the wage bill, the committee signed proven striker James Logan from Newcastle in a final attempt to lift themselves off the foot of the table. A proven goalscorer, Logan had scored a hat-trick for Notts County during their 4-1 triumph over Bolton Wanderers in the 1894 FA Cup Final. Remarkably it worked. Logan revitalised the team and helped secure the Luffs' highest placing, 12th, in the Second Division, winning seven of their last ten games.

Logan's career and life ended in tragic circumstances. Loughborough, on their way to play Newton Heath on 4 April 1896, discovered that their kit had been lost. Unable to borrow any shirts, they had to take to the field wearing their ordinary clothes. Rain fell heavily throughout the 90 minutes, and at the end of a 2-0 defeat Loughborough's players had to return home wearing the very clothes they had played the match in. Logan caught a cold, which he managed to shake off, but not long after scoring in a 4-1 victory in the final game of the season against Crewe Alexandra, he relapsed. He developed pneumonia and died on Monday, 25 May 1896, with his father present, just one month short of his 26th birthday.

While in Loughborough, Logan rented a room from John Berry, the Luffs full-back, at 108 Leopold Street. According to his obituary in the *Leicester Journal* in May 1896: 'Logan, like so many other league players, belonged to Scotland, having been brought up on the Duke of Portland's estate in Ayrshire. He crossed the border five or six seasons ago, becoming engaged to the Sunderland club. From the north he came to the Midland district, joining the ranks of Aston Villa. At about this period of his career he gave great promise of developing into a fine player.

'He was, however, not long at Birmingham, his services being transferred to Notts County, and it was while wearing the colours of this club that he attracted most attention. He it was who scored the winning goal for Notts County when they secured the FA Cup at Everton on March 31st, 1894.

'In that season which was Logan's best he scored 60 goals for Notts. His position was then centre-forward. The beginning of last season found Logan in the north again, Newcastle United obtaining command of his services. In the first week of the new year, however, he returned to these parts. Loughborough succeeding in gaining his transfer from Newcastle. It was hoped that in Logan the local club had captured just the centre-forward they wanted, and certainly some excellent performances were accomplished subsequent to his admission into the home ranks. He was of a quiet and retiring disposition and made many friends wherever he went.

'The football world will lie all the poorer for his untimely decease. His loss will be keenly felt in Loughborough, as the club had signed him on again for next season, so satisfied were the committee of his displays in the Town colours. A large sum of money was paid by the club for his transfer from Newcastle.

'As a mark of respect, the Midland League championship flag was hoisted half-mast high at the Athletic Grounds. The unexpected death of so bright an ornament in the professional football ranks casting a gloom in sporting circles. Logan's many connections having caused him to be widely known and highly respected.'

Although a large number of people attended the funeral, John Berry was the only member of the first team present. The rest had already left town to return to their homes for the summer break. Also in attendance were Jimmy's widow Mary, his father James and the wife of David Calderhead, his ex-team-mate and captain at Notts County. He lies in an unmarked grave in Loughborough cemetery.

Leicester, like the Luffs, also staged a revival and finished eighth, comfortable in mid-table, after the return of their old hero Billy Dorrell from Aston Villa in March. Dorrell missed his train for the Rotherham Town home fixture, which a hastily reorganised forward line won 8-0. The season ended on a rather disappointing note as Grimsby striker Tommy McCairn put six goals past Thraves in a humiliating 7-1 defeat at the Mariners' Abbey Park ground.

The *Leicester Chronicle*, in its review of Fosse's season, commented, 'At the beginning of last September, then, the prospects of a brilliant season were quite the reverse of obscure, but the Walnut Street crowd were not long in discovering the unwelcome fact that some of the changes at any rate were for the worse. The loss of five matches out of the seven played during September bought this home in startling fashion, but the troubles of the executive were then only commencing. It was quickly evident that the whole and sole fault lay with the forwards, who, however, were changed about, displayed an irritating inability to reach the desired height of combination and power. The intermediate and rear divisions were undoubtedly as strong and perhaps stronger than formerly, but so feeble was the scoring department that the defence naturally could not continually stand the strain.

'A few of the newcomers were quickly relegated to the second team, an obscurity from which they have never emerged, while some of the recognised first 11 professors shaped throughout in a style far from satisfactory. The inevitable search for new blood was attended by no more, happy results, and what with accidents to players and other causes which it is not desirable to specify, the executive found their position a most difficult one. So, the first half of the season passed, and when new year came Fosse had won only five out of 11 league games; and what was of perhaps as much importance at that particular stage, had, been disgracefully beaten in the FA Cup matches [defeated 2-1 at home by Kettering] even before they entered the competition proper.

'Two or three short spells of success, brilliant while they lasted, invariably gave way to these disappointing relapses, and so the season dragged on. The re-engagement of a player [Dorrell] who had much to do with the early rise of the club lent a flip up to the proceedings towards the end, but the spurt was short-lived and the feelings of the club's supporters at the present time are not entirely enthusiastic. The five cup competitions in which the first team entered were especially disastrous. Excepting the three purely village teams beaten in the earlier stages of the national competition, not a single cup match was won; not even one final was reached; on the contrary, the club's cup-fighting abilities were proved to be wretchedly weak.

'With such an unreliable combination to represent the ambitious Fossils, it is a matter for surprise that the club has attained even eighth position in the league list. One or two matches have been splendidly won, notably Liverpool, Newton Heath, and Notts County, but contemplation of these meritorious performances – showing plainly that the men had the ability if they would but utilise it – only deepens the regret that at least four presumably easy matches were simply thrown away.

'Happily, the end of the season brings with it an opportunity, previously impossible, of ridding the club of that appreciable proportion of the staff that has simply acted as a brake to its progress. With a practical footballer now, to all intents, at the head of affairs, we may fairly suppose that the egregious blunders of the past will not be repeated. The constitution of the team for next year, having regard to the experiences of the period just passed, is a work of much difficulty and delicacy. Many other clubs, ill-favoured like the Fosse in the selection of their players, are striving to improve their strength, and the search for worthy men is exceedingly keen, but we can only hope that the professors the executive have in view will prove a more reliable lot than those who are now severing their connection with Leicester.'

The Fosse balance sheet at the end of the season showed a total turnover of £3,979 9s 8.5d; the overdraft stood at £457 13s 7.5d against £383 17s 1d at the end of the previous season. On the income side of the accounts, the gate money amounted to £2,373 19s 7d, membership subscriptions were at £883 16s 6d, £150 had been accrued from the sports day of the previous season and £47 from transfer fees. The least productive Second Division gate, the match with Crewe Alexandra, amounted to £49 10s and the friendly with the Luffs bought in a further £21 4s 6d.

At the AGM held in May, it was stated that McMillan, signed for the following season, 'was a good man in the centre position, and that they had some good reports of the former Luff, Carnelley', who had also agreed to play for the Fosse. During the meeting, a telegram was received to the effect that William Freebairn had just been signed from Partick Thistle, as an outside-right.

Season ticket prices for 1896/97 were 12s 6d for the covered stand, or 17s 6d including a lady's ticket, while in the reserved stand a single ticket was 20s or 25s including a lady's ticket.

The Luffs' finances were in an even worse state. The cost of bringing Football League football to Loughborough had been high, resulting in an end-of-season deficit of £652 9s 3d. This included the sale of Benjamin Bull to Liverpool and William Owen to Wolves for £40 and £50 respectively. During the season there had been something like 40-plus professionals on the club's books. Players' wages were in excess of £36 a week. The treasurer was surprisingly upbeat at the AGM, 'Looking at the whole concern, the loss sustained during the year was easily accounted for, and another year, I have no hesitation in saying, instead of a financial loss the club would be able to show a profit.' This meant that a desire to make the club into a limited company had to be put on hold until the debt was cleared. A range of fundingraising activities was organised, including a fete, bazaar, gala, and a shilling subscription in an attempt to improve the club's finances.

In May 1896, the Loughborough and District Amateur Football League was established, with its 12 clubs including Loughborough Victoria, Loughborough Emmanuel, Loughborough Park, Thrussington, Mountsorrel St Peter's, Whitwick Albion, Barrow Excelsior and Mountsorrel Castle. The annual subscription was 5s.

1896/97

The big news in the summer of 1896 was the £100 transfer of left-back George Swift from Loughborough to Leicester Fosse. Although legitimate, the move caused a huge row between the two clubs over the size of the fee. The Football League did not help the situation by refusing to arbitrate, while the Loughborough press did not take the loss of their influential captain well, remarking, 'This sort of thing savours of white slavery.' Swift was a great signing for the Fosse, an ever-present in four of his six seasons as captain. As a full-back he had an impressive kick and scored several spectacular goals, including one from the halfway line for Leicester against Walsall in 1901. For several seasons he was also Fosse's penalty-taker and he was later awarded a benefit game before moving to Notts County. On retirement from professional football, he became a trainer.

Other new Fosse summer signings included John Leighton from Hibernian, John Freebairn from Abercorn, Thomas Lonie of Stoke, Derby County's John McMillan, and Albert Carnelley, who had scored a hat-trick against the Fosse in a Midland League for Loughborough in November 1891. Another former Luff, John Jackson, was appointed trainer after Joe Newton took up a similar role in Dundee. In the search for quality players, the Fosse executive arranged for amateur trial matches to be played against scratch teams of men anxious to play in Fosse colours. About 30 applications had been received in response to the invitation to take part. The first part of each session was devoted to ball practice with the professionals, while trial matches commenced at 4pm. Several players were identified and two signed professional forms.

A week before the season started, Walnut Street staged a match between mixed teams of the club's 1896/97 squad. The A' team was made up of Thraves in goal; Davy and Bailey as the backs; Jones, Lord and Bevans at half-back; Curtis, Manson, Harris, Trainer and Bishop as the forwards. The 'B' team was Howe in goal; Thompson and an unnamed player as the backs; Brow, Walker and Leighton at half-back; Dorrell, Freebairn, Lonie, Carnelley and McMillan in the forward positions.

Of the previous season's players, Loughborough retained nine for 1896/97: two goalkeepers, one back, two half-backs and four forwards. They secured six other players, including Robert Thompson from Tow Lane and Joseph Blackett from Willington Athletic. Due to the lack of photographs in newspapers, the age, height, and weight of new players were listed. Joseph Blackett, was 21 years old, standing 5ft 9in and weighing 11st 4lb. His sprinting abilities were reputedly exceptional and he could run 100 yards in 11 seconds. McBride was signed from Ayr and Mumford from Sheffield Wednesday. In addition, two trialists – full-back Harry Whitehead from Barlestone and Robert Miller, a forward formerly of Bolton who had moved to Loughborough having obtained work in the town – were signed. The players who had signed Football League forms prior to the start of the season were goalkeepers Hugh Monteith and Fred Fould, backs Jack Berry, Robert Thompson and Harry Whitehead, half-backs Walter Hardy, Jack Hamilton and Henry Middleton, plus Arthur Roulston, William Andrews, Robert McBride, William Jones, Walter Ward, Robert Miller and Joseph Blackett. Jack Berry was appointed captain. The signings met the approval of the local press, with one report noting, 'The club's outlook appears considerably better than it did this time last year.'

Leicestershire football fans did not have long to wait for the first Football League derby of the season, on 26 September 1896. Loughborough went into the game pointless on the back of four consecutive defeats. No fewer than six players had made their debut in Leicester's opening game of the season against Darwen, with three of them scoring in an impressive 4-1 win. This was followed by defeats against Notts County and Burton Swifts.

George Swift was cordially cheered as he led the Fosse men on to the field against his old club at the Nottingham Road ground in bright sunshine and the Luffs were equally well received. Fosse won the toss and chose to attack the entrance end, the kick-off taking place punctually. Billed by the press as 'the fight for the wooden spoon' rather than the championship of Leicestershire, the game opened in a 'spirited and exciting manner' with both sides playing a combined passing game. If anything, Loughborough started better, and were effective on the right wing, with Roulston twice causing the Fosse defence some anxiety in the opening few minutes. Fosse opened the scoring on 15 minutes against the run of play when McMillan placed a shot beyond the reach of Monteith. Fosse piled on the pressure with an impressive display of attacking football, and within a minute Blackett had the hardest of luck in not scoring, with a beautiful long-range effort just going wide. Then McMillan beat Monteith again in precisely the same manner as his first goal, doubling Fosse's lead. Play went back and forth between the two goalmouths, but Loughborough were let down by poor shooting, and Blackett and Andrews played an individual game much to the detriment of their team-mates.

The second half by comparison was poor, characterised by robust play and excessive fouling predominantly by the Loughborough team, who had clearly decided to adopt a more physical approach. Fosse were by far the better side and it was clear to all who witnessed the game that Loughborough would need to significantly invest in new players to stand any chance of avoiding the prospect of re-election. The football correspondent of the *Leicester Daily Post* stated, 'A couple of years ago Loughborough people were mad on football and are now cynical and have entered on a downward course.'

After beating Lincoln to record their first league win of the season the Saturday after losing against the Fosse, Loughborough began another run of defeats. This included losses against Walsall home and away, Notts County, Burton Swifts and an 8-1 thrashing away at Grimsby Town. A humiliating 2-1 defeat by Mansfield Town in the third qualifying round of the FA Cup in November was claimed by the local press to be a 'disgrace to both the club and players'.

Financially, the weekly wage bill of more than £30 was slowly strangling the club. Just to make matters worse, there was crowd trouble at the home game against Walsall on 10 October. A section of the 2,000 attendance were furious at a series of decisions by the referee, Mr Pennington, and when the match ended they rushed towards him, with several blows aimed at his head. Luckily, they missed, and he left the ground badly shaken but unharmed. A charge of disorderly conduct on the Athletic Grounds was bought by Mr Pennington. After an extensive investigation and hearing held at the Victoria Coffee house in Leicester, the Football Association committee unanimously arrived at the following decisions:

- 'While finding that disorderly proceedings did occur … The executive are not of the opinion that it was of such character as to justify the extreme course being taken of closing the ground.'
- 'The executive finds that Loughborough FC have not taken all precaution necessary to carry out the game in an orderly manner.'
- 'That Loughborough FC be severely censured and cautioned and ordered to publish further bills of caution to be submitted to the association and that an assurance be given to this association of the extra precautions having been taken to prevent reoccurrence.'
- 'That the whole of the expenses of the inquiry be borne by Loughborough FC.'
- ' That Mr C. Larkin of the Loughborough committee be suspended from taking any official part in connection with football until 1 May 1897, for accusing the referee of dishonourable motives, and that he apologise forthwith in writing through this association to Mr Pennington.'
- 'That the Loughborough FC committee be called upon as a committee to apologise to Mr Pennington for general misconduct towards him.'

Athletic Grounds attendances dropped to around 1,000, generating receipts of around £15 to £16 per game. Supporters were disgruntled and held a special meeting at the Corn Exchange in Loughborough on Christmas Eve 1896 to discuss the financial situation of the club. Much of the problem was down to the size of Loughborough as a town and its inability to command the number of people at their matches as larger towns. Mr Thompson, a committee member, not surprisingly wanted the Football League to change the rules, so that home and away gates should be split equally between both competing clubs. This comment was greeted with rapturous applause. Clearly the Fosse, based in a town of 211,000, had a huge advantage over Loughborough, with a population of 21,000 [1901 Census]. It is perhaps worth noting at this point that Loughborough attendances on a Saturday afternoon at the Athletic Grounds accounted for anything between 20 and 50 per cent of the total population of the north Leicestershire town – a remarkable achievement.

In a rallying cry to his team, many of whom were present at the meeting, Mr Thompson appealed to them never to 'take up the wooden spoon again'. Councillor Mato said it was a great pity that a town like Loughborough could not pay the debts of the club, while Councillor Wootton stated that it was a 'disgrace to the town that such a debt had been allowed to accumulate'. After much discussion, it was agreed to raise money for the club through a bazaar and an organising committee was formed. A canvass of the audience was made for subscriptions and this resulted in promises of over £200, including £50 from Mr Johnson-Ferguson MP, £20 from Midland Brewery Company, and £20 from Messrs. H.L. Dormer, among many others. This additional income allowed the Luffs to sign two more players, Alfred Shelton, and J. Brailsford, who combined with devastating effect in perhaps the most famous fixture ever witnessed in Loughborough on 12 December 1896 – the 8-0 demolition of Arsenal – which still stands as the Londoners' record defeat in the Football League.

In vile conditions, with rain having fallen for most of the day, Loughborough opened the scoring after just three minutes when Hamilton followed up a shot and kicked through the uprights. The lead was doubled after just seven minutes of play when a move between Brailsford, Ward and Andrews led to Jones banging the ball into the net. Luffs' backs weathered an onslaught by Arsenal and scored a sensational third when Ward broke away, beat the half-backs, ran between the backs, and hit an unstoppable shot into the top corner. Bearing down again, Jones, who had been a prominent figure, ran clean through the visitors' defence and brought the score to 4-0 at the interval. Loughborough hit the framework and had a goal ruled offside before a short and sharp passing move resulted in Ward scoring the fifth. There was no holding the Loughborough forwards and, although Brailsford had what seemed a perfectly legitimate goal disallowed, he was successful shortly afterwards for the sixth home score. The enthusiasm of the spectators had now practically given way to merriment, for it was only a question of what the final total would be. Straight from the kick-off after the sixth goal, Jones headed over from a cross when it seemed easier to score. A minute later, he made up for the miss with a beautiful shot into the net that Talbot never moved an inch to check. In spite of these severe reverses, the Woolwich forwards were game to the last and put the Loughborough defence to the test on several occasions only to see Jones score the eighth from a corner and Ward hit the bar during the last few moments.

The result was unexpected. Arsenal were in the top half of the table and an entertaining side to watch, their 12 previous games averaging five goals. Loughborough, meanwhile, had scored a total of just four goals in their previous 14 games. The Football Association had insisted that Woolwich Arsenal play Leyton in the FA Cup on the same day, a tie they won 5-0. But the first team were at Loughborough. The team had three changes from their previous league game, on 5 December. Two of these were regular first-team players, but Carver made his debut at left-back. A resounding home win was not the scoreline envisaged. Arsenal however, had their revenge a few years later, humiliating the Luffs 12-0 in March 1900.

There was a huge turnout for Leicester Fosse's first Christmas Day home fixture against Loughborough. Officially 11,000 people passed through the turnstiles, including season ticket holders, with receipts of about £220, which accounted for ten per cent of that season's gate revenue. The actual attendance, however, was significantly higher, as the gatesmen were overwhelmed, with hundreds gaining admission without paying. Football became an integral part of Christmas for many with tickets for Christmas Day games often given to children as presents. Festive double-headers developed, with local rivals playing each other twice in 48 hours in front of bumper Christmas crowds. Attitudes began to change, and as public transport declined on Christmas Day, so did attendances and the fixtures eventually disappeared from the football calendar. The final 25 December programme of games in England was in the 1957/58 season, when Leicester lost 5-1 at Blackpool.

Leicester went into 1896 festive battle with their arch rivals without McMillan and Leighton, who had been out through a knee injury, replaced by Lord on the right wing. The visitors fielded their full-strength team. Although the ground was heavy after persistent rain, the game was played in cold, dry weather. Loughborough won the toss just before 2.30pm and elected to attack the town end. McDonald opened the scoring with a header for Leicester from a cross by Trainer in the first five minutes. Fosse totally dominated, forwards passing between themselves helping to create space for Dorrell and then Freebairn to score. Brailsford pulled one back for the Luffs before half-time with a low shot that beat Thraves for pace, but Fosse were by far the 'cleverer' side and were 3-1 up at the interval.

Fosse's domination continued into the second half. Within minutes of the restart, Dorrell centred after a 'grand sprint' and the remaining Fosse forwards went for the goal as a unit, with the ball eventually being bundled through and Freebairn very prominent in the rush. The Loughborough crossbar and the upright were rattled three times in quick succession as Fosse pressed for a fifth, but Luffs reduced the lead to two goals after 70 minutes. Following a passing movement on the left wing, the ball went to Swift, who struggled to clear the ball as he got stuck in the mud and Jones pounced to score. Although Thraves was at fault for the first Luffs goal, he certainly wasn't for the second. Fosse were worthy winners at 4-2 and could rightly claim to be the 'champions of Leicestershire'.

The Luffs performed much better in the second half of the season, finishing 13th in the 16-team league on 25 points, winning 12, losing 17 and drawing just one. Thanks to a combination of a 'gift' from Mr Johnson-Ferguson, the local MP and committee member, and that year's sports subscriptions and bazaar, the previous debt of £652 was cleared. However, they still posted a loss of £301 for the season.

In the league, Fosse accumulated 30 points, winning 13, losing 13, and drawing four, scoring 59 goals, and having 57 scored against them. Overall, in all competitions and friendlies, they played 54, won 20, lost 20 and drew nine, with 110 goals for and 95 against. The chief scorers were Dorrell with 25 and McMillan with 20. In the 1895/96 season, they had gates which realised an average of £55, compared to £46 per game the previous season. The deficit increased to over £900. Apart from the kindness of the club's vice-presidents, who each paid £25 each, and the new committee men twho paid £10 on election, the club would have folded before the 1896/97 season even started. Fosse had two departures during the season – Tom Lonie was released and David Manson joined Lincoln City – and no fewer than six key players were laid on their backs at the time when their services were most required.

During the AGM in May 1897, members commented that the club's 'want of success, financially and otherwise', was due to nothing other than bad play. The annual report presented was scathing, pointing out that there were men in the team, without naming them, '[who] did not know how to play away from home, and another season these men would not be found in the ranks of the players. Further reasons for failure was the exceptionally wet season which they had experienced. That did not of course account for the bad play, because the players seemed to thrive on the worst grounds.'

A proposal was made to form the club into a limited company. It was stated that if the committee decided not to do so, then two things would happen – first bankruptcy, and the second would mean finding £719 to clear past deficits, and something like £200 a year to ensure the continuance of the club. Not surprisingly, the membership voted strongly in favour of the motion and initiated the necessary financial and legal registration processes.

Several well-known Fossils sought pastures new at the end of the season – Harry Trainer (Sheppey United), Harry Davy (Bristol City), David McDonald (Dundee), Albert Carnelley (Bristol City), John Leighton (destination unknown) and Jimmy Thraves (Long Eaton Rangers). In addition to the continued engagement of Cecil Wood, Bob Thompson, and Harry Bailey, only three new players – Roderick McLeod (West Bromwich Albion), Dick Jones (South Shore) and Alf Ball (Kettering Town) – had been signed by the end of May.

1897/98

Fosse started the 1897/98 season as a limited company with a board of directors. Mr Hudson was club chairman, and William Clark was appointed as club secretary. Formerly of Derby County, Mr Clark was instrumental in promoting in late August an exhibition game of baseball at Walnut Street and a series of 100-yard handicap races for professional footballers. About 2,000 people witnessed Palace beat Derby by 15 runs to 12 with an innings to spare in the baseball encounter. Only 14 runners competed for the £10 first prize in the handicapped sprint event. Billy Dorrell won the final in a time of 9.45s from fellow Fossil Johnny McMillan, in a run-off after the first race ended in a dead heat.

A reshaped Fosse side were Luton Town's first opponents in the Football League, in a 1-1 draw, with William Freebairn scoring Leicester's first goal of the season. In a disappointing start, only two points were accumulated in the opening five games. Encouraging wins at Woolwich Arsenal (3-0) and at home to Blackpool (4-1) gave the Fosse some confidence to meet their Leicestershire rivals.

Loughborough were as usual in a financial mire. In an attempt to clear their debt, the club's committee slashed their largest expenditure – player salaries, which were in excess of £1,000 a year. Out went Hugh Monteith, William Jones, and John Hamilton, who all joined Bristol City, and Joseph Blackett moved to Wolverhampton for £50. They were replaced by William Hodgkin from Castle Donington, Arthur White from Heanor and Arthur Ward from Barrow Rising Star, with the club announcing that local talent would be given a chance. Horace Pike and Arthur Shaw from Nottingham Forest were also signed as the new season approached.

Optimism within the club was uncharacteristically high as Shaw scored twice on his home debut, in the 2-1 win against Walsall. However, the fixture failed to fire the enthusiasm of local fans, and only attracted 1,500 spectators. If the public would not come to the ground then the club decided it should go to the public. Collection boxes were placed in public houses and clubs with some success. However, five consecutive defeats – 3-0 at Manchester

1886/87: Back: Hurndall, Hassell, W Johnson, Taylor (umpire), H Johnson, De Ville, Knight; Middle: Smith, Ashmole, Gardner, West; Front: J Johnson, Bankart, E Johnson. Reproduced with the kind permission of Leicester City FC

1888/89. Reproduced with the kind permission of Leicester City FC

1889/90: Back: Gardiner (Secretary), Rowson, Walker, Davis, Cooper (umpire); Middle: Squire, J Johnson, Murdoch, Perry, Vickers; Front: Bentley, Thompson, West, E Johnson, Atter. Reproduced with the kind permission of Leicester City FC

1892/93: Back: Marson (Secretary), Carter, Lord, Bailey, Silvester, Smith (Trainer); Middle: Thraves, Lowe, Nuttall, Slack, Webb; Front: Dorrell, Taylor. Reproduced with the kind permission of Leicester City FC

LEICESTER FOSSE F.C., 1893-4
This was the last season of the Fosse First Team in the Midland League

1893/94: Back: Marson (Secretary), Taylor, Smith, Thraves, Bailey, Brown (Trainer); Middle: Ashwell (President), Hill, Seymour, Henrys, Lord, Dorrell; Front: Miller, Worrall, Slack. Reproduced with the kind permission of Leicester City FC

1893/94: (With various committee members): Back: unknown, Hartopp, Lee, Curtis; Second Row: Jones, Cooper, W Brown, Smith, Thraves, Bailey, unknown, Ashwell, Porter, Seddon; Third Row: Kilby, Marson (Secretary), Hughes, J Brown, McArthur, Henrys, Lord, Gardner; Front: Hill, Priestman, Miller, Dorrell. Reproduced with the kind permission of Leicester City FC

1894/95: Back: Lee (Secretary), Smith, Chappel, Priestman, Bailey, Whitelaw, Miller,Brown (Trainer); Front: Hill, Hughes, McArthur, Brown, Thraves, Skea, Gallacher; On Ground: Seymour, Henrys. Reproduced with the kind permission of Leicester City FC

1895/96: Back: Lee (Secretary), Baird, Atherton, Thompson, Strachan, Lord, Walker, Bailey, Newton (Trainer); Middle: Hogan, Manson, Thraves, Davies, Pickard, Gallacher, Henrys; Front: McArthur, Trainer, Skea, Brown. Reproduced with the kind permission of Leicester City FC

1896/97: Back: J Jackson (Trainer), Lord, Davy, Bailey, Swift, Dorrell, H Jackson (Secretary); Middle: Brown, Lonie, Carnelly, Thraves, Leighton, Walker; Front: Freebairn, McMillan, Manson. Reproduced with the kind permission of Leicester City FC

1897/98: Back: Clarke (Secretary), Gillies, Bailey, Walker, Ball, Leese, Rowell, Howes, Jackson (Trainer); Middle: McLeod, Proudfoot, Lord, Swift, Jones, Dorrell, Smith; Front: King, Flanagan, McMillan, Freebairn. Reproduced with the kind permission of Leicester City FC

1898/99: Back: Ball, Galbraith, Watkins, Beardsley, Dorrell, Dunmore (Trainer); Middle: Johnson (Secretary), Brown, Eaton, Swift, Walker, McMillan; Front: Jones, King. Reproduced with the kind permission of Leicester City FC

Action from the 1890s

Two action shots from Walnut Street, 1890s

City, 2-0 at home to Small Heath, 2-1 at Darwen, 3-0 at home to Manchester City and the same scoreline away at Walsall – dampened spirits both on and off the pitch. The home game with Manchester City attracted a crowd of 5,000, indicating that the support was there if the club could provide a team that the town could be proud of. A 2-0 home win against Luton, with goals from Walker and Pegg, followed by a 3-2 win away at Lincoln, and a narrow defeat away at Small Heath gave the Luffs some hope for the first derby of the season.

A little of the old excitement was infused into the first encounter of the season between Loughborough and the Fosse at the Nottingham Road ground on 13 November. Upwards of 5,000 people witnessed the game despite the poor form of both sides and the damp surroundings. Many travelled from Leicester, who were firm favourites. The home XI did not include Godfrey Beardsley, the Luffs' first-choice goalkeeper, who was suffering from an ankle injury. Kick-off took place a minute or two before 2.30pm, Loughborough losing the toss and starting towards the Moor Lane goal. Rough tactics were adopted by both sides.

Mr Green, the referee, made it known that he would stand for none of it and his timely nipping in the bud of foul play had a salutary effect. There was much giving and taking in the first half, without any goals. Perhaps if anything the Fosse had the lion's share of the play but they struggled to break down a resolute Luffs defence. Crossing over at half-time, Loughborough took control and 17 minutes after the restart the great majority of the crowd were 'electrified' by a Luffs goal. Walker feebly sent the ball in the direction of the home goal and it travelled up to Charlie Saer, in the Fosse goal, who stood waiting very coolly with his legs wide apart and his hands down. Much to the amazement and delight of the home crowd, Saer allowed the greasy ball to roll leisurely between his legs out of his grip, and into the net. Although such a 'muff' as this was enough to take the heart out of the visitors, instead it had the opposite effect as they set about making amends and a determined onslaught on the Luffs goal brought dividends and the equaliser was scored within five minutes. The goal resulted from a goalmouth scrimmage, McLeod skilfully placing the ball over the heads of the defenders and into the net, high out of reach. It was now the turn of the 'Fossilised' supporters to cheer and cheer they did. McLeod made other efforts, as the fans chanted 'Roddie, Roddie, Roddie', to pop the ball through, but he failed as did other Fossils. Loughborough at the other end were equally unsuccessful, although they were persistent triers, the match ending in well-contested draw.

Loughborough secured their first and only double of the season in the following fixture, a 4-2 home win against Lincoln City. The run-up to the festive clash with the Fosse at Walnut Street, was dreadful, including a 7-0 destruction at Grimsby and a 1-0 home defeat to a Darwen team who were almost as terrible as they were. The local press crucified them. Fosse's form was steady between derby days, drawing 1-1 at home with Newton Heath, followed by a 3-2 victory at Burton Swifts, completing the double over Arsenal at Walnut Street, a 2-1 defeat at Manchester City and a narrow 2-1 win at home to Darwen.

The Fosse-Loughborough game on Christmas Day in 1897 was the only outdoor attraction in Leicester, resulting in an additional £243 to the home club's funds. The game was one-sided, with Loughborough being on the defensive for almost the whole game. George Swift won the toss for Leicester and decided to play with the wind. Mumford, Hardy and White defended their lines well. The only goal of the first half was secured by McMillan after Smith had hit the crossbar. In the second half the Fosse forwards gave an exhibition of football, with goals being scored by Smith, McLeod and Freebairn. The credit for the latter's goal, however, belonged to Dorrell who went on one of his characteristic sprints up the wing, in which he left Hardy yards behind, and centred for the right winger to score right in front of goal.

The defence was the best part of the Loughborough side, with Mumford in goal putting on a simply outstanding display, his only mistake being when he misjudged a shot from which McLeod scored low down in the corner. Tich Smith was clearly at sea against the combination of Dorrell and McMillan, while most of the forward line showed the form of a third-rate club. On the Fosse side, goalkeeper Saer had only three shots to deal with. Swift kicked splendidly, and Walker as in previous games came to the fore. The halves had no real difficulties in holding the Loughborough forwards in check, and consequently had plenty of opportunities for supplying their own front line. This they did in good style, allowing McLeod and his fellow forwards to shine. Smith, who appeared for the first time since his accident, again showed how difficult it was for an opposing half to rob him of the ball. Dorrell and McMillan made the most effectual wing play, and it was strange that the former, who was by far the best forward on the field, was the only one not to score.

There was still a glimmer of hope for the new year as the Luffs won the final fixture of 1897 at the Athletic Grounds against Burton Swifts, with Hodgkin, Pike and Pegg scoring in a 3-2 thriller. Loughborough then lost 11 consecutive games, including a 7-0 thrashing at Luton Town, and conceding nine at Burnley. In the last five league games of the season they managed to claim three points, including a rare win, at home to Grimsby, and nine days later an uninspiring 0-0 draw to Newton Heath at the Athletic Grounds. Perhaps not surprisingly they finished bottom of the league, with the same number of points, 14, from 30 games, but with an inferior goal average to Darwen. With just six wins all season, and just two points from 15 away games, they scored only 24 goals. Ernest 'Dick' Pegg finished as top scorer in the league with seven, followed by Walker with four, and Roulston and Shaw with three each. 'Lougburian', the local newspaper football reporter, summed up the thoughts of many Luff fans, when he commented, 'It was a positive relief to many enthusiasts in Loughborough that the curtain has been rung down on what has probably been the most disastrous season in the history of Loughborough Town Football Club.' Little did he know that much worse was to follow.

Loughborough again suffered the humiliation of seeking re-election, along with Lincoln City and Darwen. The other applicants were Burslem Port Vale, Bristol City, Nelson, and New Brighton. At the Football League meeting held on 21 May 1898, they voted as follows: Lincoln City 21, Burslem Port Vale 18, Loughborough 16, Darwen 15, New Brighton 13, Nelson 3, Bristol City 1. Loughborough were thus re-elected, by just one vote, along with Lincoln

City and Burslem Port Vale. The expansion of the Second Division from 16 to 18 clubs, and Burnley gaining promotion to the First Division through Test Matches, created three vacancies. At an adjourned meeting of the league the following week, Glossop, Barnsley, and New Brighton were elected to complete the Second Division for the 1898/99 season.

At the AGM, it was announced that Loughborough recorded a loss of about £150 in 1897/98, increasing the club's deficit to £459 6s 4d. They owed £270 12s 11d to the bank, £93 3s 2d to tradesmen and £25 10s 3d to committee and players. The committee were surprised to receive an application from the Fosse for the transfer of their two amateurs, Beardsley and Bailey. The committee were very strongly of the opinion that if they could prevent the transfers then they would do so. Mr Dormer, a Committee member, thought it was extremely unkind of the Fosse to wish to lure these two players away. Loughborough also decided to investigate the possibility of forming the club into a company with limited liability.

Fosse's season ended as it started with a series of highs and lows, eventually securing mid-table mediocrity. Prior to the home fixture against lowly Darwen on 5 February 1898, a 440-yard challenge race was staged between Billy Dorrell and visiting half-miler C.H. Kilpatrick, which the Fosse winger won to claim the £10 prize. Fosse lost the game 1-0, not helped presumably by fielding their tired star player. Six players had been suspended indefinitely by the club for alcohol-related indiscipline and insubordination. Southern League Southampton knocked Fosse out of the FA Cup, the first time the club had been automatically entered into the first round proper. Fosse's trainer employed a 'paper chase' as an unusual prematch training session. A critical review in the press read, 'Looking back at the past eight months' work of the Fosse club, one scarcely knows whether to blame the club all round that they are not in the First Division and have not yet won the FA Cup, or to sympathise with them because so many other clubs with the same aspirations have gone one better than they. Certain it is that for the past three seasons the Walnut Street people have made exceedingly little progress as far as the results are concerned.'

Operations required to move towards becoming a limited liability company revealed that the club had been rapidly drifting and all season the directorate had been crippled in their efforts due to a formidable overdraft. The wage bill was close to £60 a week. Given the financial status at the start of the season, the results from a playing point of view were by no means bad. A slight improvement had been made in the league compared to the previous two seasons with 33 points, following 32 and 30, respectively but still some way from the 38 points and fourth spot achieved when the Fosse were first elected members of the Football League. Fosse played 30 matches in the Second Division, winning 13, losing ten and drawing seven, with 46 goals scored and 35 conceded. Walker, Swift and Saer played consistently throughout. Forward deficiency came chiefly from the unreliability of the extreme wings, and the lack of a centre-forward to occupy Smith's place after the latter's serious and prolonged injury. For more than half the season the XI 'carried a passenger', so to speak, in Freebairn. Dorrell did not come up to the standard of previous seasons.

McLeod, although openly criticised by supporters and the press, ended the season as top scorer, with 13 league goals. McMillan following with nine, Dorrell seven, Freebairn four, Smith four, King three, Keech three, Coulson one and Watkins one, while Dorrell kicked one in from the penalty spot.

1898/99

The fixture list for the 1898/99 season was determined for the first time using a system developed by a Birmingham gentleman, Mr Fletcher. Matches were nearly all home and away on alternate Saturdays, and in the case of two clubs hailing from the same locality, they never played at home on the same Saturday. Thus, the Fosse and Loughborough played at home on alternate Saturdays.

Facilities at the Athletic Grounds were enhanced in preparation for the 1898/99 season. Drainage was improved, raised banking was constructed around the pitch and significant enhancements were made to the stand and the press box.

Leicester's trainer Jackson left to join Brighton United and was replaced by Bob Dunmore. Compared with previous seasons' transfer activity was limited.

However, it was events off the pitch that dominated the beginning of the 1898/99 campaign as Fosse club secretary William Clark's dealings came under serious scrutiny during early September. First there was the Beardsley affair and then the Rowley affair.

Leicester Fosse endeavoured to induce goalkeeper George Beardsley and other players for that matter to play for them. Beardsley, having either a real grievance or an imaginary one with the Luffs committee, was persuaded to leave and join the Fossils. Discussions took place in public houses in Loughborough between Beardsley and Fosse committee members. Not surprisingly, Loughborough felt somewhat aggrieved and when the Fosse asked for Beardsley's transfer it was refused, and a price was put upon the head of the amateur. Beardsley later formally requested to leave, but that request was also turned down. The Luffs made a formal complaint of 'poaching' against the Fosse to the Football League. The hearing was due to be held on 14 October 1898, but the Football League received a wire withdrawing the charge. It was therefore deemed that Beardsley should be eligible forthwith for the Fosse, and that Loughborough were required to provide an explanation as to why the charge was withdrawn. Henry T. Dunn, Loughborough's secretary, was prepared to produce evidence in support of the poaching charge. However, when he received the wire notifying him of the date of the Management Committee hearing he was on the Isle of Wight, having been recommended by his medical advisor to take a holiday for the benefit of his health.

Mr Dunn immediately wired back stating that he would return home. He arrived the day before the meeting, but found that William Clarke, the Fosse secretary, had been to Loughborough with a view to arranging an amicable settlement and getting the charge withdrawn. An appointment was made at Leicester and just 24 hours before the hearing was due to commence, Messrs. Vickers and Dormer, chairman and ex-chairman of the Loughborough committee had a conference with the Fosse committee. The matter was discussed, and it was agreed that the issue could be settled by Fosse giving Loughborough a cheque for £50 and guarantee match of £25 on 27 December (a Football League fixture) and half the gate over £50. The Fosse also had to pay Loughborough's expenses.

Mr Dunn stated that it was the intention to produce evidence to substantiate the charge of poaching and that he had no hand in the settlement of the matter with the Fosse, and was not therefore personally answerable to the Football League for the course adopted. The arrangement was intended by the Fosse to be of a private and confidential nature. After much discussion and deliberation, the league's Management Committee were thoroughly satisfied that the case of 'poaching' had been established, and the Fosse were told that if it had been proved that the directors were aware of what had been done by their secretary Mr Clarke then the club would have been suspended. Mr Clarke did not put in an appearance and was suspended from all connection with league football with immediate effect. The decision of the committee in no way affected the transfer of Beardsley, and Fosse were compelled to abide by the arrangement already entered into. Having had his authority challenged, Mr Dunn, felt he had no alternative but to resign as the Luffs' secretary.

The Beardsley affair cost the Fosse a pretty penny – a £50 transfer, a £50 fine, and another fine of £10 in respect of William Rowley, who was engaged as a substitute for Beardsley, and the various costs and expenses incurred. To give an indication of the severity of the fine, Fosse were still applying for more time to pay in November. If Fosse had approached Loughborough in a business-like manner, it seems likely that they would have acquired the services of Beardsley for a much lower sum, indeed it would have paid them to have given the Luffs £100 for his services. Loughborough came out of the affair with almost a clean sheet, a small sum of £5 5s and displaying a much 'better spirit towards the Fosse than the Fosse had shown towards Loughborough'. However, as we shall see, the affair in the longer term had a hugely detrimental impact on the club.

Controversy was never too far away; Fosse's signing of Rowley bought the club into conflict yet again with the football authorities. The former England goalkeeper was Stoke City's charismatic wheeler-dealer secretary when he transferred himself in August 1898 and even negotiated a signing-on fee, prior to making his one and only appearance for the Fosse, at home to Lincoln City. Having retired, Rowley had to seek reinstatement as an amateur before he could be appointed as Stoke's secretary. To pay an amateur was a capital offence as far as the Football Association was concerned. Rowley's signing caused an uproar and all parties concerned felt the force of the FA's wrath. The Fosse were fined £10, and Rowley and William Clarke, Fosse's secretary-manager, were each suspended for 12 months for unethical practice.

The fall-out from the affairs rocked both clubs to their very foundations. Leicester's chairman, Samuel Hudson, resigned in January 1899 and director Arthur Staines was suspended for eight months from April when Clarke's first appeal against his sentence was unsuccessful. The Beardsley affair also had a huge impact on Loughborough. Not only did they lose of one of their best players, but also their highly respected club secretary Harry Dunn. Although not immediately apparent, the loss of the latter, even as it turned out not for long, was more damaging to the club than anyone could have imagined.

On the pitch, things were no better. Loughborough had a disastrous start to the season with a 7-0 thrashing by Walsall on the opening day. In fact, they only won one game and accumulated just four points in the eight matches leading up to the first derby day in November. Included in this poor run were 6-1 and 6-0 thumpings away at Newton Heath and Lincoln respectively.

George Johnson, appointed as replacement secretary at Leicester, somehow managed to galvanise the side into serious promotion challengers after an uninspiring start. The Fosse were clear favourites to be crowned 'champions of Leicestershire' again. More than 3,000 spectators, including several hundred Fosse supporters who travelled by Midland Railways, were at the Athletic Grounds for the first Leicester derby of the 1898/99 season, on Saturday 26 November.

The game initially was one-sided; with the Fosse forwards attacking the Loughborough goal in prolonged waves. McMillan scored the opening goal of the game after seven minutes for Leicester after seizing on a clearance from Mumford in the Luffs goal, and with a smart shot hit the back of the net after the ball rebounded off the upright. Loughborough's backs played well, but the forward line could make no headway. Play was fast and furious, and as time progressed Fosse's combination play deteriorated to the level of Loughborough's. Individually Fosse were cleverer than Loughborough, some of whose players lost their heads, with muffed shots, foul play and miskicks. The ball travelled rapidly between the two ends, as players of both sides kicked the ball aimlessly towards their opponents' goal. Loughborough forwards were guilty of missing several easy chances.

McMillan deliberately kicked a Luffs player with a back heel and was immediately reprimanded by the referee, but less than a minute later he committed the same offence. Loughborough back Ward mis-kicked, and left King with a good chance, but Mumford cleared. From a corner by Fulwood, Mumford jumped to clear, and the ball touched the tips of his fingers or the crossbar – or both – and dropped just inside the goal, doubling Fosse's lead. Minutes later, King ran through the Luffs defence to score after an appeal for offside was refused. Free kicks abounded as the game became rough, with Fosse being the main offenders. Mumford stopped a splendid shot before Beardsley cleared after a ferocious scrimmage in the Leicester goalmouth, as the final whistle blew, with Leicester winning 3-0.

After the fixture, it was rumoured that it would be the last game Loughborough would play in the Second Division and that the bank had confiscated the takings of the gate. Many fans regarded the rumours as ridiculous, but they were nevertheless concerned. An announcement in the newspapers on the Monday after derby day confirmed the truth, 'After the league match with Leicester Fosse on Saturday it was understood that Loughborough had finished its career as a Second Division club.

'It was well known in local circles that the end was not far off. It is stated on good authority than an official announcement will probably be made today or tomorrow. The agents of several well-known clubs were spectators of the game on Saturday and that negotiations for Loughborough players were opened. With a view of ascertaining the true position of affairs our representative called upon some of the members of the Loughborough committee on Monday and as a result of the inquiries found that at any rate the announcement of the club's decease was premature.

'No meeting of the club executive was held after the match and there was absolutely no truth in the statement that the receipts of the match were taken by the bank or other creditors, the fact that the bank were protected by guarantees for the overdraft being sufficient to render such action of their part totally unnecessary. The receipts were taken by the committee and were deposited at the bank, a meeting of the committee being called for Monday evening to coincide the question of their disposal. We were informed that the bank have lately submitted that it was time the overdraft was reduced or paid off.

'The committee had been looking forward to Saturday's match to obtain the money requisite for current expenses, and, in view of the bank's intimidation, the club were undoubtedly faced with a serious crisis, as the cash received could not serve both purposes. The takings for the match in consequence of the miserable weather were much less than anticipated ... some £78.'

The club had been in a much worse financial position previously and pulled through, but the complication of adverse circumstances rendered the difficulty more awkward than usual. The latest crisis began with the humiliating defeat at lowly Kettering in the FA Cup on 19 November 1898, which robbed Loughborough of the half-gate of the match with Fosse in the next round of the competition. The share was fully expected to realise £100 and would have practically saved the club. Then came the action of the bank, who 'called in' the overdraft and the committee found themselves obliged to hand over the greater part, if not all, of the receipts of the Fosse fixture, which left them with no cash whatever to pay current expenses or the players' wages.

The players met on the Monday evening and discussed the position and the course they should take in view of the club's financial situation. They came to the conclusion that unless there was some guarantee of their wages being forthcoming the committee could not rely on them to fulfil the club's fixture at Darwen on the Saturday. This was communicated to a meeting of the committee held later in the evening, and it was resolved that the payers should be asked to defer their final decision until later in the week. Mr J.E. Johnson-Ferguson MP, club president, saved the day yet again. He paid his three-month £25 subscription early, which paid the players' wages. A couple of days later, right-winger Bosworth moved to Derby County for a transfer fee in the region of £100, which relieved the club's immediate financial embarrassment, but sadly not for long. The executive sought local players to both replace Bosworth and strengthen the squad.

The first derby game was Leicester's sixth in the club's record-breaking seven consecutive wins in all competitions that began on 22 October with a 4-2 at home against Glossop and ended with a 1-1 draw away to Kettering in the FA Cup on 15 December – during which they scored 26 and conceded just four goals. Meanwhile, the Luffs managed to accumulate just two points in the five league games between derby days – beating a side that was even worse than them – Darwen – away from home.

There was a poor gate for the return league match between the Fosse and the Luffs on the Tuesday after Christmas, 27 December 1898, at Walnut Street. Ward was unfit for the Luffs, severely weakening their defence, while the old Loughburian George Swift was missing at the back for Fosse, as was King at centre-forward. Davis made his first Loughborough appearance on the wing. Early on, Luffs keeper Albert Mumford saved a shot from Robinson that struck Ball's head in transit. Being hampered, the Loughborough goalkeeper carried the ball several yards and was promptly penalised. The 'free' resulted in a corner, and after both Moore and Mumford had cleared, Ball hammered in a shot that struck the underside of the bar and dropped into the net. Incidentally, Mumford was signed from Sheffield Wednesday in 1896 as a centre-forward, and Loughborough gave him a new lease of life which fully exploited his versatility. Minutes later, Ball again hit the crossbar, this time his effort bouncing over, while another shot by the same player went just wide.

After a period of sustained pressure by the Luffs, the Fosse again returned to besiege their opponent's goal. Galbraith, standing close under the bar, applied the finishing touch, but the goal was disallowed for offside. Each time Loughborough forwards travelled into their opponents' half they were penalised either for offside or a foul. With the number of free kicks awarded in their favour, the Fosse were able to continually press, but were foiled again and again mainly through the clever goalkeeping of Mumford. Loughborough's frustrations continued into the second half. Each time they seemed to be on the verge of a breakthrough they were penalised or yet again found themselves offside. Leicester had a couple of opportunities to double their lead, but the best chance of the half came with just seconds to go when a shot from a cross missed the corner of the goal by inches. The exciting encounter ended with a victory, by the narrowest of margins, for the Fosse.

The local press urged people to save Loughborough by attending home fixtures in an article early in 1899, 'Spectators should be loyal, and those who absent themselves from matches week after week cannot honestly call themselves. The gate last Saturday [v Walsall on 31 December 1898] was disgraceful and if this sort of thing continues the spectators will themselves be directly responsible for the club's failure.'

It was not just non-attendance that hampered the club's future, but also the supporters' behaviour. They bought further shame to the club at a Leicester Senior League encounter between Loughborough Athletic (Luffs' reserve team) and Coalville Town at the Athletic Grounds. The visitors took an early lead, but following some 'dubious' decisions by Mr Carpenter, the referee, the home supporters expressed 'considerable dissatisfaction'. Feeling threatened for his own safety by the intolerable abuse he was receiving, Mr Carpenter, who was also the secretary of Leicestershire Football Association, abandoned the game before half-time. The club were found guilty of gross misconduct by the council of the Leicestershire Football Association, the executive closed the Athletic Grounds for two weeks until 6 February, and the club was banned from playing within a radius of six miles. The Loughborough chairman threatened to call the membership together with the intention of closing down the club. A better way out of the difficulty, however, was afterwards arrived at.

The executive of Leicester Fosse generously placed the Walnut Street enclosure at the Loughborough club's disposal for their home fixture against Blackpool on Saturday 4 February. Sympathy with Loughborough was strong in Leicester and as the Fosse were riding high in the Second Division, it was the least they could do to lend help to their neighbours. The Fosse reserve team's match took place at 1.30pm and the Loughborough game at 3pm. Admission charged was for both fixtures, and after expenses Loughborough took two-thirds of the gate. Fosse also agreed to a collection being made for the benefit of the Loughborough club. Donation boxes were placed at the entrances. Fosse also loaned the Luffs a couple of players – Maurice Parry and William Keech. Fosse reserves beat Mexborough 2-1 in the warm-up game and by the time the main event began, around 5,000 spectators, the vast majority being Fosse fans, greeted the Luffs players with a huge cheer. Leicester's football supporters turned up in sufficient numbers to realise a £100 gate, while a sum of £11 was collected to further assist Loughborough in their financial difficulties.

At a meeting of the Loughborough club held at the Greyhound Hotel prior to the Blackpool match, Mr Dunn was unanimously asked to resume as secretary, replacing Mr Harriman, who had resigned on 19 January. Mr Dunn accepted and said that he had received a telegram from Manchester City stating that they were forwarding a cheque for £10. Newton Heath had already promised to consider providing financial assistance. Blackpool wrote expressing sympathy for Loughborough for the 'unjust suspension', and the following letter, published by the local press was received from local rivals Notts County, written by T.E. Harris, 'An old club which has successfully emerged from a long period of adversity, we have every sympathy with your club in the trouble you are passing through, and to show the same in a practical manner we beg your acceptance of the enclosed cheque for £10.

'It is not a large amount, but we hope it may be of some use to you in your difficulties.

'With every good wish for the future.'

The generous gift aroused much grateful feeling among Luff supporters, as besides demonstrating true sportsmanlike sympathy, it was unsolicited.

The two Fosse loanees, Parry and Keech, made a remarkable impact on the fortunes of the club. They were instrumental in a club record Football League win of 10-0 over Darwen on April Fool's Day, against opponents who were in even more trouble than the Luffs. The 'Salmoners' arrived with only ten men and after a spirited first-half performance where they conceded twice, they were destroyed in the second period and shipped eight goals. Pegg scored five and Parker two in front of just 1,500 at the Athletic Grounds.

Trouble, however, was never too far away from Loughborough. At the end of a home fixture against Gainsborough Trinity on Easter Monday, 3 April 1899, which ended 0-0, spectators mobbed referee Mr Shelton. Luffs fans were furious with his inability to clamp down on rough play by Gainsborough and that he had disallowed what appeared to be a fine goal by new signing Walter Allan for offside. The incident was reported by the match officials to the Football Association who delegated the investigation of the charge of serious misconduct to the Leicestershire executive. On Tuesday, 25 April, after hearing evidence from the referee and Mr Thomson from the club, it was decided to close the Athletic Grounds up to 11 September and the club not be allowed to play matches within a six-mile radius. Loughborough were also required to provide better arrangements for referees leaving the field of play and were ordered to pay the expenses of the inquiry. Loughborough finished the season in 17th, with nine points more than bottom side Darwen.

A special meeting of Loughborough supporters was held on Friday, 5 May 1899 to decide whether the club should seek re-election to the Second Division. Although during the first three months of the 1898/99 season they looked like a sinking ship, the club had much improved its position both financially and on the field. Under the secretaryship of Henry Dunn, debts had been reduced by an impressive 75 per cent. In the last seven matches of 1898/99, Loughborough secured eight points out of 14 and scored 23 goals, conceding ten, which was an average that few clubs in the Second Division managed. If this form had been maintained through the season, they would have been fighting the Fosse for a position in the First Division. Loughborough's chairman said that as much as they hated each other he was genuinely sorry that Fosse did not succeed but was also glad as well because Loughborough would have the pleasure of meeting them again. Finally, he and the committee believed that they could do a great deal better by securing young and promising players than by paying transfer fees for players 'who were getting used up'.

The Loughborough committee decided to seek re-election, along with Blackpool. Darwen, who suffered 18 consecutive defeats, which remains a Football League record, and conceded 141 goals – also a record – did not reapply and joined the Lancashire League. Other applicants were Ashton North End, Chesterfield, Chorley, Stockport County, Coventry City, Wigan County and Middlesbrough. Much to the delight of Leicestershire football followers, Loughborough received the highest number of votes (28) at the AGM of the Football League held towards the end of May. Making up the remaining places in the Second Division for 1899/1900 were Middlesbrough and Chesterfield.

Meanwhile, Leicester Fosse had begun 1899 full of hope and optimism with promotion to the First Division a distinct possibility. After beating Arsenal at home in the first game of 1899, they demolished Luton 6-1 at Dunstable Road. The Luton game was effectively over as a contest after a few minutes through the disablement of Ekins, the home team having to play nearly the whole game with only ten men. Sadly, the match was marred by the attempts of the Luton supporters to assault the referee. As a result, the ground was closed for two weeks. A 3-1 home win on 21 January 1899 the following week against Barnsley St Peters sent the Fosse to the top of the Second Division for the first time in their history. A record crowd of 14,000 (generating gate receipts of £344) watched the Fosse draw 1-1 at home against Manchester City. This followed a series of four draws in six games that cost them promotion. Fosse finished in third, just one point adrift of second-placed Glossop, in the first season that automatic promotion and relegation took place instead of Test Matches. They won 18, drew nine and lost seven of their league fixtures, scoring 64 goals – averaging almost two per game, while conceding 42. Three forwards – Rab King (16), Tommy Galbraith (17) and Alf Watkins (13) – scored more than ten league goals.

It was reported by the *Leicester Chronicle* that at the annual meeting of Fosse's shareholders, held at the Victoria Coffee House in mid-June 1899, club president Sir John Rolleston referred to the tremendous progress that had been made during the 1898/99 season. He stated, 'The success [financial] that had been experienced could scarcely fail to be gratifying to each and every shareholder, and all that was wanted to place the club upon a sounder basis was the shareholders' assistance in getting more shares taken up. If they looked back upon the state of affairs which prevailed not so long ago and realised how the club had emerged from its troubles in such encouraging style, and that he and the other shareholders would render all the assistance they possibly could to the directors in their efforts to get the club into the First Division.'

No details of the finances were reported.

1899/1900

The final season of the 19th century would sadly be the last for Leicestershire Football League derby games. Loughborough started the 1890s as the champions of Leicester, but as it ended, they had reached rock bottom, and would shortly become extinct. But again, we are getting ahead of ourselves.

Fosse made only two additions to their squad for the start of the turn-of-the-century season – centre-half Herbert Dainty, and centre-forward Tommy Brown. The centre-half, signed from Kettering, made over 50 appearances for the Fossils during two spells. He became somewhat of a Dundee legend as a player and even returned there as a player-manager during World War I. Brown, who came south from Glenbuck Cherrypickers in Ayrshire, was a goal machine and was Fosse's top scorer for three consecutive seasons, scoring 38 goals from 72 league appearances and three goals in five FA Cup outings. One notable difference was a change in playing strip – out went white shirts and black breeches and in came 'Cambridge' blue shirts and dark blue shorts. There was also a name change as Fosse's home ground became officially known as Filbert Street.

Loughborough retained their former goalkeeper and versatile player, Albert Mumford, as trainer for the 1899/1900 season, and among the principal players signed were goalkeeper Francis Stubbs, backs Walter Hardy, Frederick Bailey and Arthur Roulston, half-backs William Hodgkin, Walter Rose, Charles Rose, Josiah Adcock, and forwards Parker, George Wileman, Thomas Harrison, George Clifford, Arthur Earl and John Tebbs. The committee believed that a 'fairly good team' should be available, which would be improved if supporters turned up in sufficient numbers.

Stubbs was a giant of a man in the William 'Fatty' Foulke mould, attracted the attention of the Luffs after helping Coalville Albion win the Leicestershire Senior League. The team was inexperienced with the exception of the Rose brothers, who were past their best, and Roulston, who was the only player to appear in each of the Luffs' five seasons in the Football League. Nevertheless, the committee felt upbeat. Much of the optimism was based on the performance of Hardy, Hodgkin, Parker and Tebbs in trial matches. John Tebbs, a local outside-left, shone in a match between the first team defence (stripes) and the first team forwards (blues), scoring twice for the stripes and setting up a third, all before half-time.

Loughborough, although undoubtedly short of funds, which handicapped efforts in securing players, started the season with both spirit and enthusiasm. The club's chairman, Mr Fearn, said in a press statement a couple of days before the new season, 'Over-enthusiasm has compelled us to play our first home match at Leicester owing to the suspension of the Loughborough ground and hence on 2 September Loughborough will engage Bolton Wanderers, who have descended from the higher region, on the Fosse Ground, for which we are indebted to the Fosse committee. The kick-off is timed for 3.45pm, and prior to that the Fosse Reserves are engaged in a friendly with Barrow Rising Star. As it is the opening match both Fosse and Loughborough spectators should turn up in great numbers.'

More than 5,000 spectators turned out on a showery autumn afternoon to watch what turned out to be a close and exciting fixture. Luffs twice equalised through Tebbs and Clifford before Jack scored the winner for the Trotters. The following game was against another side relegated from the First Division, Burton Wanderers, which resulted in a 3-1 loss, before Luffs managed a 0-0 draw at home against would-be champions The Wednesday. From then onwards, it was clear from quite early on that the team assembled on a shoestring in the summer, including the return of former players Dolly Rose and George Ward, was simply not up to the task. In the first ten games they accumulated just three points, conceding 20 and scoring only seven times.

The difference in fortunes between the two giants of Leicestershire football could not be starker. While Loughborough were firmly rooted to the bottom of the table, Leicester Fosse were flying high. The Fosse started with three straight victories at Woolwich Arsenal, and against Barnsley and Burton Swifts at home, although on the latter two occasions their attack was poor, and the winning goals in each instance were scored by a defender. At Luton, a disjointed game resulted in a disappointing draw, but the following Monday, 23 September 1899, a victory over Walsall was particularly pleasing on account of Beardsley being unable to play, and a shift having to be made for a goalkeeper at practically the last moment. A draw at home with Burslem Port Vale the previous season was upgraded to a win this time around and one of the newcomers to the Football League, Middlesbrough, went down heavily at Filbert Street, in spite of scoring first. At Chesterfield, another goalless draw ensued, and a 2-2 draw came from Fosse's visit to Bolton Wanderers, where the Leicester team gave a praiseworthy display.

Next came the first Leicestershire derby day of the season. Although the weather was dreadful throughout the morning, the game was witnessed by a good crowd of 4,000 at the Athletic Grounds. Loughborough's chances seemed poor given that they were stuck at the bottom of the table. Nevertheless, Luffs fans came out in numbers eagerly awaiting the 'supreme delight of taking it out of the county town once again as in the old days'. Allan reappeared for the Luffs and Fosse included Beardsley and Swift, two ex-Luffs players – the former a Loughborough native. Swift attracted shouts of derision from the Luffs fans each time he kicked the ball. Instead of putting him off his game, it seemed to spur him on, and he even saved Fosse from disaster. From a free kick, the home forwards got right through to within a couple of yards of the goal. The ball was at the feet of two Luffs forwards and while they stopped to think, Swift gyrated on his heel and effected an incredibly lucky clearance, Loughborough having thrown away the softest of soft chances.

There was little between the sides. Stubbs made two outstanding saves, but to the obvious disappointment of the majority of the crowd, he then allowed a shot to pass through his fingers and between his legs into the back of the net. The goal was credited to Wragg, whose shot should have required little effort to clear. Fosse, encouraged by this fluke, bombarded the Loughborough goal. One of the Fosse forwards charged Stubbs right in the mouth of the goal, one of the backs stepping back to clear close to the goal line. No penalty was given. Stubbs tipped a shot over the bar and then made a series of impressive stops resulting in consecutive corners. Loughborough felt aggrieved to go into the break one down, as they had missed a sitter and conceded a soft goal.

During the interval, a brass band played 'Soldiers of the Queen' and other 'inspiriting' tunes, then luck remained with the Fosse in the second half, with Beardsley tipping a stinging shot on to the crossbar and Swift yet again coming to the rescue to prevent a certain goal with a last-second clearance. The home team continued to press, Beardsley charging down several shots and safely negotiating long efforts that rained in on him. To rub salt into Loughborough's wounds, Fosse doubled their lead with yet another lucky goal. As Stubbs kicked away a shot, the ball accidentally struck Brown, and it rolled into the back of the net. The game ended with a 2-0 victory to the Fosse.

A rare fast fight with The Wednesday the following Saturday, in front of a record 12,000 crowd at Filbert Street, produced yet another goalless draw. The Fosse had gone the first 11 games unbeaten, conceding just four goals in the process. Then on 2 December came the first defeat – at Lincoln, on a day when the Fosse forwards were very disappointing. A point was picked up at New Brighton, followed by three wins at home against Grimsby, Loughborough, and Walsall and just a point from Woolwich Arsenal.

It somehow seems fitting that the final Leicestershire derby took place on the last Christmas Day of the 19th century. One week later was the first day of the 20th century and within a period of just a few months Loughborough FC would no longer exist, and Leicester supporters would have to seek out new rivals. At Filbert Street, it came as no surprise to anyone with an ounce of football knowledge that the Fosse won the game with ease, given that the Luffs were dead and buried by Christmas, having gained just two points from their opening 13 matches. There appeared to be no lack of interest among the Fosse faithful, as about 7,000 witnessed the game. It is difficult to gauge the major attraction of the fixture: the fact it was played on Christmas Day, that it was against the 'auld enemy' or that a Fosse win seemed a certainty. Maybe a mixture of all three, is most likely.

As predicted from the outset there was only one team in it and the Leicester keeper Beardsley, a former Luff, had nothing to do. Even if there had been no Fosse goalkeeper on the field, they would still have won the game with ease. Stubbs, the Luffs' custodian, although making some excellent saves, also made some costly errors. The visitors' halves and backs were poor as they had been all season. Dolly Rose, who led the Loughborough side, was run ragged. Fosse captain George Swift, another former Luff, was by far best player on the pitch. It must have hurt the Luffs fans to be thrashed 4-0 by a team whose backbone was composed of former Loughborough talent.

Loughborough's first win of the season eventually did arrive in the first league fixture of the new century, with a 2-1 home victory against Burton Swifts. Attendances plummeted as the season progressed, with only 400 diehards present for the Luffs' first two-pointer. This victory proved to be the only highlight of a dreadful season. Loughborough only picked up one more point in the remaining 18 games as defeat followed defeat. They suffered their record loss, 12-0 at Woolwich Arsenal on Monday 12 March 1900, after the original game on Boxing Day was abandoned after 75 minutes due to fog. Arsenal had forwarded the necessary travel expenses to transport the players to London. The 11 players only included four regulars, the others being amateurs who had played for the reserve team in the Leicestershire Football League. Two of the players had not even played for several weeks. Loughborough were never in it, with Arsenal scoring four times in front of 800 onlookers at Plumstead in the first half and eight times in the second. Things did not improve as Bolton and Barnsley both put seven past the hapless Luffs, who conceded their 99th and 100th league goals of the season against Gainsborough in their final competitive game, on 28 April 1900, witnessed by only 100 spectators.

At the end of March 1900, the Athletic Grounds was closed for the third time in a short period of time for crowd trouble. At the home game against Woolwich Arsenal on 3 March, the crowd hotly disputed Arsenal's winning goal by Logan in an exciting 3-2 encounter, with the referee Mr Price 'receiving a hostile demonstration' from the 800 spectators present. Loughborough were found guilty, were required to close the Athletic Grounds for a month and were not allowed to play within a radius of six miles. A further charge was made by Mr Wallis, the linesmen, against Loughborough secretary Henry Dunn for 'making observations reflecting upon him as a linesman'. Mr Dunn was found guilty and suspended for a month from taking part in football or football management.

Loughborough's committee virtually collapsed with the loss of Mr Dunn, who had worked tirelessly to keep the club afloat. Players took charge, selecting the team, organising matchdays and paying themselves through the meagre home game gate receipts. Rooted firmly to the bottom of the league, the club haemorrhaged support, with gates rapidly diminishing from 800 for the Middlesbrough game down to 500 for the following week's fixture against Luton.

Loughborough finished bottom of the Second Division, winning only a single game and collecting just eight points from a possible 68, arguably the worst record in the history of the Football League – only Doncaster Rovers have an equally low points record, set in 1904/05, but they had a somewhat better goal average. The Luffs conceded 100 goals in 34 league games, scoring just 18. Loughborough-born John Tebbs finished as the club's top scorer with just three goals. William Hodgkin had the dubious honour of scoring the Luffs last goal in the club's swansong Football League fixture, a 2-1 defeat at home to Gainsborough Trinity. Despite shipping 97 goals, Francis Stubbs moved to First Division side The Wednesday in a £50 transfer. He would later become mayor of Loughborough during the early 1940s.

On a miserable January afternoon at Barnsley – where one end was steadily qualifying as a duckpond – the Fosse won and promotion to the top tier of English football seemed to be a distinct possibility. But at Burton the following week disaster awaited, the Swifts winning 2-0. Eaton then scored both goals as the Fosse beat Burslem Port Vale 2-0 at Corbridge, as they had done the previous season, before 17 February became a date to be remembered since it was the occasion of the Middlesbrough match, at the Linthorpe Road ground, where the pitch was more like a ploughed field.

A great storm had raged that week, paralysing telegraphic transmissions, the Fosse fans having to be content with the bare result – which was good news – instead of a full press report, as their team won 1-0. Although the result was fully deserved it was a lucky goal. Scorer Brown had been offside just a moment before, only a Middlesbrough man happened to touch the ball on its way into the net, making Brown onside.

Chesterfield, who had proved such a tough opponent, were as challenging at home in another drawn game, then a visit to Gainsborough was pointless and a 3-0 defeat ensued. 'Wild' football was played by both sides when Fosse hosted Bolton Wanderers. Waller, the Richmond amateur – the 'Richmond gem' – was, nevertheless, excellent in goal for the Trotters, as he made a series of outstanding saves, one in particular from King in the last ten minutes going on record as one of the best things seen at the ground. That match ended goalless, Newton Heath were beaten 2-0 at Filbert Street, and even by late March Fosse were still in with a shout for a promotion place. Sadly, a 2-0 defeat at Hillsborough, then known as the Owlerton Stadium, by The Wednesday finally ended the 'great fight for promotion'.

Although the players were crushed, Fosse managed to pull themselves together and beat Lincoln City 2-0 the following Saturday. They then had a punishing schedule, playing four league games in just five days. They lost twice away in two days, 3-2 at Newton Heath and 4-1 at Small Heath, on Friday, 13 and Saturday, 14 April respectively, before destroying Gainsborough 5-0 on the Monday. The following day Fosse beat Small Heath 2-0 at Filbert Street. But on the last Saturday of the season, Fosse lost on their own ground for the first time in two seasons, New Brighton doing the damage with a 2-1 victory. In the final game, at Grimsby, Leicester were beaten 6-1, their worst league defeat.

Rab King finished as Fosse's top scorer with 14, followed by Johnny McMillan with 12 and new boy Tommy Brown with nine. The best two home gates of the season were against The Wednesday (£291 4s 6d) and Bolton Wanderers (£288 8s 3d). The record gate for a league match was against Manchester City the previous season when the attendance yielded £344. Leicester finished in fifth place, nine points from runners-up Bolton Wanderers and 11 points from The Wednesday, who were both automatically promoted to the First Division. The gulf between Fosse and Loughborough was an astonishing 35 points.

At the end of the season, the Loughborough committee, with Mr Dunn back at the helm after his ban, formally sought re-election along with Barnsley and Luton, the three teams who made up the bottom three. Given the number of issues both on and off the pitch Loughborough only received the support of three clubs at the annual meeting of the Football League held on 21 May 1900 and failed to be re-elected along with Luton. The clubs elected were Blackpool, Barnsley, and Stockport County. A week later, Loughborough were elected back to the Midland League. Preparations were made to establish a new committee to run the club. Sadly, there was not the interest within the town to save Loughborough FC.

On 29 June 1900, at a meeting held in Loughborough, it was decided that the club was defunct. In one last-ditch attempt at salvation, Henry Dunn called an 'important general meeting' on 3 July 1900 at the Greyhound Hotel. Few people attended and as there seemed no prospect of a satisfactory meeting, no attempt was made to hold one. Not a single member of the club committee put in an appearance. Mr Dunn stated to the small gathering present that the Midland League were anxious to know whether the club would fulfil their 1900/01 fixtures, by which had already been published. They wanted to know by the end of that week, so that arrangements could be made with other clubs as to the fixtures. Mr Dunn unfortunately had little choice but to decline the offer to join the Midland League. The local press reported, 'It seems that Loughborough Football Club is dead' – indeed it was an incredibly sad end to a once proud club. The final debt was just £200, which was much lower than it had been in previous years.

It is difficult to say with any degree of certainty what killed Loughborough FC. There was some bad luck and occasional mismanagement, but it was probably the lack of support and the limited catchment area that ultimately bought the club to an untimely end. Although by comparison with Leicester Fosse and other local Football League clubs, attendances at the Athletic Grounds were low, it must be remembered that in the late 19th century Loughborough had a population of around 22,000, so to attract crowds of up to 10,000 was a remarkable achievement. The running costs, in particular the wage bill, spiralled out of control as the club rapidly rose from regional football to the second tier of professional football in England.

Loughborough FC will never be forgotten. Although they were only in existence for less than 20 years, they were the first Leicestershire club to complete in the FA Cup and in a league competition; they inflicted the record Football League defeat on the mighty Arsenal in 1896, and last but by no means least, Leicester Fosse versus Loughborough 'derby day' encounters provided hitherto unknown intense interest and excitement to football supporters across the county throughout the 1880s and 1890s.

Leicester Fosse, who became Leicester City after the county town was granted city status in 1919, have remained ever since Leicestershire's only Football League club. City's history has had many lows and highs – promotions, relegations, League Cup wins, FA Cup Final defeats and ultimately a victory in 2021, administration and a magnificent new home, the King Power Stadium. But no one who has ever shown any interest in football will ever forget 5,000/1 Leicester City winning the Premier League title in 2016 and parading the trophy through the city before more than 250,000 cheering supporters. Described by many newspapers as the greatest sporting shock ever, the team were dubbed 'The Unbelievables', paying homage to 'The Invincibles' – the undefeated teams of Preston North End (1888/88) and Arsenal (2003/04). Reacting to Leicester winning the title, the Premier League's executive chairman, Richard Scudamore, said, 'If this was a once in every 5,000-year event, then we've effectively got another 5,000 years of hope ahead of us.'

5
Statistics

	Date	Match	Result	Score	Goalscorers	Venue	Attd	Comp
1	5 February 1887	Loughborough v Leicester Fosse	W	4-1		Athletic Grounds, Loughborough		Friendly
2	26 March 1887	Leicester Fosse v Loughborough	W	3-0	Knight (3)	Victoria Park, Leicester		Friendly
3	30 September 1888	Loughborough v Leicester Fosse	W	4-0	**Lowe, Smith (2), Cross**	Athletic Grounds, Loughborough		Friendly
4	17 November 1888	Loughborough v Leicester Fosse	W	3-1	**Rodgers, Gibson, A N Other** / Webb	Athletic Grounds, Loughborough		Friendly
5	23 February 1889	Loughborough v Leicester Fosse	W	2-0	**Smith, Gibson**	Athletic Grounds, Loughborough	800	Leicestershire Challenge Cup R3
6	1 March 1890	Leicester Fosse v Loughborough	W	4-0	Bentley, Webb, Johnston, Murdoch	Sports Grounds, Coalville		Leicestershire Challenge Cup SF
7	13 December 1890	Leicester Fosse v Loughborough	D	1-1	Murdoch / **Cross**	Mill Lane, Leicester	3,000	Friendly
8	29 December 1890	Leicester Fosse v Loughborough	D	1-1	Lomas / **Lowe**	Belgrave Cycle and Cricket Ground, Leicester	3,000	Friendly (charity)
9	7 February 1891	Loughborough v Leicester Fosse	W	3-1	**Freestone, Smith, A.N. Other** / A.N. Other	Athletic Grounds, Loughborough	2,500	Friendly

	Date	Match	Result	Score	Goalscorers	Venue	Attd	Comp
10	14 November 1891	Loughborough v Leicester Fosse	W	6-2	**Carnelley (3), Lowe, Freestone, A.N. Other** / Mouel, Atter	Athletic Grounds, Loughborough	4,000	Midland League
11	28 November 1891	Leicester Fosse v Loughborough	W	1-2	Mouel/ **Freestone, Carnelley**	Walnut Street, Leicester	2,000	Midland League
12	16 January 1892	Loughborough v Leicester Fosse	W	4-1	**Jackson, Smith, Carnelley (2)** / Nuttall	Athletic Grounds, Loughborough	1,500	Friendly
13	23 April 1892	Leicester Fosse v Loughborough	W	1-2	Mouel / **Freestone, Lowe**	Walnut Street, Leicester		Friendly
14	12 November 1892	Loughborough v Leicester Fosse	W	2-1	**Carnelley, Start/** Slack	Athletic Grounds, Loughborough	7,000	Midland League
15	18 March 1893	Leicester Fosse v Loughborough	D	1-1	Dorrell / **Start**	Walnut Street, Leicester	8,000	Midland League
16	5 April 1893	Loughborough v Leicester Fosse	W	4-1	**Freestone, Carnelley (2), Farmer** / Dorrell	Athletic Grounds, Loughborough	5,000	Friendly
17	29 April 1893	Leicester Fosse v Loughborough	W	5-1	Worrall, Slack, Paton, Lowe (2) / **Farmer**	Walnut Street, Leicester	10,000	Friendly

	Date	Match	Result	Score	Goalscorers	Venue	Attd	Comp
18	7 October 1893	Loughborough v Leicester Fosse	W	1-0	**Storer**	Athletic Grounds, Loughborough	6,000	Midland League
19	16 December 1893	Loughborough v Leicester Fosse	W	0-1	Dorrell	Athletic Grounds, Loughborough	8,000	FA Cup
20	6 January 1894	Leicester Fosse v Loughborough	W	4-0	Dorrell, Hill, Brown, Lord	Walnut Street, Leicester	6,000	Midland League
21	30 March 1894	Loughborough v Leicester Fosse	D	1-1	**A.N.Other**/Dorrell	Athletic Grounds, Loughborough	2,000	Friendly
22	14 April 1894	Leicester Fosse v Loughborough	W	6-0	McArthur (3), Priestman (2), Dorrell	Walnut Sreet, Leicester		Friendly
23	15 December 1894	Leicester Fosse v Loughborough	D	1-1	Hill / **Edge**	Walnut Street, Leicester	10,000	FA Cup
24	19 December 1894	Loughborough v Leicester Fosse	D	2-2	**Edge (2)** / Skea, Gallacher	Athletic Grounds, Loughborough	5,000	FA Cup
25	22 December 1894	Leicester Fosse v Loughborough	W	3-0	Gallacher, Hill, Skea (pen)	Walnut Street, Leicester		FA Cup

	Date	Match	Result	Score	Goalscorers	Venue	Attd	Comp
26	11 March 1895	Leicester Fosse v Loughborough	W	3-1	Brown, Skea Gallacher/ **Owen**	North Street, Kettering	2,000	Kettering Challenge Cup SF
27	5 October 1895	Leicester Fosse v Loughborough	W	5-0	Brown, Skea, McArthur, Gallacher (2)	Walnut Street, Leicester	7,000	Second Division
28	16 November 1895	Loughborough v Leicester Fosse	W	1-4	**Davy OG** / Bishop, Davies (2), Lynes	Athletic Grounds, Loughborough	7,000	Second Division
29	18 February 1896	Leicester Fosse v Loughborough	D	2-2	Manson, Gallacher / **Clarke, Logan**	Walnut Street, Leicester	500	Friendly
30	17 March 1896	Loughborough v Leicester Fosse	D	0-0		Athletic Grounds, Loughborough	500	Friendly
31	26 September 1896	Loughborough v Leicester Fosse	W	0-2	McMillan (2)	Athletic Grounds, Loughborough	5,000	Second Division
32	15 October 1896	Leicester Fosse v Loughborough	W	4-2	Fairbairn (2), Carnelley (2) / **Blackett, Jones**	Walnut Street, Leicester	200	Friendly

	Date	Match	Result	Score	Goalscorers	Venue	Attd	Comp
33	25 December 1896	Leicester Fosse v Loughborough	W	4-2	McDonald, Dorrell, Freebairn (2)/ **Brailsford, Jones**	Walnut Street, Leicester	11,000	Second Division
34	31 March 1897	Loughborough v Leicester Fosse	D	0-0		Athletic Grounds, Loughborough		Friendly
35	13 November 1897	Loughborough v Leicester Fosse	D	1-1	**Walker**/ McLeod	Athletic Grounds, Loughborough	5,000	Second Division
36	25 December 1897	Leicester Fosse v Loughborough	W	4-0	Freebairn, McMillan, Smith, McLeod	Walnut Street, Leicester	9,000	Second Division
37	24 February 1898	Leicester Fosse v Loughborough	W	4-0	Keech (3) McLeod	Walnut Street, Leicester		Friendly
38	26 November 1898	Loughborough v Leicester Fosse	W	0-3	Eaton, Fulwood, King	Athletic Grounds, Loughborough	3,000	Second Division
39	27 December 1898	Leicester Fosse v Loughborough	W	1-0	Ball	Walnut Street, Leicester	2,000	Second Division

	Date	Match	Result	Score	Goalscorers	Venue	Attd	Comp
40	25 March 1899	Leicester Fosse v Loughborough	W	1-2	Lyon / **Allan, Pegg**	Walnut Street, Leicester	1,000	Friendly
41	11 November 1899	Loughborough v Leicester Fosse	W	0-2	Wragg, Brown	Athletic Grounds, Loughborough	5,000	Second Division
42	25 December 1899	Leicester Fosse v Loughborough	W	5-0	Bradshaw, King (2), Galbriath, Allen	Filbert Street, Leicester	7,000	Second Division

Note: Loughborough scorers are in bold

Friendly Games and Local Cup Competitions

Games	22
Fosse wins	7
Draws	6
Loughborough wins	9
Fosse goals	41
Loughborough goals	37

Midland League

Games	6
Fosse wins	1
Draws	1
Loughborough wins	4
Fosse goals	9
Loughborough goals	12

FA Cup

Games	4
Fosse wins	2
Draws	2
Loughborough wins	0
Fosse goals	7
Loughborough goals	3

Football League

Games	10
Fosse Wins	9
Draws	1
Loughborough wins	0
Fosse goals	31
Loughborough goals	4

Overall

Games	42
Fosse Wins	19
Draws	10
Loughborough wins	13
Fosse Goals	88
Loughborough Goals	56

Leading Scorers in Leicestershire Derby Games

Leicester Fosse		Loughborough	
Billy Dorrell	7	Albert Carnelley	10
Hugh Gallacher	6	William Freestone	5
Jimmy Brown	4	Smith	5
Willie McArthur	4	William Lowe	4
David Skea	4	Unknown players	3
Fairbairn	3	Robert Edge	3
William Keech	3	William Cross	2
Rab King	3	Oscar Farmer	2
Knight	3	Walter Gibson	2
Johnny McMillan	3	William Jones	2
Albert Carnelley	2	John Start	2
William Lowe	2		
Roddie McLeod	2		
Jimmy Murdoch	2		

Highest Aggregate Score

Loughborough 6 Leicester Fosse 2, 14 November 1891, Midland League

Largest Winning Margin

Leicester Fosse 6 Loughborough 0, 14 April 1894, Friendly

Largest Fosse Wins (Midland League, Football League, FA Cup)

05.10.1895	5-0	Second Division
25.12.1899	5-0	Second Division
25.12.1897	4-0	Second Division
06.01.1894	4-0	Midland League
05.10.1895	5-0	Second Division

Largest Loughborough Wins (Midland League, Football League, FA Cup)

14.11.1891	2-6	Midland League
07.10.1893	0-1	Midland League
12.11.1892	1-2	Midland League
28.11.1891	1-2	Midland League

Players who have scored for Leicester Fosse and Loughborough in derby games:

Jimmy Brown
Albert Carnelley
William Lowe

Players who have played for both Leicester Fosse and Loughborough:

Godfrey Beardsley
Joseph Blackett,
Jimmy Brown
Albert Carnelley
Bertina Carris
John Hamilton
William Harris
William Keech
William Lowe
Maurice Parry
Arthur Roulston
Charles Shelton
George Swift
Henry Whitehead

6

Complete Records

NOTES:
- A: away
- H: home
- All Leicester Fosse home games designated as (H) were played at Walnut (Filbert) Street, Leicester, unless labelled otherwise
- All Loughborough home games designated as (H) were played at Athletic (Hubbards) Grounds, Nottingham Road, Loughborough
- Bel: Belgrave Cricket and Cycle Ground, Leicester
- M: Mill Lane Ground, Leicester
- GR: Aylestone Cricket Ground (Grace Road), Leicester
- VP: Victoria Park, Leicester
- No friendly games other than encounters between Fosse and Loughborough are given after 1890/91
- Only Midland League, Football League and FA Cup goals are included in the seasonal top scorers
- P: postponed
- Aban: abandoned

1884/85
Leicester Fosse

Date	Opposition	Result	Score	Scorers	Competition
01.11.1884	Syston Fosse (Fosse Rd)	W	5-0	West (2), Digley, H. Johnson (2)	Friendly
08.11.1884	Wyggeston Boys School (VP)	D	1-1		Friendly
15.11.1884	Mill Hill House (VP)	L	1-2	W. Johnson	Friendly
22.11.1884	Syston St Peters (A) (12-a-side game)	W	2-1	A.N. Other, W. Johnson	Friendly
29.11.1884	Mill Hill House (VP)	D	0-0		Friendly
06.12.1884	Belgrave 2nd Team (A)	L	0-2		Friendly
03.01.1885	Melbourne Hall (VP)	W	2-0	West, Lewitt	Friendly
10.01.1885	Syston Fosse (A)	Aban (rain)	1-0	J. Johnson	Friendly
24.01.1885	St Marys (VP)	W	1-0		Friendly
31.01.1885	Mill Hill House (VP)	D	1-1		Friendly
07.02.1885	Syston St Peters (VP) (12-a-side game)	W	2-0	H. Johnson, Coleman	Friendly

07.03.1885	Wyggeston Boys School (VP)*	L	0-1		Friendly
14.03.1885	Mill Hill House (VP)	W	2-0	West, H. Johnson	Friendly
21.03.1885	St Marys (VP)	W	1-0		Friendly

*It was discovered after the game that the school team had 13 players

1885/86
Leicester Fosse

Date	Opposition	Result	Score	Scorers	Competition
03.10.1885	Trinity Band of Hope (VP)	W	6-0	J. Johnson (2), West (2), Coleman, Lewitt	Friendly
17.10.1885	Wyggeston Boys School (VP)	W	4-1		Friendly
24.10.1885	Market Harborough 2nd Team (VP)	D	1-1		Friendly
07.11.1885	Mill Hill House (VP)	L	0-1		Friendly
14.11.1885	Belgrave (played on private ground)	W	3-0	J. Johnson, E. Johnson, West	Friendly
21.11.1885	St Marys (VP)	W	3-0		Friendly

30.01.1886	Mill Hill House (VP)*	W	3-0	J. Johnson (2), E. Johnson	Friendly
06.02.1886	Wyggeston Boys School (V)	W	1-0		Friendly
13.02.1886	Syston Wreake Valley (A)	W	2-1	J. Johnson, E. Johnson	Friendly
20.02.1886	Belgrave (VP)	W	1-0	Gardner	Friendly
17.04.1886	Leicester Town (VP)	W	2-0	Bankart (2)	Friendly

* Mill Hill House played with one player short

1886/87
Leicester Fosse

Date	Opposition	Result	Score	Scorers	Competition
16.10.1886	Leicester Association (VP)	W	2-1	A.N. Other, Simpson	Friendly
23.10.1886	Barwell (A)	D	1-1	West	Friendly
30.10.1886	Leicester Wanderers (VP)	L	0-2		Friendly
06.11.1886	Coalville (A)*	Aban	0-0		Friendly
13.11.1886	Wyggeston School Past and Present (VP)	W	5-0	Johnson, Brown, Knight (3)	Friendly

20.11.1886	Belgrave (A)	W	2-0	J. Johnson, Roberts	Friendly
27.11.1886	Leicester Association (A)	L	0-1		Friendly
04.12.1886	St Marks (VP)	D	2-2		Friendly
11.12.1886	Leicester Wanderers (VP)	W	3-0	OG, J. Johnson, A.N. Other	Friendly
22.01.1887	Coalville (VP)*	W	3-0	Knight, A.N. Other, Brown	Friendly
29.01.1887	Wigston (VP)	W	6-0		Friendly
05.02.1887	Loughborough (A)	L	1-4		Friendly
12.02.1887	Belgrave (VP)	W	5-0		Friendly
19.02.1887	Barwell (VP)	W	2-0		Friendly
26.02.1887	Notts St Saviours (A)	D	1-1		Friendly
05.03.1887	Market Harborough (VP)	L	0-1		Friendly
19.03.1887	Wyggeston School Past and Present (VP)	W	9-0		Friendly
26.03.1887	Loughborough (VP)	W	3-0	Knight (3)	Friendly
09.04.1887	Mill Hill House Past and Present (VP)	W	1-0		Friendly

* Coalville players walked off the pitch

Loughborough FC

Date	Opposition	Result	Score	Scorers	Competition
25.09.1886	Derby County Wanderers (H)	D	1-1	Gadsby	Friendly
02.10.1886	Castle Donington (A)	L	0-5		Friendly
09.09.1886	Kegworth St Andrews (H)	D	2-2		Friendly
23.09.1886	Coalville (A)	D	1-1		Friendly
30.09.1886	Long Eaton Athletic (H)	L	1-5		Friendly
06.11.1886	Melbourne Town (H)	W	4-3	Lockwood (2), Gadsby (2)	Friendly
13.11.1886	Sheepshed Town (H)	D	3-3	Smalley, A.N. Others	Friendly
20.11.1886	Leicester Town (A)	D	0-0		Friendly
27.11.1886	Loughborough Liberal Club (H)	W	8-1		Friendly
02.12.1886	Melbourne Town (A)	L	0-2		Friendly
18.12.1886	Long Eaton Athletic (H)	W	2-1	Gadsby, Burton	Friendly
25.12.1886	Loughborough Olympic (H)	W	7-0		Friendly
26.12.1886	Keyworth (H)	D	2-2		Friendly
08.01.1887	Sheepshed Town (A)	P			Friendly

15.01.1887	Keyworth (A)	W	3-1		Friendly
22.01.1887	Sheepshed (H)	L	1-2		Friendly
05.02.1887	Leicester Fosse (H)	W	4-1		Friendly
19.02.1887	Coalville (H)	W	2-0		Friendly
12.03.1887	Sheepshed (A)	D	5-5	Cockain, A.N. Others	Friendly
26.03.1887	Leicester Fosse (A)	L	0-3		Friendly

1887/88
Leicester Fosse

Date	Opposition	Result	Score	Scorers	Competition
01.10.1887	Market Harborough (VP)	W	4-0	Wright, Knight (3)	Friendly
08.10.1887	Mill Hill House (VP)	W	2-0	Wright, A.N. Other	Friendly
15.10.1887	Wellingborough (A)	L	0-3		Friendly
22.10.1887	Notts County Reserves (Bel)	L	0-5		Friendly
29.10.1887	St Saviours (Bel)	W	4-2	Bankart, James, Hassell, Knight	Leicestershire Challenge Cup R1

05.11.1887	Burton Swifts (Bel)	L	0-4		Friendly
12.11.1887	Kettering (Bel)	L	2-4	E. Johnson, Ashmole	Friendly
26.11.1887	St Saviours (Bel)	W	5-0	James, Thompson (2), Bentley (2)	Leicestershire Challenge Cup R1 replay
19.11.1887	Market Harborough (A)	D	2-2		Friendly
03.12.1887	Leicester Wanderers (Bel)	W	1-0	James	Friendly
15.12.1887	Leicester Banks (VP)	L	4-6	Bentley, Ashmole, James, Knight	Friendly
24.12.1887	Sheepshed (A)	D	3-3	Thompson (2), Knight	Leicestershire Challenge Cup R2
26.12.1887	Leicester Association (Bel)				Friendly
07.01.1888	Notts County Reserves (A)	L	0-1		Friendly
14.01.1888	Mill Hill House (Bel)	L	0-2		Friendly
21.01.1888	Shepshed (A)	D	2-2		Leicestershire Challenge Cup R2 replay
26.01.1888	Thursday Half Holiday XI (VP)				Friendly
28.01.1888	Shepshed (A)	L	1-2	Knight	Leicestershire Challenge Cup R2 2nd replay

04.02.1888	Leicester Association (VP)				Friendly
11.02.1888	Kettering (A)	L	0-3		Friendly
03.03.1888	Burton Swifts (A)	D	0-0		Friendly
10.03.1888	Leicester Association (VP)	W	2-0		Friendly
15.03.1888	Leicester Banks (VP)				Friendly
24.03.1888	Mill Hill House Past and Present (Bel)				Friendly
31.03.1888	Leicester Wanderers (VP)	D	1-1	Thompson	Friendly
07.04.1888	Rushden (Bel)				Friendly
21.04.1888	Coalville Town (A)	W	3-1	Thompson, Knight, E. Johnson	Friendly
05.05.1888	Coalville Town (A)	L	1-5		Friendly

Loughborough FC

Date	Opposition	Result	Score	Scorers	Attd	Competition
22.09.1887	Sheepshed Town (H)	W	2-1	Kelham, Simpson		Friendly
31.09.1887	Notts County Reserves (H)	L	1-6	Kelham		Friendly
08.10.1887	Notts St Catherines (H)	L	0-1			Friendly
15.10.1887	Grantham Rovers (A)	L	3-5			Friendly
22.10.1887	Notts Olympic (H)	W	9-1			Friendly
05.11.1887	Notts St Catherines (H)	W	5-0	Dawson, Kelham (2), A.N. Others		Friendly
11.11.1887	Sheepshed Town (H)	W	9-2			Friendly
12.11.1887	Grantham Rovers (H)	L	1-3			Friendly
19.11.1887	Kegworth St Andrews (H)	W	6-1			Leicestershire Challenge Cup R1
26.11.1887	Derby County Reserves (H)	W	3-0	Shannon, Brewin, A.N. Other	300	Friendly
05.12.1887	Notts County Reserves (A)	L	3-5	Shannon, Brewin, A.N. Other		Friendly
12.12.1887	Aston Villa Reserves (H)	W	8-1			Friendly

19.12.1887	Lincoln City (A)	L	2-5			Friendly
26.12.1887	Beeston St Johns (H)	L	4-5			Friendly
31.12.1887	Long Eaton Rangers (H)	W	3-0			Friendly
07.01.1888	Burton Alma (A)	W	2-0			Friendly
14.01.1888	Notts United Amateurs (H)	D	2-2	Rodgers, A.N. Other		Friendly
21.01.1888	Notts Olympic (H)	L	3-4	Shannon (2), A.N. Others		Friendly
04.02.1888	Aston Villa Reserves (H)	L	1-4	Shannon	1,000	Friendly
11.02.1888	Burton Alma (H)	W	1-0			Friendly
18.02.1888	Castle Donington (H)	D	2-2	Cross, A.N. Other		Friendly
25.02.1888	Burton Swifts (H)	L	2-3			Friendly
03.03.1888	Leicester St Saviours Inst. (H)	L	1-2			Friendly
10.03.1888	Sheepshed Town (A)	W	3-1			Friendly
31.03.1888	Notts Olympic (A)	W	4-3			Friendly

1888/89
Leicester Fosse

Date	Opposition	Result	Score	Scorers	Competition
16.09.1888	Long Eaton Midland (A)	L	1-4		Friendly
22.09.1888	Nottingham Forest Reserves (VP)	L	0-3		Friendly
30.09.1888	Loughborough (A)	L	0-4		Friendly
06.10.1888	Leicester Teachers (V)	W	5-0		Friendly
13.10.1888	Coalville Town (VP)	W	4-0	Bentley, E. Johnson (2), Knight	Friendly
20.10.1888	Shepshed (A)	D	2-2	Webb, A.N. Other	Friendly
27.10.1888	Market Harborough (A)	W	6-0	Webb, A.N. Others	Friendly
03.11.1888	Kettering (A)	W	2-1	Johnson, Draper	Friendly
10.11.1888	Syston Wreake Valley (VP)	W	12-1	Glover, Webb (6), Knight (4), E. Johnson	Leicestershire Challenge Cup R1
17.11.1888	Loughborough (A)	L	1-3	Webb	Friendly
24.11.1888	Nottingham Forest Reserves (A)	L	1-2	Webb	Friendly
01.12.1888	Kettering (VP)	L	0-1		Friendly

08.12.1888	Mill Hill House (A)	W	3-0		Friendly
15.12.1888	Wellingborough (VP)	D	0-0		Friendly
22.12.1888	Beeston St Johns (VP)				Friendly
29.12.1888	Notts County Reserves (A)	D	0-0		Late arrival of Fosse; 30 mins each half
05.01.1889	Market Harborough (VP)	D			Friendly
12.01.1889	Bulwell United (H)	D	0-0		Friendly
19.01.1889	Sawley United (A)	W	3-1	Webb (2), Knight	Friendly
26.01.1889	Long Eaton Midland (VP)	L	2-3		Friendly
02.02.1889	Notts County Reserves (VP)	L	1-2		Friendly
09.02.1889	Wellingborough (A)				Friendly
16.02.1889	Notts St Johns (A)	D	2-2		Friendly
23.02.1889	Loughborough (A)	L	0-2		Leicestershire Challenge Cup R3
09.03.1889	Leicester Teachers (VP)	W	2-1		Friendly
16.03.1889	Wellingborough (A)	W	8-2	Webb (4), E. Johnson (2), Knight, Sudbury	Friendly

23.03.1889	Shepshed (VP)	W	3-2		Friendly
30.03.1889	Leicester Teachers (VP)	W	2-0	Gardner, West	Friendly
06.04.1889	Bulwell United (A)	D	0-0		Friendly
13.04.1889	Mill Hill House (A)	W	3-2	E. Johnson, Perry, Knight	Leicester Children's Hospital Fund
20.04.1889	Coalville (A)	W	1-0	Gardner	Friendly

Loughborough FC

Date	Opposition	Result	Score	Scorers	Attd	Competition
22.09.1888	Castle Donington (A)	W	4-1			Friendly
30.09.1888	Leicester Fosse (H)	W	4-0	Lowe, Smith (2), Cross		Friendly
06.10.1888	Derby Midland (H)	W	1-0			Friendly
20.10.1888	Coalville Town (H)	P				Friendly
27.10.1888	Derby Junction (A)	L	1-5			Friendly
03.11.1888	Derby Junction (H)	W	6-2	OG, Rodgers (2), Peters		Friendly
09.11.1888	Castle Donington (H)	W	5-0			Friendly

Date	Opponent	Result	Score	Scorers	Att	Competition
10.11.1888	Kettering Town (H)	W	7-2	Bailey, Cross, A.N. Other		Friendly
17.11.1888	Leicester Fosse (H)	W	3-1	Rodgers, Gibson, A.N. Other		Friendly
24.11.1888	Derby St Lukes (H)	Aban (bad light)	3-1			Friendly
01.12.1888	Grantham Rovers (H)	W	5-2	Bailey, A.N. Others		Friendly
08.12.1888	Belper (A)	L	4-6			Friendly
08.12.1888	*Leicester Wanderers (H)	W	8-2		300	Leicestershire Challenge Cup R2
15.12.1888	Derby St Lukes (A)	L	2-3	Bailey, Swifts		Friendly
22.12.1888	Rotherham Swifts (A)	L	0-3			Friendly
24.12.1888	Sheffield Heeley (H)	W	3-0	Kelham, Cross, A.N. Other		Friendly
25.12.1888	Notts Wanderers (H)	L	1-2	Taylor		Friendly
26.12.1888	Birmingham Excelsior (H)	W	10-2	Bailey (2), Gibson, Taylor, Rodgers (2), A.N. Others		Friendly
30.12.1888	Nottingham Swifts (H)	W	5-1	Gadsby, Smith, A.N. Others		Friendly

05.01.1889	Burton Wanderers (A)	L	0-3			Friendly
12.01.1889	Kettering Town (A)	W	7-3	Smith, A.N. Others		Friendly
19.01.1889	Small Heath Alliance (A)	L	0-6		3,000	Friendly
26.01.1889	Burton Wanderers (H)	W	2-0	Gibson, A.N. Other		Friendly
02.02.1889	Kettering Town (A)	W	2-0	Bailey (2)		Kettering Challenge Cup R2
16.02.1889	Belper (H)	W	4-1	Rodgers, Gadsby, AN Others		Friendly
23.02.1889	Leicester Fosse (H)	W	2-0	Smith, Gibson	800	Leicestershire Challenge Cup R3
05.03.1889	Grantham Rovers (at Kettering Town FC)	L	0-3			Kettering Challenge Cup SF
30.03.1889	Mill Hill House (at Coalville)	W	3-0	Rodgers, Gibson, Smith	1,800	Leicestershire Challenge Cup Final

*This game against Leicester Wanderers was contested by Loughborough Athletic (reserve team)

1889/90
Leicester Fosse

Date	Opposition	Result	Score	Scorers	Competition
28.09.1889	Bullwell Forest (A)	L	0-3		Friendly
05.10.1889	Mill Hill House (M)	W	3-1	A.N. Other, Webb, Murdoch	Friendly
12.10.1889	Grantham (A)	L	0-2		Friendly
19.10.1889	Notts Mapperley (A)	L	0-2		Friendly
26.10.1889	Leicester Teachers (M)	W	6-2		Friendly
02.11.1889	Coalville Town (A)	W	3-1	Murdoch, Webb (2)	Friendly
09.11.1889	Market Harborough (M)	W	9-0		Friendly
16.11.1889	Long Eaton Midland (A)	L	0-2		Friendly
23.11.1889	Nottingham Forest Reserves (M)	L	0-1		Friendly
30.11.1889	Shepshed (M)	W	6-1		Kettering Charity Cup R1
14.12.1889	Leicester Teachers (H)	W	2-0	Webb, E. Johnson	Leicestershire Challenge Cup R2
21.12.1889	Grantham Rovers (A)	L	0-3		Friendly

26.12.1889	Stafford Rangers (A)	L	1-2	Webb	Friendly
11.01.1890	Notts County Reserves (M)	L	1-2	Murdoch	Friendly
18.01.1890	Kettering (A)	L	2-4	Thompson, Atter	Friendly
25.01.1890	Beeston St Johns (A)	L	1-5		Friendly
01.02.1890	Beeston St Johns (M)	W	4-0		Friendly
08.02.1890	Kettering (A)	D	2-2		Kettering Charity Cup R3
22.02.1890	Kettering (M)	L	1-3		Kettering Charity Cup R3 replay
01.03.1890	Loughborough (A) (played at Sports Ground, Coalville)	W	4-0	Bentley, Murdoch, Webb, E Johnson	Leicestershire Challenge Cup SF
08.03.1890	Bulwell (H)	W	5-0	Atter (2), Webb (2), E Johnson	Friendly
15.03.1890	Coalville Town (M)	D	1-1		Friendly
29.03.1889	Coalville Town (A) (played at Loughborough)	D	1-1	Webb	Leicestershire Challenge Cup Final
04.04.1890	Gresley Rovers (A)				Friendly
05.04.1890	Notts County Reserves (M)	L	2-3	Webb, OG	Friendly

| 08.04.1890 | Sheffield Montrose (M) | W | 2-0 | Gardner, AN Other | Friendly |
| 12.04.1890 | Coalville Town (A) (played at Loughborough) | W | 4-0 | Rowson, Murdoch, F Gardner, Thompson | Leicestershire Challenge Cup Final replay |

Loughborough FC

Date	Opposition	Result	Score	Scorers	Competition
21.09.1889	Notts Olympic (A)	W	4-1	Kelham, Gibson, Cross, A.N. Other	Friendly
28.09.1889	Notts County Reserves (H)	L	2-6	Vessey (2)	Friendly
05.10.1889	Beeston (H)	W	5-1	Cross, Vessey, A.N. Others	Friendly
12.10.1889	Grantham Rovers (A)	L	0-3		Friendly
19.10.1889	Belper (A)	L	2-3		Friendly
26.10.1889	Derby St Lukes *	W	2-1	Coltman, Simpson	FA Cup 2QR
02.11.1889	Rotherham Swifts (A)	L	1-4		Friendly
09.11.1889	Derby St Lukes	L	0-2		FA Cup 2QR

16.11.1889	Sheepshed Town (A)	W	8-2	Angrave, Rodgers (2), Gibson, OG, A.N. Others	Friendly
17.11.1889	Everton Reserves (H)	W	7-0		Friendly
21.11.1889	Leicester Wanderers (A)	W	5-1	Cross, A.N. Others	Friendly
28.11.1889	Notts Olympic (H)	W	2-1	Rodgers, Cross	Friendly
14.12.1889	Leicester Wanderers (H))	W	4-0	Cross (2), Wiseman (2)	Friendly
23.12.1889	Leicester Wanderers (H)	W	Wanderers failed to turn up, the tie was awarded to L'boro		Leicestershire Challenge Cup R2
26.12.1889	London Casuals (H)	L	1-2		Friendly
28.12.1889	Hathern Britannia (H)	W	2-1		Friendly
04.01.1890	Derby St Lukes (H)	L	1-3	Palmer	Friendly
11.01.1890	Leicestershire XI (H)	D	4-4	Palmer, Wiseman, A.N. Others	Friendly
25.01.1890	Notts Jardines (H)	L	1-4	Cross	Friendly
01.02.1890	Rotherham Swifts (H)	L	0-7		Friendly
08.02.1890	Newark (H)	W	2-1	Rodgers, Gibson	Friendly

22.02.1890	Matlock (H)	D	3-3	Rodgers, Cross, Wiseman	Friendly
25.02.1890	Matlock (A)	L	1-2		Friendly
01.03.1890	Leicester Fosse (A) (at the Sports Ground, Coalville)	L	0-4		Leicestershire Challenge Cup SF
15.03.1890	Heanor (H)	D	3-3	Peters, Angrave, Rodgers	Friendly
22.03.1890	Long Eaton Athletic (H)	D	0-0		Friendly
19.04.1890	Notts Jardines (A)	D	3-3		Friendly

* Game ordered to be replayed due to Loughborough fielding an ineligible player

1890/91
Leicester Fosse

Date	Opposition	Result	Score	Scorers	Competition
06.09.1890	Boston United (A)	W	7-4	E. Johnson, Webb (3), Nuttall, A.N. Others	Friendly
13.09.1890	Singers (M)	W	5-3	Bird (2), Webb, Bentley, Johnson	Friendly
20.09.1890	Northampton (M)	W	10-0		Friendly
25.09.1890	Wellingborough Grammar School (A)	W	4-2	Webb (3), E. Johnson	Friendly

Date	Opponent	Result	Score	Scorers	Competition
27.09.1890	Notts Mapperley (M)	W	3-0		Friendly
04.10.1890	Burton Wanderers (M)	L	0-4		FA Cup 1QR
11.10.1890	Long Eaton Athletic (M)	W	3-2	Atter, E. Johnson, Webb	Friendly
16.10.1890	Nottingham Forest Reserves (M)	W	3-2	Nuttall, Atter, Webb	Friendly
18.10.1890	Burton Casuals (A)	L	0-1		Friendly
25.10.1890	Wellingborough Grammar School (M)	W	4-1		Friendly
01.11.1890	Beeston St John (M)	W	4-1	Webb (2), Atter, Murdoch	Friendly
08.11.1890	Notts County Reserves (A)	W	4-3	Atter, Murdoch (2), Webb	Friendly
15.11.1890	Aston Villa Reserves (M)	L	2-3	Flint, Webb	Friendly
24.11.1890	Finedon (A)	L	0-1		Kettering Charity Cup R1
06.12.1890	Derby County Wanderers (M)	W	3-1	Webb (3)	Friendly
13.12.1890	Loughborough (M)	D	1-1	Murdoch	Friendly
26.12.1890	Stafford Rangers (A)	D	1-1		Friendly
26.12.1890	London Casuals (M)	W	1-0	E. Johnson	Friendly

29.12.1890	Loughborough (Bel)	D	1-1	Lomas	Charity match
03.01.1891	Kettering Town (A)				Friendly
17.01.1891	Melton Rovers (A)	W	6-2		Friendly
24.01.1891	Melton Rovers (M)	W	10-0	Davis, Flint, Murdoch (2), Webb (2), E. Johnson (2), Atter (2)	Leicestershire Challenge Cup R1
31.01.1891	Leicester Teachers (M)	W	8-0	Atter, Webb (3), Murdoch, Flint, A.N. Others	Friendly
07.02.1891	Loughborough (A)	L	1-3	A.N. Other	Friendly
14.02.1891	Stafford Rangers (M)	L	0-2		Friendly
21.02.1891	Leicester Teachers (A) (played at Coalville)	W	3-1	Webb, Atter (2)	Leicestershire Challenge Cup SF
28.02.1891	Notts County Reserves (M)	D	3-3		Friendly
07.03.1891	Grantham Rovers (A)	L	2-3	A.N. Other, Webb	Friendly
14.03.1891	Nottingham Forest Reserves (M)	L	2-3	E. Johnson, Hanford	Friendly
21.03.1891	Gresley Rovers (A) (played at Loughborough)	W	2-0	Webb, E. Johnson	Leicestershire Challenge Cup Final

28.03.1891	Notts Olympic (M)	W	5-0	Webb (3), A.N. Others	Friendly
30.03.1891	Burton Wanderers (M)	D	2-2	Webb, A.N. Other	Friendly
31.03.1891	Nottingham Forest Reserves (M)	W	1-0		Friendly
04.04.1891	Sheffield Attercliffe	L	2-3	E. Johnson, R. Smith	Friendly
11.04.1891	Long Eaton Athletic (A)*	W	3-0	Bennett (2), Atter	Friendly
11.04.1891	Kettering Town (H)*	W	3-2		Friendly
13.04.1891	Leicester Teachers/YMCA Select (M)	W	2-1		Friendly
18.04.1891	Stafford Rangers (M)	W	1-0	Webb	Friendly
25.04.1891	Burton Alma (M)	W	5-1	Webb (2), E. Johnson (2), Flint	Friendly
27.04.1891	Notts County (M)	D	2-2	Webb, Atter	Friendly

*Mixed team – two games played on the same day

Midland Alliance League 1890/91

		P	W	D	L	F	A	Pts
1	Notts County Reserves	14	9	4	1	33	17	22
2	Doncaster Rovers	14	9	1	4	43	19	17
3	**Loughborough**	**14**	**7**	**2**	**5**	**35**	**23**	**16**
4	Grantham Rovers	14	5	4	5	33	30	14
5	Heanor Town	14	5	2	7	32	41	12
6	Newark	14	4	4	6	26	37	12
7	Notts Olympic	14	3	3	8	20	39	9
8	Sheffield	14	3	2	9	23	37	8
9	Notts Jardine	9	1	2	6	13	28	4
10	Rotherham Swifts	6	1	0	5	8	22	2

Note: Notts Jardines and Rotherham Swifts resigned during the season. All results expunged.

Notts Olympic deducted two points for playing an ineligible player.

Loughborough FC

Date	Opposition	Result	Score	Scorers	Attd	Competition
13.09.1890	Beeston (A)	W	4-3	Smith, Rodgers, Freestone, Kelham		Friendly
21.09.1890	Doncaster Rovers (A)	L	0-4			Midland Alliance
28.09.1890	Sheffield (A)	L	1-2			Midland Alliance
04.10.1890	Derby Midland (H)	W	3-2	Smith, Lowe, Cross	1,000	FA Cup 1QR
11.10.1890	Notts Jardines (A)	W	3-1	Plackett, Kelham (2)		Midland Alliance

18.10.1890	Heanor Town (H)	D	3-3	Lowe, Freestone, A.N. Other		Midland Alliance
25.10.1890	Burton Wanderers (H)	W	8-1	Freestone (2), Kelham, Lowe, Smith, A.N. Others		FA Cup 2QR
01.11.1890	Newark (A)	L	0-1			Midland Alliance
08.11.1890	Notts Olympic (H)	W	3-1	Lowe (2), A.N. Other		Midland Alliance
15.11.1890	Belper Town (H)*	W	5-2	Lowe, Kelham (2), Plackett, A.N. Other	1,500	FA Cup 3QR
22.11.1890	Rotherham Swifts (A)	L	1-3			Midland Alliance
29.11.1890	Notts County Reserves (A)	D	1-1			Midland Alliance
06.12.1890	Sheffield United (A)**	L	1-6	Smith		FA Cup 4QR
13.12.1890	Leicester Fosse (A)	D	1-1	Cross	3,000	Friendly
20.12.1890	Sheffield (H)	W	7-2	Lowe, Freestone, Smith, A.N. Others		Midland Alliance
26.12.1890	London Casual (H)	W	4-2		1,000	Friendly
29.12.1890	Leicester Fosse (A)	D	1-1	Lowe	3,000	Charity match
03.01.1891	Doncaster Rovers (H)	W	3-0	Cross, Kelham, Lowe		Midland Alliance
10.01.1891	Grantham Rovers (H)	W	3-1	Smith, Kelham, A.N. Other		Midland Alliance

263

17.01.1891	Notts Jardines (H)	W	3-0	Kelham, Smith A.N. Other		Midland Alliance
24.01.1891	Notts Olympic (A)	W	5-0			Midland Alliance
31.01.1891	Rotherham Swifts (H)	W	4-1			Midland Alliance
07.02.1891	Leicester Fosse (H)	W	3-1	Freestone, Smith, A.N. Other	2,500	Friendly
14.02.1891	Notts County Reserves (H)	L	2-4			Midland Alliance
21.02.1891	Heanor Town (A)	L	1-2			Midland Alliance
28.02.1891	Beeston (H)	W	7-0	Kelham, Smith (3), Plackett, Freestone, A.N. Other		Friendly
07.03.1891	Derby St Lukes (H)	W	5-1			Friendly
21.03.1891	Kettering (A)	W	3-0	Smith, Plackett, Freestone		Friendly
27.03.1891	Newark (A)	W	6-2	Plackett (2), Kelham, Cross, Smith, A.N. Other		Midland Alliance
01.04.1891	Bury Wanderers (H)	W	3-0	Plackett, Kelham (2)	800	Charity Match
11.04.1891	Matlock (A)	L	1-2			Friendly
18.04.1891	Grantham Rovers (A)	L	1-4	Cross		Midland Alliance

Notes: * The cup tie was drawn to be played at Belper but switched to Loughborough's ground on the payment of a cash inducement.

** The cup tie was drawn to be played at Loughborough but switched to Sheffield United's Bramall Lane on the payment of a cash inducement.

1891/92
Midland League

		P	W	D	L	F	A	Pts
1	Rotherham Town	20	13	1	6	70	41	27
2	Gainsborough Trinity	20	12	2	6	49	31	26
3	Burslem Port Vale	20	11	1	8	49	33	23
4	Wednesbury Old Athletic	20	9	5	6	49	41	23
5	Burton Wanderers	20	10	2	8	48	32	22
6	Doncaster Rovers	20	8	5	7	30	36	21
7	Grantham Rovers	20	6	6	8	29	37	18
8	**Loughborough**	**20**	**8**	**1**	**11**	**42**	**46**	**17**
9	Long Eaton Rangers	20	5	7	8	32	46	17
10	Derby Junction	20	4	5	11	21	41	13
11	**Leicester Fosse**	**20**	**5**	**3**	**12**	**21**	**56**	**13**

Leicester Fosse

Date	Opposition	Result	Score	Scorers	Attd	Competition
12.09.1891	Derby Junction (GR)	W	1-0	Atter		Midland League
03.10.1891	Small Heath (GR)	L	2-6	Nuttall, Herrod	4,000	FA Cup (1QR)
10.10.1891	Grantham Rovers (GR)	W	3-1	Lord, Webb, Atter	2,000	Midland League
17.10.1891	Burton Wanderers (A)	L	0-6		2,000	Midland League
14.11.1891	Loughborough (A)	L	2-6	Mouel, Atter	3,000	Midland League
28.11.1891	Loughborough (H)	L	1-2	Mouel	2,000	Midland League
05.12.1891	Wednesbury Old Athletic (A)	W	4-3	Hufton, Mouel, Atter, Webb	2,000	Midland League

19.12.1891	Grantham Rovers (A)	L	0-2			Midland League
26.12.1891	Doncaster Rovers (A)	L	0-1		1,000	Midland League
02.01.1892	Burton Wanderers (H)	L	1-6	Bennett	1,000	Midland League
09.01.1892	Rotherham Town (H)	W	4-1	Atter (2), Mouel (2)	800	Midland League
16.01.1892	Loughborough (A)	L	1-4	Nuttall	1,500	Friendly
23.01.1892	Long Eaton Rangers (A)	L	1-5	Bennett		Midland League
30.01.1892	Wednesbury Old Athletic (H)	W	1-0	Johnson		Midland League
13.02.1892	Gainsborough Trinity (H)	L	0-3			Midland League
12.03.1892	Derby Junction (A)	D	0-0			Midland League
19.03.1892	Gainsborough Trinity (A)	L	0-1			Midland League
09.04.1892	Long Eaton Rangers (H)	D	0-0			Midland League
16.04.1892	Rotherham Town (A)	L	0-11			Midland League
19.04.1892	Burslem Port Vale (H)	L	1-3	Bailey	4,000	Midland League
23.04.1892	Loughborough (H)	W	1-2	Mouel		Friendly
28.04.1892	Burslem Port Vale (A)	L	0-4		3,000	Midland League
30.04.1892	Doncaster Rovers (H)	D	0-0		3,000	Midland League

Loughborough FC

Date	Opposition	Result	Score	Scorers	Attd	Competition
21.09.1891	Burslem Port Vale (A)	L	1-7		1,500	Midland League
10.10.1891	Doncaster Rovers (H)	W	11-2	Smith (3), Freestone (2), Carnelley (4), Cross, Lowe		Midland League
17.10.1891	Grantham Rovers (H)	L	1-3	Carnelley		Midland League
24.10.1891	Hereford Association (H)	W	7-0	Carnelley (5), Smith, Freestone	2,000	FA Cup 2QR
31.10.1891	Gainsborough Trinity (H)	L	0-5			Midland League
07.11.1891	Long Eaton Rangers (A)	L	0-2			Midland League
14.11.1891	Leicester Fosse (H)	W	6-2	Carnelley (3), Lowe, Freestone, Shelton	4,000	Midland League
14.11.1891	Brierley Hill Alliance (A) *	L	0-7		2,500	FA Cup 3QR
21.11.1891	Staveley (A)	L	0-2			Midland League
28.11.1891	Leicester Fosse (A)	W	2-1	Freestone, Carnelley	2,000	Midland League
12.12.1891	Rotherham Town (A)	L	1-6	Freestone		Midland League
19.12.1891	Derby Junction (H)	W	2-1	Lowe, Kelham	300	Midland League

26.12.1891	Wednesbury Old Athletic (H)	W	5-1	Smith, Freestone (2), Carnelley (2)	2,000	Midland League
02.01.1892	Gainsborough Trinity (A)	W	2-1	Lowe, Freestone		Midland League
09.01.1892	Burton Wanderers (H)	L	2-3	Freestone, Carnelley	1,500	Midland League
16.01.1892	Leicester Fosse (H)	W	4-1	Jackson, Smith, Carnelley (2)	1,500	Friendly
23.01.1892	Rotherham Town (H)	W	3-1	Smith, Carnelley (2)		Midland League
30.01.1892	Grantham Rovers (A)	L	0-1			Midland League
06.02.1892	Long Eaton Rangers (H)	W	2-0	Freestone, Farmer	1,000	Midland League
13.02.1892	Burton Wanderers (A)	L	0-1			Midland League
27.02.1892	Doncaster Rovers (A)	D	0-0			Midland League
12.03.1892	Burslem Port Vale (H)	L	1-2	Freestone		Midland League
19.03.1892	Wednesbury Old Athletic (A)	L	2-5			Midland League
15.04.1892	Derby Junction (A)	L	1-2	Lowe		Midland League
23.04.1892	Leicester Fosse (A)	W	2-1	Freestone, Lowe		Friendly

Note: * Loughborough Athletic contested this cup tie as the first team played Leicester Fosse in the Midland League

1891/92 Top Scorers

Leicester Fosse		Loughborough	
James Atter	6	Ernest Carnelley	19
Ernest Mouel	5	William Freestone	12
Arthur Bennett	2	Smith	6
Harry Webb	2		

1892/93 season
Midland League

		P	W	D	L	F	A	Pts
1	Rotherham Town	24	19	3	2	80	28	41
2	Burton Wanderers	24	15	4	5	49	33	34
3	**Loughborough**	**24**	**15**	**3**	**6**	**64**	**30**	**33**
4	**Leicester Fosse**	**24**	**12**	**3**	**9**	**50**	**37**	**27**
5	Doncaster Rovers	24	11	4	9	47	44	26
6	Gainsborough Trinity	24	12	1	11	51	34	25
7	Kettering	24	11	3	10	48	41	25
8	Grantham Rovers	24	10	2	12	46	43	22
9	Wednesbury Old Athletic	24	8	3	13	41	51	19
10	Long Eaton Rangers	24	6	6	12	34	53	18
11	Mansfield Town	24	7	2	15	26	70	16
12	Newark	24	6	3	15	34	62	15
13	Derby Junction	24	3	5	16	32	76	11

Leicester Fosse

Date	Opposition	Result	Score	Scorers	Attd	Competition
17.09.1892	Mansfield Town (A)	L	1-4	Lowe		Midland League

26.09.1892	Rotherham Town (A)	L	1-6	Freeman		Midland League
01.10.1892	Newark (H)	W	7-1	Slack (3), Freeman (2), Silvester, Dorrell	3,000	Midland League
08.10.1892	Kettering Town (A)	W	4-0	Webb (3), OG	1,500	Midland League
15.10.1892	Rushden (H)	W	7-0	Lowe, Webb (3), Dorrell (3)	3,000	FA Cup (1QR)
22.10.1892	Derby Junction (H)	W	4-0	Lowe, Dorrell, Freeman, Webb		Midland League
29.10.1892	Notts Olympic (A)	D	3-3	Lowe, Freeman, OG		FA Cup (2QR)
05.11.1892	Notts Olympic (H)	W	7-0	Dorrell (4), Webb (2), Slack	4,000	FA Cup (2QR)
12.11.1892	Loughborough (A)	L	1-2	Slack	7,000	Midland League
19.11.1892	Buxton (H)	L	1-2	Freeman	5,000	FA Cup (3QR)
26.11.1892	Grantham Rovers (H)	W	2-0	Mabbutt, Slack	2,000	Midland League
17.12.1892	Doncaster Rovers (A)	W	1-0	Freeman	1,000	Midland League
24.12.1892	Wednesbury Old Athletic (A)	L	2-3	Hardy, Slack		Midland League
07.01.1893	Doncaster Rovers (H)	L	0-1		4,000	Midland League
14.01.1893	Burton Wanderers (H)	L	1-2	Hardy		Midland League
21.01.1893	Gainsborough Trinity (A)	W	2-1	Carter, Slack		Midland League

28.01.1893	Grantham Rovers (A)	W	2-1	Dorrell, Lowe		Midland League
04.02.1893	Wednesbury Old Athletic (H)	W	3-1	Lowe (2), Slack		Midland League
18.02.1893	Gainsborough Trinity (H)	W	2-1	Taylor, Lowe		Midland League
25.02.1893	Burton Wanderers (A)	L	0-3			Midland League
04.03.1893	Rotherham Town (H)	D	1-1	Lowe		Midland League
11.03.1893	Long Eaton Rangers (A)	L	1-2	Nuttall		Midland League
18.03.1893	Loughborough (H)	D	1-1	Dorrell	8,000	Midland League
01.04.1893	Newark (A)	D	3-3	Dorrell, Nuttall, Lowe		Midland League
03.04.1893	Long Eaton Rangers (H)	L	0-1			Midland League
05.04.1893	Loughborough (A)	L	1-4	Dorrell	5,000	Friendly
08.04.1893	Kettering Town (H)	W	3-1	Dorrell (2), Slack		Midland League
22.04.1893	Mansfield Town (H)	W	5-1	Worrall, Lowe, Priestman (2), Slack		Midland League
27.04.1893	Derby Junction (A)	W	3-1	Webb (2), Dorrell		Midland League
29.04.1893	Loughborough (H)	W	5-1	Worrall, Slack, Paton, Lowe (2)	10,000	Friendly

Loughborough FC

Date	Opposition	Result	Score	Scorers	Attd	Competition
03.09.1892	Burton Wanderers (H)	L	0-1			Midland League
10.09.1892	Newark Town (A)	W	2-1			Midland League
17.09.1892	Doncaster Rovers (H)	L	1-4	Carnelley		Midland League
24.09.1892	Long Eaton Rovers (A)	D	0-0			Midland League
01.10.1892	Rotherham Town (H)	D	2-2	Butterworth, Start		Midland League
08.10.1892	Mansfield Town (H)	W	6-0	Kent, Culley, Farmer (2), Start, Carnelley		Midland League
15.10.1892	Ridings (H)	W	8-1	Farmer, Butterworth, Start, Smith, Carnelley, A.N. Others		FA Cup 1QR
29.10.1892	Heanor Town (H)	W	3-1	Freestone, Farmer, Start	3,000	FA Cup 2QR
12.11.1892	Leicester Fosse (H)	W	2-1	Carnelley, Start	7,000	Midland League
19.11.1892	Kettering Town (A)	W	2-1	OG, Farmer		FA Cup 3QR
26.11.1892	Wednesbury Old Athletic (H)	W	2-1	Farmer (2)		Midland League
03.12.1892	Grantham Rovers (A)	L	2-3	Carnelley (2)	3,000	Midland League
10.12.1892	Buxton (A)*	W	6-0	Start, Carnelley (2), Butterworth	1,500	FA Cup 4QR

17.12.1892	Mansfield Town (A)	W	1-0	Farmer		Midland League
24.12.1892	Grantham Rovers (H)	W	2-1	Farmer, Butterworth		Midland League
26.12.1892	Doncaster Rovers (A)	W	3-1		1,500	Midland League
31.12.1892	Buxton (A)	W	3-0	Spibey, Carnelley, Start		FA Cup 4QR
07.01.1893	Long Eaton Rangers (H)	W	5-0	Smith, Start (3), Farmer	1,000	Midland League
21.01.1893	Northwich Victoria (H)	L	1-2	Carnelley	5,000	FA Cup R1
04.02.1893	Gainsborough Trinity (H)	W	3-2	Farmer (2), Carnelley		Midland League
11.02.1893	Gainsborough Trinity (A)	L	2-3			Midland League
18.02.1893	Derby Junction (A)	W	6-2	Carnelley (3), Start (2), Smith	500	Midland League
25.02.1893	Newark Town (H)	W	7-0	Carnelley (3), Sharpe, Farmer, Start, Plackett		Midland League
04.03.1893	Burton Wanderers (A)	L	1-2	Carnelley		Midland League
11.03.1893	Kettering (H)	W	2-0	Start, Carnelley		Midland League
18.03.1893	Leicester Fosse (A)	D	1-1	Start	8,000	Midland League
01.04.1893	Wednesbury Old Athletic (A)	W	3-1	Butterworth, Freestone, Farmer		Midland League

04.04.1893	Derby Junction (H)	W	7-0	Butterworth (2), Carnelley, Farmer (3), Smith	2,000	Midland League
05.04.1893	Leicester Fosse (H)	W	4-1	Freestone (2), Carnelley, Farmer	5,000	Friendly
08.04.1893	Rotherham Town (A)	L	1-3	Sharpe	4,000	Midland League
22.04.1893	Kettering Town (A)	W	3-1			Midland League
29.04.1893	Leicester Fosse (A)	L	1-5	Farmer	10,000	Friendly

* Ordered to be replayed due to the state of the pitch

1892/93 Top Scorers

Leicester Fosse		Loughborough	
Billy Dorell	15	Albert Carnelley	20
William Lowe	11	Oscar Farmer	14
Alf Slack	11	John Start	14
Harry Webb	11		

1893/94
Midland League

		P	W	D	L	F	A	Pts
1	Burton Wanderers	20	17	3	0	82	12	35
2	**Leicester Fosse**	20	15	2	3	49	13	32
3	**Loughborough**	20	12	6	2	52	22	30
4	Grantham Rovers	20	9	4	7	35	33	22
5	Mansfield Greenhalghs	20	9	3	8	43	54	21
6	Long Eaton Rangers	20	7	4	9	43	44	18
7	Doncaster Rovers	20	5	4	11	27	48	14
8	Newark	20	6	2	12	28	55	14
9	Kettering	20	4	5	11	26	59	13
10	Gainsborough Trinity	20	5	1	14	28	46	11
11	Mansfield Town	20	2	4	14	27	54	8

Leicester Fosse

Date	Opposition	Result	Score	Scorers	Attd	Competition
09.09.1893	Burton Wanderers (H)	L	1-2	Worrall	5,000	Midland League
23.09.1893	Long Eaton Rangers (H)	W	3-0	Hill, Worrall, Henrys	4,000	Midland League
30.09.1893	Gainsborough Trinity (A)	D	0-0		2,000	Midland League
07.10.1893	Loughborough (A)	L	0-1		6,000	Midland League
21.10.1893	Mansfield Town (H)	W	4-0	Miller, Dorrell, Seymour, Edwards	3,000	Midland League

04.11.1893	Mansfield Town (H)	W	1-0	Dorrell	4,000	FA Cup 2QR
18.11.1893	Doncaster Rovers (H)	W	2-1	Brown, Dorrell	2,000	Midland League
25.11.1893	Mansfield Greenhalghs (A)	W	5-0	Brown, Hill, Lord, Miller, OG	5,000	FA Cup 3QR
02.12.1893	Newark (H)	W	3-0	Hill (2), Miller	3,000	Midland League
09.12.1893	Mansfield Greenhalghs (H)	W	4-2	Dorrell, Brown (3)	2,000	Midland League
16.12.1893	Loughborough (A)	W	1-0	Dorrell	8,000	FA Cup 4QR
23.12.1893	Grantham Rovers (H)	W	4-0	Miller (2), Brown (2)		Midland League
06.01.1894	Loughborough (H)	W	4-0	Dorrell, Hill, Brown, Lord	6,000	Midland League
13.01.1894	Gainsborough Trinity (H)	W	3-1	Brown, Edwards, Hill	3,000	Midland League
20.01.1894	Doncaster Rovers (A)	W	2-1	Slack, OG	1,500	Midland League
27.01.1894	South Shore (H)	W	2-1	Hill, Brown	4,000	FA Cup R1
03.02.1894	Long Eaton Rangers (A)	W	2-0	Miller, OG	1,000	Midland League
10.02.1894	Derby County (H)	D	0-0		12,000	FA Cup R2
17.02.1894	Derby County (A)	L	0-3		4,000	FA Cup R2 replay
24.02.1894	Kettering Town (H)	W	4-0	Brown, Hill, Miller, OG	4,000	Midland League

03.03.1894	Mansfield Greenhalghs (A)	W	3-0	Hill, Brown (2)		Midland League
10.03.1894	Burton Wanderers (A)	L	1-2	Dorrell	3,500	Midland League
17.03.1894	Newark (A)	W	2-0	Dorrell (2)		Midland League
24.03.1894	Kettering Town (A)	D	1-1	Brown	2,000	Midland League
30.03.1894	Loughborough (A)	D	1-1	Dorrell	3,000	Friendly
04.04.1894	Mansfield Town (A)	W	3-0	Lord, Priestman, Brown		Midland League
14.04.1894	Loughborough (H)	W	6-0	McArthur (3), Priestman (2), Dorrell		Friendly
28.04.1894	Grantham Rovers	W	3-2	Miller, Brown, Dorrell		Midland League

Loughborough FC

Date	Opposition	Result	Score	Scorers	Attd	Competition
02.09.1893	Mansfield Town (A)	D	3-3	Carnelley (2), Farmer		Midland League
09.09.1893	Mansfield Town (H)	W	2-1	Mills, Mellors	2,500	Midland League
23.09.1893	Burton Wanderers (H)	D	1-1	Carnelley	3,000	Midland League
30.09.1893	Long Eaton Rangers (A)	D	3-3	Farmer (2), Carnelley		Midland League

07.10.1893	Leicester Fosse (H)	W	1-0	Storer	6,000	Midland League
14.10.1893	Kettering Town (H)	W	4-1			FA Cup 1QR
30.10.1893	Kettering Town (H)	D	1-1	Sharpe		Midland League
04.11.1893	Newark Town (H)	W	4-0	Storer, Mills, Carnelley (2)		FA Cup 2QR
11.11.1893	Long Eaton Rangers (H)	W	6-0	Mills, Storer, Sharpe, Plackett, Carnelley (2)		Midland League
18.11.1893	Mansfield Greenhalghs (A)	W	5-1	Mills (2), Storer (2), Smith		Midland League
25.11.1893	Rushden (H)	W	1-0	Carnelley		FA Cup 3QR
02.12.1893	Grantham Rovers (H)	W	3-1	Plackett, Carnelley, Farmer	2,000	Midland League
16.12.1893	Leicester Fosse (II)	L	0-1		8,000	FA Cup 4QR
23.12.1893	Gainsborough Trinity (H)	W	1-0			Midland League
31.12.1893	Doncaster Rovers (A)	Aban (fog)	1-0	Storer		Midland League
06.01.1894	Leicester Fosse (A)	L	0-4		6.000	Midland League
03.02.1894	Burton Wanderers (A)	L	1-2			Midland League
10.02.1894	Doncaster Rovers (H)	W	3-1			Midland League

17.02.1894	Newark Town (H)	W	6-2	Plackett, A.N. Others		Midland League
24.02.1894	Gainsborough Trinity (A)	W	2-0	Farmer, Carnelley		Midland League
23.03.1894	Kettering Town (A)	D	1-1	Weightman	1,200	Midland League
24.03.1894	Mansfield Greenalgh's (H)	W	8-0	Mills (2), OG, Weightman, Farmer, A.N. Others		Midland League
30.03.1894	Leicester Fosse (H)	D	1-1		3,000	Friendly
07.04.1894	Grantham Rovers (A)	D	0-0			Midland League
14.04.1894	Leicester Fosse (A)	L	0-6			Friendly
19.04.1894	Doncaster Rovers (A)	W	3-1			Midland League
21.04.1894	Newark Town (A)	W	4-0	Sharpe, OG, Farmer, Mills		Midland League

1893/94 Top Scorers

Leicester Fosse		Loughborough	
Jimmy Brown	16	Albert Carnelley	11
Billy Dorrell	10	Samuel Mills	8
Jacky Hill	9	Oscar Farmer	7

1894/95
Football League Second Division

			HOME				AWAY						
		P	W	D	L	F	A	W	D	L	F	A	G Ave	Pts
1	Bury	30	15	0	0	48	11	8	2	5	30	22	2.36	48
2	Notts County	30	12	2	1	50	15	5	3	7	25	30	1.67	39
3	Newton Heath	30	9	6	0	52	18	6	2	7	26	26	1.77	38
4	**Leicester Fosse**	**30**	**11**	**2**	**2**	**45**	**20**	**4**	**6**	**5**	**27**	**33**	**1.36**	**38**
5	Grimsby Town	30	14	0	1	51	16	4	1	10	28	36	1.52	37
6	Darwen	30	13	1	1	53	10	3	3	9	21	33	1.72	36
7	Burton Wanderers	30	10	3	2	49	9	4	4	7	18	30	1.72	35
8	Woolwich Arsenal	30	11	3	1	54	20	3	3	9	21	38	1.29	34
9	Manchester City	30	9	3	3	56	28	5	0	10	26	44	1.14	31
10	Newcastle United	30	11	1	3	51	28	1	2	12	21	56	0.86	27
11	Burton Swifts	30	9	2	4	34	20	2	1	12	18	54	0.70	25
12	Rotherham Town	30	10	0	5	37	22	1	2	12	18	40	0.89	24
13	Lincoln City	30	8	0	7	32	27	2	0	13	20	65	0.57	20
14	Walsall Town Swifts	30	8	0	7	35	25	2	0	13	12	67	0.51	20
15	Burslem Port Vale	30	6	3	6	30	23	1	1	13	9	54	0.51	18
16	Crewe Alexandra	30	3	4	8	20	34	0	0	15	6	69	0.25	10

Leicester Fosse

Date	Opposition	Result	Score	Scorers	Attd	Competition
01.09.1894	Grimsby Town (A)	L	3-4	Skea (2), McArthur	5,000	Division Two
08.09.1894	Rotherham Town (H)	W	4-2	Skea (3), Gallacher	4,000	Division Two

15.09.1894	Burton Wanderers (H)	L	1-2	Skea	8,000	Division Two
22.09.1894	Newton Heath (H)	L	2-3	Skea, McArthur	6,000	Division Two
29.09.1894	Newcastle United (A)	L	0-2		5,000	Division Two
06.10.1894	Notts County (A)	L	0-3		10,000	Division Two
13.10.1894	Notts Olympic (A)	W	13-0	Skea (3), Miller (4), McArthur (4), Hill (2)	2,000	FA Cup 1QR
20.10.1894	Newcastle United (H)	D	4-4	McArthur, Henrys, Miller (2)	8,000	Division Two
27.10.1894	Newton Heath (A)	D	2-2	Skea (2)	3,000	Division Two
03.11.1894	Kimberley (H)	W	7-2	Gordon (2), Skea, Gallacher (2), McArthur, Hill, A.N.Other	1,000	FA Cup 2QR
10.11.1894	Darwen (H)	W	2-1	Hill, McArthur	5,000	Division Two
17.11.1894	Burton Swifts (H)	D	2-2	Skea, OG	6,000	Division Two
24.11.1894	Rushden (A)	W	3-2	Seymour, Gallacher, Skea	1,000	FA Cup 3QR
01.12.1894	Notts County (H)	W	5-1	Skea (3), Gordon, McArthur	5,000	Division Two
08.12.1894	Walsall (A)	W	3-1	McArthur (2), Skea	2,000	Division Two
15.12.1894	Loughborough (H)	D	1-1	Hill	10,000	FA Cup 4QR

19.12.1894	Loughborough (A)	D	2-2	Skea, Gallacher	5,000	FA Cup 4QR replay
22.12.1894	Loughborough (H)	W	3-0	Gallacher, Hill, Skea (pen)		FA Cup 4QR 2nd replay
25.12.1894	Bury (A)	L	1-4	McArthur	5,000	Division Two
05.01.1895	Walsall (H)	W	9-1	McArthur, Gordon (2), Brown, Skea (2) Gallacher, Seymour, OG	2,000	Division Two
07.01.1895	Woolwich Arsenal (H)	W	3-1	McArthur, Gordon, Hill	3,000	Division Two
12.01.1895	Crewe Alexandra (A)	D	2-2	Gallacher (2)	600	Division Two
15.01.1895	Darwen (A)	L	2-8	Skea, Gordon	500	Division Two
26.01.1895	Rotherham Town (A)	W	1-0	McArthur	2,000	Division Two
02.02.1895	Bury (A)	L	1-4	McArthur		FA Cup R1
09.02.1895	Burton Wanderers (A)	D	1-1	Brown		Division Two
18.02.1895	Crewe Alexandra (H)	W	4-0	McArthur, Priestman, Stirling, Gordon	1,000	Division Two
23.02.1895	Burslem Port Vale (A)	D	1-1	Priestman	5,000	Division Two
02.03.1895	Burton Swifts (A)	W	5-0	Hughes, Skea, Gallacher (2), McArthur	3,000	Division Two

04.03.1895	Lincoln City (H)	W	2-1	Skea, Gallacher		Division Two
09.03.1895	Woolwich Arsenal (A)	D	3-3	McArthur, Gordon, Skea	4,000	Division Two
11.03.1895	Loughborough (A) (North Road, Kettering)	W	3-1	Brown, A.N. Others	2,000	Kettering Charity Cup SF
16.03.1895	Manchester City (H)	W	3-1	Gordon, Hughes, McArthur	4,000	Division Two
23.03.1895	Burslem Port Vale (H)	W	2-1	Gordon, Skea	3,000	Division Two
30.03.1895	Manchester City (A)	D	1-1	Gordon	4,000	Division Two
06.04.1895	Lincoln City (A)	W	2-1	Gallacher, McArthur		Division Two
15.04.1895	Grimsby Town (H)	W	1-0	Skea	3,000	Division Two
20.04.1895	Bury (H)	W	1-0	Gordon	3,000	Division Two

Midland League

		P	W	D	L	F	A	Pts
1	**Loughborough Town**	26	19	4	3	84	25	42
2	Stoke Swifts	26	14	7	5	90	33	35
3	Derby County Reserves	26	12	8	6	46	27	32
4	Gainsborough Trinity	26	14	4	8	55	36	32
5	Kettering	26	13	6	7	59	45	32
6	Ilkeston Town	26	13	5	8	53	46	31
7	Mansfield	26	12	5	9	46	37	29
8	Heanor Town	26	9	5	12	49	48	23
9	Rushden Town	26	10	3	13	47	70	23
10	Long Eaton Rangers	26	7	5	14	41	55	19
11	Newark	26	6	6	14	37	63	18
12	Doncaster Rovers	26	6	6	14	35	70	18

Loughborough FC

Date	Opposition	Result	Score	Scorers	Attd	Competition
08.09.1894	Stoke Swifts (H)	W	2-1	Booth, Edge		Midland League
13.10.1894	Kettering Town (H)	W	4-0	Edge (2), Dewey (2)		FA Cup 1QR
15.09.1894	Kettering Town (H)	D	2-2	Booth, A.N. Other		Midland League
22.09.1894	Newark Town (H)	W	8-0	Dewey (3), Booth, OG, Edge, Kidger, Owen		Midland League
29.09.1894	Rushden (A)	W	6-1	Edge (2), Tucker, Mills (2), Owen		Midland League

Date	Opponent	Result	Score	Scorers	Attendance	Competition
06.10.1894	Doncaster Rovers (H)	W	6-1	Edge (3), Mills, Tucker, OG		Midland League
20.10.1894	Long Eaton Rangers (A)	W	2-1	Mills, Edge		Midland League
27.10.1894	Derby County Reserves (H)	W	2-0	Mills, Dewey		Midland League
04.11.1894	Hucknall St Johns	W	4-1	Booth, Owen, Mills, Saxton		FA Cup 2QR
11.11.1894	Long Eaton Rangers (H)	W	3-1	Owen, OG, Mills		Midland League
18.11.1894	Stoke Swifts (A)	D	1-1	A.N. Other	2,800	Midland League
24.11.1894	Newark	W	1-0	Smith		FA Cup QR3
08.12.1894	Matlock (H)	W	7-0	Mills, Edge, Dewey (2), Middleton, A.N. Others		Midland League
15.12.1894	Leicester Fosse (A)	D	1-1	Edge	10,000	FA Cup 4QR
19.12.1894	Leicester Fosse (H)	D	2-2	Edge (2)	5,000	FA Cup 4QR replay
22.12.1894	Leicester Fosse (A)	L	0-3			FA Cup 4QR 2nd replay
26.12.1894	Heanor Town (A)	Aban (bad light)	2-0	Saxton, Berry		Midland League
05.01.1895	Rushden (H)	W	7-1	Edge (2), Mills, Smith, Saxton, A.N. Others		Midland League
12.01.1895	Newark Town (A)	W	3-1	Smith, Edge, Mills		Midland League

26.01.1895	Grantham Rovers (H)	W	4-0	Edge (2), Owen, Dewey		Midland League
02.02.1895	Gainsborough Trinity (A)	D	0-0			Midland League
23.02.1895	Kettering Town (A)	W	4-1	Dewey, Bull, Saxton, Edge	4,000	Midland League
02.03.1895	Ilkeston (H)	W	7-1	Bull, Saxton (3), Dewey (2), Rose	3,500	Midland League
11.03.1895	Leicester Fosse (A) (North Street, Kettering)	L	1-3	Owen	2,000	Kettering Charity Cup SF
23.03.1895	Mansfield Town (H)	W	1-0	Dewey		Midland League
30.03.1895	Grantham Rovers (A)	L	0-1		400	Midland League
06.04.1895	Gainsborough Trinity (H)	W	5-3	Middleton, A.N. Others		Midland League
12.04.1895	Matlock (A)	W	5-2	Saxton, Owen, Bull (2), Mills	2,000	Midland League
13.04.1895	Heanor Town (H)	W	3-0	Cotterill, Middleton, A.N. Other		Midland League
15.04.1895	Rest of the League	W	2-1	Bull, Preston		Championship Fixture
16.04.1895	Ilkeston (A)	W	2-0	Saxton, Mills	4,000	Midland League
17.04.1895	Heanor Town (A)	D	1-1	Preston		Midland League
20.04.1895	Mansfield Town (A)	W	2-0	Cotterill, A.N. Other		Midland League
27.04.1895	Doncaster Rovers (A)	L	0-1			Midland League
30.04.1895	Derby County Reserves (A)	L	1-4	Owen	1,500	Midland League

1894/95 Top Scorers

Leicester Fosse		Loughborough	
David Skea	31	Robert Edge	15
Willie McArthur	22	Joseph Dewey	13
Bob Gordon	14	Samuel Mills	12
Hugh Gallacher	10		

1895/96
Football League Second Division

			HOME					AWAY						
		P	W	D	L	F	A	W	D	L	F	A	G Ave	Pts
1	Liverpool	30	14	1	0	65	11	8	1	6	41	21	3.31	46
2	Manchester City	30	12	3	0	37	9	9	1	5	26	29	1.66	46
3	Grimsby Town	30	14	1	0	51	9	6	1	8	31	29	2.16	42
4	Burton Wanderers	30	12	1	2	43	15	7	3	5	26	25	1.73	42
5	Newcastle United	30	14	0	1	57	14	2	2	11	16	36	1.46	34
6	Newton Heath	30	12	2	1	48	15	3	1	11	18	42	1.16	33
7	Woolwich Arsenal	30	11	1	3	42	11	3	3	9	16	31	1.38	32
8	**Leicester Fosse**	30	10	0	5	40	16	4	4	7	17	28	1.30	32
9	Darwen	30	9	4	2	55	22	3	2	10	17	45	1.07	30
10	Notts County	30	8	1	6	41	22	4	1	10	16	32	1.06	26
11	Burton Swifts	30	7	2	6	24	26	3	2	10	15	43	0.57	24
12	Loughborough	30	7	3	5	32	25	2	2	11	8	41	0.61	23
13	Lincoln City	30	7	1	7	36	24	2	3	10	17	51	0.71	22
14	Burslem Port Vale	30	6	4	5	25	24	1	0	14	18	54	0.55	18
15	Rotherham Town	30	7	2	6	27	26	0	1	14	7	71	0.35	17
16	Crewe Alexandra	30	5	2	8	22	28	0	1	14	8	67	0.32	13

Leicester Fosse

Date	Opposition	Result	Score	Scorer	Attd	Competition
07.09.1895	Burton Swifts (H)	W	2-1	Gallacher, Skea	5,000	Division Two
14.09.1895	Manchester City (A)	L	0-2		9,000	Division Two
21.09.1895	Darwen (A)	L	1-4	Skea	1,000	Division Two
28.09.1895	Burton Wanderers (H)	L	1-3	McArthur	6,000	Division Two
05.10.1895	Loughborough (H)	W	5-0	Brown, Skea, McArthur, Gallacher (2)	7,000	Division Two
12.10.1895	Hinckley Town (H)	W	4-0	Trainer (2), Bishop, McArthur	2,500	FA Cup 1QR
19.10.1895	Burton Wanderers (A)	D	0-0		2,000	Division Two
26.10.1895	Darwen (H)	L	2-3	Trainer, Davies	5,000	Division Two
02.11.1895	Hucknall St Johns (H)	W	3-1	Manson, Hibbert, Trainer		FA Cup 2QR
09.11.1895	Liverpool (A)	L	1-3	Bishop	7,000	Division Two
16.11.1895	Loughborough (A)	W	4-1	Bishop, Davies (2), Lynes	7,000	Division Two
23.11.1895	Kimberley (A)	W	3-1	McArthur (2), OG		FA Cup 3QR

30.11.1895	Liverpool (H)	W	2-0	Davies, McArthur	8,000	Division Two
07.12.1895	Woolwich Arsenal (A)	D	1-1	Lynes	5,000	Division Two
14.12.1895	Kettering Town (H)	L	1-2	Trainer	7,000	FA Cup 4QR
21.12.1895	Crewe Alexandra (H)	W	4-1	Skea (2), McArthur, OG	3,000	Division Two
01.01.1896	Newcastle United (A)	L	0-1		7,000	Division Two
04.01.1896	Newton Heath (H)	W	3-0	McArthur (2), Mnson	7,000	Division Two
11.01.1896	Notts County (H)	W	2-1	Manson, Skea	10,000	Division Two
18.01.1896	Rotherham Town (A)	L	0-2		1,000	Division Two
25.01.1896	Woolwich Arsenal (H)	W	1-0	Lynes	6,000	Division Two
03.02.1896	Newton Heath (A)	L	0-2		1,000	Division Two
08.02.1896	Notts County (A)	W	2-1	McArthur, Manson	11,000	Division Two
15.02.1896	Lincoln City (A)	W	3-2	McWhirter, Manson, OG	2,000	Division Two
18.02.1896	Loughborough (H)	D	2-2	Manson, Gallacher	500	Friendly
22.02.1896	Crewe Alexandra (A)	D	1-1	McArthur	3,000	Division Two
29.02.1896	Lincoln City (H)	L	1-3	Trainer	3,000	Division Two
07.03.1896	Burslem Port Vale (A)	D	1-1	OG	1,500	Division Two

17.03.1896	Loughborough (A)	D	0-0		500	Friendly
21.03.1896	Burslem Port Vale (H)	W	5-0	Lord (2), Gallacher, Trainer, Dorrell	5,000	Division Two
28.03.1896	Burton Swifts (A)	W	2-0	McArthur, Gallacher	3,000	Division Two
03.04.1896	Rotherham Town (H)	W	8-0	Trainer (5), McArthur, Manson, OG	5,000	Division Two
04.04.1896	Manchester City (H)	L	1-0	McArthur	4,000	Division Two
06.04.1896	Grimsby Town (H)	L	1-2	Dorrell	4,000	Division Two
07.04.1896	Newcastle United (H)	W	2-0	Trainer (2)	5,000	Division Two
11.04.1896	Grimsby Town (A)	L	1-7	Manson	3,000	Division Two

Loughborough FC

Date	Opposition	Result	Score	Scorers	Attd	Competition
07.09.1895	Newcastle United (A)	L	0-3		6,000	Division Two
14.09.1895	Newton Heath (H)	D	3-3	Cotterill (2), Clark	2,500	Division Two
21.09.1895	Liverpool (H)	L	2-4	Middleton, Swift	3,500	Division Two
28.09.1895	Burton Swifts (A)	W	2-1	Gordon, Middleton		Division Two
05.10.1895	Leicester Fosse (A)	L	0-5		7,000	Division Two

12.10.1895	Bulwell United (H)	W	5-2			FA Cup 1QR
26.10.1895	Lincoln City (H)	W	3-0	Middleton, Clark, Bull		Division Two
02.11.1895	Newstead Byron (H)	D	0-0			FA Cup 2QR
06.11.1895	Newstead Byron (A)	W	1-0	Rose		FA Cup 2QR replay
09.11.1895	Lincoln City (A)	L	1-4	Cotterill	2,000	Division Two
15.11.1895	Burton Wanderers (H)	D	1-1	Smith		Division Two
16.11.1895	Leicester Fosse (H)	L	1-4	OG	7,000	Division Two
23.11.1895	Kettering Town (A)	L	1-2	Ward		FA Cup 3QR
30.11.1895	Grimsby Town (A)	L	0-2			Division Two
07.12.1895	Liverpool (A)	L	0-1		1,000	Division Two
21.12.1895	Grimsby Town (H)	L	0-1			Division Two
25.12.1895	Notts County (A)	L	0-2			Division Two
26.12.1895	Burton Swifts (H)	D	2-2	Dickson, Middleton		Division Two
28.12.1895	Notts County (H)	L	1-3	Middleton		Division Two
04.01.1896	Woolwich Arsenal (A)	L	0-6			Division Two
20.01.1896	Burton Wanderers (A)	L	0-4		800	Division Two

01.02.1896	Manchester City (H)	L	2-4	Hamilton, Logan	1,500	Division Two
18.02.1896	Leicester Fosse	D	2-2	Clarke, Logan	500	Friendly
22.02.1896	Darwen (A)	D	1-1	Logan	300	Division Two
24.02.1896	Manchester City (A)	L	1-5	Logan	2,000	Division Two
29.02.1896	Woolwich Arsenal (H)	W	2-1	Clark, Roulston	2,500	Division Two
07.03.1896	Newcastle United (H)	W	1-0	Rose	2,000	Division Two
14.03.1896	Rotherham Town (A)	L	0-4			Division Two
17.03.1896	Leicester Fosse (H)	D	0-0		500	Friendly
21.03.1896	Darwen (H)	W	4-1	Roulston, Logan, Andrew, A.N. Other	2,500	Division Two
03.04.1896	Crewe Alexandra (A)*	W	2-1	Ward, Jones		Division Two
04.04.1896	Newton Heath (A)	L	0-2		4,000	Division Two
06.03.1896	Rotherham Town (H)	W	3-0	Andrews, Jones, Hamilton	3,000	Division Two
07.04.1896	Burslem Port Vale (A)	D	1-1	Andrews		Division Two
11.04.1896	Burslem Port Vale (H)	W	3-0	Jones, Roulston, Berry	1,000	Division Two
18.04.1896	Crewe Alexandra (H)	W	4-1	Andrews, Jones, Logan, A.N. Other	1,500	Division Two

* Played at Sandbach since Crewe's ground had been closed due to crowd trouble

1895/96 Top Scorers

Leicester Fosse		Loughborough	
William McArthur	14	James Logan	5
Harry Trainer	14	Henry Middleton	5
David Manson	6	William Andrews	4

1896/97
Football League Second Division

		P	W	D	L	F	A	W	D	L	F	A	G Ave	Pts
1	Notts County	30	12	1	2	60	18	7	3	5	32	25	2.14	42
2	Newton Heath	30	11	4	0	37	10	6	1	8	19	24	1.65	39
3	Grimsby Town	30	12	2	1	44	15	5	2	8	22	30	1.47	38
4	Small Heath	30	8	3	4	36	23	8	2	5	33	24	1.47	37
5	Newcastle United	30	13	1	1	42	13	4	0	11	14	39	1.08	35
6	Manchester City	30	10	3	2	39	15	2	5	8	19	35	1.16	32
7	Gainsborough Trinity	30	10	2	3	35	16	2	5	8	15	31	1.06	31
8	Blackpool	30	11	3	1	39	16	2	2	11	20	40	1.05	31
9	**Leicester Fosse**	**30**	**11**	**2**	**2**	**44**	**20**	**2**	**2**	**11**	**15**	**37**	**1.04**	**30**
10	Woolwich Arsenal	30	10	1	4	42	20	3	3	9	26	50	0.97	30
11	Darwen	30	13	0	2	54	16	1	0	14	13	45	1.10	28
12	Walsall	30	8	2	5	37	25	3	2	10	17	44	0.78	26
13	**Loughborough**	**30**	**10**	**0**	**5**	**37**	**14**	**2**	**1**	**12**	**13**	**50**	**0.78**	**25**
14	Burton Swifts	30	7	4	4	33	20	2	2	11	13	41	0.75	24
15	Burton Wanderers	30	8	1	6	22	22	1	1	13	9	45	0.46	20
16	Lincoln City	30	4	2	9	17	27	1	0	14	10	58	0.32	12

Leicester Fosse

Date	Opposition	Result	Score	Scorers	Attd	Competition
05.09.1896	Darwen (H)	W	4-1	McMillan, Lonie, Walker, Freebairn	4,000	Division Two
12.09.1896	Notts County (H)	L	2-3	Manson (2)	6,000	Division Two
19.09.1896	Burton Swifts (A)	L	1-2	Dorrell	4,000	Division Two
26.09.1896	Loughborough (A)	W	2-0	McMillan (2)	5,000	Division Two
03.10.1896	Blackpool (H)	W	2-1	McMillan, Carnelley	6,000	Division Two
15.10.1896	Loughborough (H)	W	4-2	Fairbairn (2), Carnelley (2)	200	Friendly
17.10.1896	Notts County (A)	L	0-6		5,000	Division Two
24.10.1896	Darwen (A)	L	1-4	Lonie	2,000	Division Two
07.11.1896	Lincoln City (H)	W	4-1	McMillan (2), Carnelley, Freebairn	2,000	Division Two
14.11.1896	Newcastle United (A)	L	1-3	McMillan	6,000	Division Two
21.11.1896	Bulwell United (H)	W	3-1	Freebairn (2), Lord	1,000	FA Cup 3QR
28.11.1896	Walsall (H)	W	4-2	Freebairn, Carnelley (2), McDonald	4,000	Division Two
05.12.1896	Grimsby Town (H)	W	4-2	McMillan (2), Dorrell, McDonald	8,000	Division Two
12.12.1896	Wellingborough (A)	W	3-2	McMillan, Dorrell, Freebairn	1,500	FA Cup 4QR

19.12.1896	Burton Wanderers (A)	L	1-2	McDonald	3,000	Division Two
25.12.1896	Loughborough (H)	W	4-2	McDonald, Dorrell, Freebairn (2)	11,000	Division Two
28.12.1896	Newton Heath (H)	W	1-0	Dorrell	8,000	Division Two
02.01.1897	Kettering Town (A)	L	1-2	Dorrell	4,000	FA Cup 5QR
09.01.1897	Newcastle United (H)	W	5-0	Trainer, McDonald (2), Carnelley, Dorrell	3,000	Division Two
16.01.1897	Burton Wanderers (H)	W	2-1	Brown, Trainer	8,000	Division Two
23.01.1897	Grimsby Town (A)	L	1-4	Dorrell	3,000	Division Two
06.02.1897	Gainsborough Trinity (A)	W	2-0	McMillan (2)	7,000	Division Two
13.02.1897	Woolwich Arsenal (H)	W	6-3	Dorrell (2), Carnelley (2), Freebairn, OG	6,000	Division Two
20.02.1897	Newton Heath (A)	L	1-2	Carnelley	8,000	Division Two
27.02.1897	Blackpool (A)	L	0-3		1,000	Division Two
06.03.1897	Burton Swifts (H)	W	3-0	Carnelley, Dorrell, Freebairn	7,000	Division Two
13.03.1897	Manchester City (A)	L	0-4		6,000	Division Two
20.03.1897	Walsall (A)	D	1-1	Wood	2,500	Division Two
27.03.1897	Small Heath (H)	L	0-1		5,500	Division Two

31.03.1897	Loughborough (H)	D	0-0			Friendly
10.04.1897	Lincoln City (A)	L	1-2	Feebairn	1,400	Division Two
12.04.1897	Manchester City (H)	D	3-3	McMillan, Carnelley, OG	1,000	Division Two
16.04.1897	Small Heath (A)	D	2-2	McDonald, Freebairn	2,000	Division Two
17.04.1897	Woolwich Arsenal (A)	L	1-2	Dorrell	5,000	Division Two
19.04.1897	Gainsborough Trinity (H)	D	0-0		2,000	Division Two

Loughborough FC

Date	Opposition	Result	Score	Scorers	Attd	Competition
02.09.1896	Grimsby Town (H)	L	1-4	McBride	2,000	Division Two
05.09.1896	Notts County (A)*	L	1-3	Ward	1,000	Division Two
12.09.1896	Burton Swifts (H)	L	0-2		2,000	Division Two
19.09.1896	Woolwich Arsenal (A)	L	0-2		9,000	Division Two
26.09.1896	Leicester Fosse (H)	L	0-2		5,000	Division Two
03.10.1896	Lincoln City (A)	W	2-0	Blackett, Ward	2,000	Division Two
10.10.1896	Walsall (H)	L	1-2	Blackett	2,000	Division Two

15.10.1896	Leicester Fosse (A)	L	2-4	Blackett, Jones	200	Friendly
17.10.1896	Grimsby Town (A)	L	1-8	Blackett	3,000	Division Two
24.10.1896	Notts County (H)	L	0-1		2,000	Division Two
31.10.1896	Walsall (A)	L	1-5	Jones	2,000	Division Two
07.11.1896	Burton Swifts (A)	L	1-3	Andrews	500	Division Two
14.11.1896	Gainsborough Trinity (H)	W	1-0	Gourlay		Division Two
21.11.1896	Mansfield Town (A)	L	1-2	Andrews		FA Cup 3QR
28.11.1896	Newcastle United (A)	L	1-4	Mumford	7,000	Division Two
05.12.1896	Gainsborough Trinity (A)	L	0-2			Division Two
12.12.1896	Woolwich Arsenal (H)	W	8-0	Hamilton, Jones (4), Ward (2), Brailsford	2,000	Division Two
19.12.1896	Small Heath (H)	W	2-0	Jones, Ward	1,000	Division Two
25.12.1896	Leicester Fosse (A)	L	2-4	Brailsford, Jones	11,000	Division Two
02.01.1897	Darwen (H)	W	4-2	Ward (2), Jones, Brailsford		Division Two
30.01.1897	Blackpool (H)	W	4-1	Jones (3), Roulston		Division Two
06.02.1897	Newton Heath (A)	L	0-6		5,000	Division Two
13.02.1897	Darwen (A)	L	1-5	Blackett	500	Division Two

20.02.1897	Newcastle United (H)	W	3-0	Roulston (2), Blackett	2,000	Division Two
06.03.1897	Lincoln City (H)	W	3-0	Blackett (2), Brailsford	4,000	Division Two
17.03.1897	Manchester City (H)	W	2-0	Roulston, Ward	1,000	Division Two
20.03.1897	Small Heath (A)	L	0-3		4,000	Division Two
27.03.1897	Blackpool (A)	L	1-4	Roulston	2,000	Division Two
31.03.1897	Leicester Fosse (A)	D	0-0			Friendly
10.04.1897	Newton Heath (H)	W	2-0	Ward, Jones	3,000	Division Two
16.04.1897	Manchester City (A)	D	1-1	Andrews	2,000	Division Two
17.04.1897	Burton Wanderers (H)	W	6-0	Andrews (3), Jones (2), Shelton		Division Two
19.04.1897	Burton Wanderers (A)	W	1-0	Blackett		Division Two

* Played at Nottingham Forest's Town Ground, as Trent Bridge was being used for cricket.

1896/97 Top Scorers

Leicester Fosse		Loughborough	
Billy Dorrell	13	William Jones	14
Willie Fairbairn	12	Arthur Ward	9
Albert Carnelley	10	Joseph Blackett	8

1897/98
Football League Second Division

		P	HOME					AWAY					G Ave	Pts
			W	D	L	F	A	W	D	L	F	A		
1	Manchester City	34	15	1	1	64	10	8	5	4	28	25	2.63	52
2	Glossop	34	12	1	4	48	13	8	5	4	28	25	2.00	46
3	**Leicester Fosse**	**34**	**12**	**5**	**0**	**35**	**12**	**6**	**4**	**7**	**29**	**30**	**1.52**	**45**
4	Newton Heath	34	12	4	1	51	14	7	1	9	14	29	1.51	43
5	New Brighton Tower	34	13	2	2	48	11	5	5	7	23	39	1.42	43
6	Walsall	34	12	5	0	64	11	3	7	7	15	25	2.19	42
7	Woolwich Arsenal	34	14	2	1	55	10	4	3	10	17	31	1.76	41
8	Small Heath	34	14	1	2	66	17	3	6	8	19	33	1.70	41
9	Burslem Port Vale	34	12	2	3	35	12	5	3	9	21	22	1.65	39
10	Grimsby Town	34	10	3	4	39	17	5	2	10	32	43	1.18	35
11	Barnsley	34	11	4	2	44	18	1	3	13	8	38	0.93	31
12	Lincoln City	34	10	5	2	31	16	2	2	13	20	40	0.91	31
13	Burton Swifts	34	7	5	5	35	25	3	3	11	16	45	0.73	28
14	Gainsborough Trinity	34	8	4	5	40	22	2	1	14	16	50	0.78	25
15	Luton Town	34	8	1	8	37	31	2	2	13	14	64	0.54	23
16	Blackpool	34	6	3	8	35	30	2	1	14	14	60	0.54	20
17	**Loughborough**	**34**	**5**	**4**	**8**	**31**	**26**	**1**	**2**	**14**	**7**	**66**	**0.41**	**18**
18	Darwen	34	2	4	11	16	32	0	1	16	6	109	0.16	9

Leicester Fosse

Date	Opposition	Result	Score	Scorer	Attd	Competition
04.09.1897	Luton Town (H)	D	1-1	Freebairn	6,000	Division Two
11.09.1897	Small Heath (A)	L	1-2	Smith	3,000	Division Two
18.09.1897	Grimsby Town (A)	D	0-0		3,000	Division Two
02.10.1897	Newton Heath (A)	L	0-2		6,000	Division Two
09.10.1897	Burnley (H)	L	0-1		6,000	Division Two
16.10.1897	Walsall (H)	W	3-1	Smith (2), King	2,500	Division Two
23.10.1897	Woolwich Arsenal (A)	W	3-0	McMillan, McLeod, King	7,000	Division Two
06.11.1897	Blackpool (H)	W	4-1	Freebairn, McLeod (2), McMillan	6,000	Division Two
13.11.1897	Loughborough (A)	D	1-1	McLeod	5,000	Division Two
20.11.1897	Newton Heath (H)	D	1-1	McLeod	1,000	Division Two
27.11.1897	Burton Swifts (A)	W	3-2	Dorrell, Freebairn, McMillan	1,000	Division Two
04.12.1897	Woolwich Arsenal (H)	W	2-1	McLeod, Dorrell	4,000	Division Two
11.12.1897	Manchester City (A)	L	1-2	McMillan	9,000	Division Two
18.12.1897	Darwen (A)	W	2-1	McLeod, McMillan	600	Division Two

25.12.1897	Loughborough (H)	W	4-0	Freebairn, McMillan, Smith, McLeod	9,000	Division Two
08.01.1898	Blackpool (A)	L	1-2	Freebairn	3,000	Division Two
15.01.1898	Burnley (A)	L	0-4		3,000	Division Two
22.01.1898	Newcastle United (A)	L	2-4	McLeod, King	10,000	Division Two
29.01.1898	Southampton (A)	L	1-2	McLeod	10,000	FA Cup R1
05.02.1898	Darwen (H)	L	0-1		5,000	Division Two
12.02.1898	Lincoln City (H)	W	3-1	Coulson, McLeod, Dorrell	3,000	Division Two
24.02.1898	Loughborough (H)	W	4-0	Keech (3), McLeod		Friendly
26.02.1898	Walsall (A)	L	1-2	McLeod	2,000	Division Two
05.03.1898	Lincoln City (A)	W	4-1	McLeod, McMillan, Dorrell, Keech	2,000	Division Two
12.03.1898	Burton Swifts (H)	D	1-1	McMillan	5,000	Division Two
19.03.1898	Gainsborough Trinity (A)	L	0-1		2,000	Division Two
26.03.1898	Small Heath (H)	W	2-0	McLeod, Keech	2,000	Division Two
02.04.1898	Manchester City (H)	D	0-0		6,000	Division Two
08.04.1898	Luton Town (A)	W	1-0	Dorrell	4,000	Division Two

09.04.1898	Newcastle United (H)	D	1-1	Dorrell (pen)	6,000	Division Two
11.04.1898	Grimsby Town (H)	W	1-0	McMillan	4,000	Division Two
16.04.1898	Gainsborough Trinity (H)	W	3-1	Dorrell, Watkins, Keech	5,000	Division Two

Loughborough FC Results

Date	Opposition	Result	Score	Scorers	Attd	Competition
04.09.1897	Walsall (H)	W	2-1	Shaw (2)	1,500	Division Two
11.09.1897	Manchester City (A)	L	0-3		9,000	Division Two
18.09.1897	Small Heath (H)	L	0-2		2,000	Division Two
25.09.1897	Darwen (A)	L	1-2	Walker		Division Two
02.10.1897	Manchester City (H)	L	0-3		5,000	Division Two
09.10.1897	Walsall (A)	L	0-3		3,000	Division Two
16.10.1897	Luton Town (H)	W	2-0	Pegg, Walker		Division Two
23.10.1897	Lincoln City (A)	W	3-2	Walker, Pegg, Roulston	1,500	Division Two
30.10.1897	Bullwell United	L	0-3		1,600	FA Cup 3QR
06.11.1897	Small Heath (A)	L	0-1		5,000	Division Two

13.11.1897	Leicester Fosse (H)	D	1-1	Walker	5,000	Division Two
27.11.1897	Lincoln City (H)	W	4-2	White, Pegg, Pike, OG	1,600	Division Two
04.12.1897	Grimsby Town (A)	L	0-7		700	Division Two
18.12.1897	Woolwich Arsenal (H)	L	1-3	Shaw	1,800	Division Two
25.12.1897	Leicester Fosse (A)	L	0-4		9,000	Division Two
27.12.1897	Burton Swifts (H)	W	3-2	Hodgkin, Pegg, Pike	2,000	Division Two
03.01.1898	Newcastle United (A)	L	1-3	Pegg	4,000	Division Two
06.01.1898	Darwen (H)	L	0-1		1,500	Division Two
15.01.1898	Luton Town (A)	L	0-7		2,000	Division Two
22.01.1898	Burnley (H)	L	0-2		2,000	Division Two
05.02.1898	Gainsborough Trinity (H)	L	0-5		1,000	Division Two
24.02.1898	Leicester Fosse (A)	L	0-4			Friendly
05.03.1898	Gainsborough Trinity (A)	L	0-4			Division Two
19.03.1898	Woolwich Arsenal (A)	L	0-4		5,000	Division Two
26.03.1898	Blackpool (H)	L	0-2			Division Two
28.03.1898	Burnley (A)	L	3-9	Roulston, Pegg (2)		Division Two
29.03.1898	Newton Heath (A)	L	1-5	Smith	2,000	Division Two

08.04.1898	Burton Swifts (A)	L	0-3			Division Two
09.04.1898	Grimsby Town (H)	W	2-1	Roulston, Hall	1,500	Division Two
11.04.1898	Newcastle United (H)	L	0-1		1,200	Division Two
16.04.1898	Newton Heath (H)	D	0-0		1,200	Division Two
23.04.1898	Blackpool (A)	L	0-4		300	Division Two

1897/98 Top Scorers

Leicester Fosse		Loughborough	
Roddie McLeod	14	Dick Pegg	7
Johnny McMillan	9	Thomas Walker	4
Billy Dorrell	7	Arthur Roulston, Arthur Shaw	3

1898/99
Football League Second Division

		P	W	D	L	F	A	W	D	L	F	A	G Ave	Pts
			HOME					AWAY						
1	Manchester City	34	15	1	1	64	10	8	5	4	28	25	2.63	52
2	Glossop	34	12	1	4	48	13	8	5	4	28	25	2.00	46
3	**Leicester Fosse**	34	12	5	0	35	12	6	4	7	29	30	1.52	45
4	Newton Heath	34	12	4	1	51	14	7	1	9	14	29	1.51	43
5	New Brighton Tower	34	13	2	2	48	11	5	5	7	23	39	1.42	43
6	Walsall	34	12	5	0	64	11	3	7	7	15	25	2.19	42
7	Woolwich Arsenal	34	14	2	1	55	10	4	3	10	17	31	1.76	41
8	Small Heath	34	14	1	2	66	17	3	6	8	19	33	1.70	41
9	Burslem Port Vale	34	12	2	3	35	12	5	3	9	21	22	1.65	39
10	Grimsby Town	34	10	3	4	39	17	5	2	10	32	43	1.18	35
11	Barnsley	34	11	4	2	44	18	1	3	13	8	38	0.93	31
12	Lincoln City	34	10	5	2	31	16	2	2	13	20	40	0.91	31
13	Burton Swifts	34	7	5	5	35	25	3	3	11	16	45	0.73	28
14	Gainsborough Trinity	34	8	4	5	40	22	2	1	14	16	50	0.78	25
15	Luton Town	34	8	1	8	37	31	2	2	13	14	64	0.54	23
16	Blackpool	34	6	3	8	35	30	2	1	14	14	60	0.54	20
17	**Loughborough**	34	5	4	8	31	26	1	2	14	7	66	0.41	18
18	Darwen	34	2	4	11	16	32	0	1	16	6	109	0.16	9

Leicester Fosse

Date	Opposition	Result	Score	Scorer	Attd	Competition
03.09.1898	Lincoln City (H)	W	3-2	Watkins (2), King	8,000	Division Two
10.09.1898	Woolwich Arsenal (A)	L	0-4		6,000	Division Two
17.09.1898	Luton Town (H)	D	1-1	King	3,000	Division Two
24.09.1898	Barnsley St Peters (A)	W	4-3	Galbraith (2), Keech (2)	3,000	Division Two
26.09.1898	Walsall (A)	D	1-1	Galbraith	2,500	Division Two
01.10.1898	Darwen (A)	L	0-3		1,500	Division Two
08.10.1898	Gainsborough Trinity (H)	W	1-0	Galbraith	4,000	Division Two
15.10.1898	Manchester City (A)	L	1-3	Eaton	8,000	Division Two
22.10.1898	Glossop (H)	W	4-2	King, Eaton, Watkins, Fulwood,	3,000	Division Two
29.10.1898	Kimberley (H)	W	9-0	King (4), Watkins (2), Fulwood, Smith, A.N.Other	2,000	FA Cup 3QR
05.11.1898	Burton Swifts (H)	W	1-0	Watkins	4,000	Division Two
12.11.1898	Burslem Port Vale (A)	W	2-0	King, Galbraith	2,000	Division Two
19.11.1898	Rushden (H)	W	2-1	Galbraith, McMillan	6,000	FA Cup 4QR
26.11.1898	Loughborough (A)	W	3-0	Eaton, Fulwood, King	3,000	Division Two

03.12.1898	Blackpool (H)	W	4-0	Galbraith (2), King, Watkins	4,000	Division Two
10.12.1898	Kettering Town (A)	D	1-1	Fulwood	5,000	FA Cup 5QR
15.12.1898	Kettering Town (H)	L	1-2	Eaton	5,000	FA Cup 5QR replay
17.12.1898	Newton Heath (H)	W	1-0	Fulwood	8,000	Division Two
24.12.1898	New Brighton Tower (A)	L	0-1		2,000	Division Two
26.12.1898	Darwen (H)	W	4-0	Eaton, Galbraith, McMillan, Watkins	5,000	Division Two
27.12.1898	Loughborough (H)	W	1-0	Ball	2,000	Division Two
31.12.1898	Lincoln City (A)	L	1-3	Robinson	1,500	Division Two
07.01.1899	Woolwich Arsenal (H)	W	2-1	King, Watkins	10,000	Division Two
14.01.1899	Luton Town (A)	W	6-1	King, Watkins, Galbraith (2), McMillan, Lyon	2,000	Division Two
21.01.1899	Barnsley St Peters (H)	W	3-1	Galbraith (2), King	3,000	Division Two
04.02.1899	Gainsborough Trinity (A)	L	0-4		1,000	Division Two
11.02.1899	Manchester City (H)	D	1-1	McMillan	10,000	Division Two
18.02.1899	Glossop (A)	W	3-1	King, Galbraith, Watkins	1,000	Division Two
25.02.1899	Walsall (H)	D	2-2	Watkins, Lyon	1,700	Division Two

04.03.1899	Burton Swifts (A)	D	1-1	McMillan	4,000	Division Two
11.03.1899	Burslem Port Vale (H)	D	1-1	McMillan	12,000	Division Two
18.03.1899	Small Heath (A)	W	3-0	Galbraith, Eaton, King	10,000	Division Two
25.03.1899	Loughborough (A)	L	1-2	Lyon	1,000	Friendly
31.03.1899	Grimsby Town (A)	L	0-1		5,000	Division Two
01.04.1899	Blackpool (A)	D	2-2	Galbraith, McMillan	2,500	Division Two
03.04.1899	Grimsby Town (H)	W	2-0	Watkins, Eaton	6,000	Division Two
15.04.1899	Newton Heath (A)	D	2-2	Bradshaw, McMillan	6,000	Division Two
22.04.1899	New Brighton Tower (H)	W	4-1	Galbraith, Bradshaw, Ball, King	10,000	Division Two
29.04.1899	Small Heath (H)	D	0-0		4,000	Division Two

Loughborough FC

Date	Opposition	Result	Score	Scorers	Attd	Competition
03.09.1898	Walsall (A)	L	0-7		2,000	Division Two
10.09.1898	Burton Swifts (H)	W	1-0	Mee		Division Two
17.09.1898	Burslem Port Vale (A)	L	0-3		3,000	Division Two

24.09.1898	Small Heath (H)	D	1-1	Bosworth	2,000	Division Two
01.10.1898	Mansfield Town (H)	W	4-0	Bosworth, Pike, Pegg, OG	2,000	FA Cup 1QR
08.10.1898	Blackpool (A)	L	1-2	Pegg	300	Division Two
15.10.1898	Rothwell Town Swifts (H)	W	7-0	Roulston (2), Pegg (3), Tuthill (2)	1,500	FA Cup 2QR
22.10.1898	Newton Heath (A)	L	1-6	Nicholl	2,000	Division Two
29.10.1898	Wellingborough (H)	D	0-0			FA Cup 3QR
31.10.1898	Wellingborough (H)	W	3-1	Roulston, Bosworth, OG		FA Cup 3QR replay
05.11.1898	Lincoln City (A)	L	0-6			Division Two
12.11.1898	Woolwich Arsenal (H)	D	0-0		2,500	Division Two
19.11.1898	Kettering Town	L	1-2	Pike	2,500	FA Cup 4QR
26.11.1898	Leicester Fosse (H)	L	0-4		3,000	Division Two
03.12.1898	Darwen (A)	W	1-0	Nicholl	750	Division Two
10.12.1898	Manchester City (H)	L	1-3	Pike	1,000	Division Two
17.12.1898	Manchester City (A)	L	0-5		4,000	Division Two
24.12.1898	Glossop (H)	L	1-3	Pike	1,900	Division Two
26.12.1898	Gainsborough Trinity (A)	L	0-3			Division Two

27.12.1898	Leicester Fosse (A)	L	0-1		2,000	Division Two
31.12.1898	Walsall (H)	D	1-1	Pike	2,000	Division Two
07.01.1899	Burton Swifts (A)	D	1-1			Division Two
14.01.1899	Burslem Port Vale (H)	L	0-3		2,000	Division Two
21.01.1899	Small Heath (A)	L	0-3		3,000	Division Two
28.01.1899	Barnsley (A)	L	0-9		2,000	Division Two
04.02.1899	Blackpool (H) *	L	1-3	Parker	4,000	Division Two
11.02.1899	Grimsby Town (A)	L	0-5		3,500	Division Two
18.02.1899	Newton Heath (H)	L	0-1		1,800	Division Two
25.02.1899	New Brighton Tower (A)	L	0-3		2,000	Division Two
04.03.1899	Lincoln City (H)	L	2-4	Pegg, Tuthill	1,300	Division Two
11.03.1899	Barnsley (H)	W	2-0	Keech, Pike		Division Two
13.03.1899	Woolwich Arsenal (A)	L	1-3	A.N. Other	2,000	Division Two
18.03.1899	Luton Town (H)	W	4-1	Keech, Allen, A.N. Others		Division Two
25.03.1899	Leicester Fosse (A)	W	2-1	Allan, Pegg	1,000	Friendly
31.03.1899	Luton Town (A)	D	2-2	Parker, Pegg		Division Two
01.04.1899	Darwen (H)	W	10-0	Pegg (5). Parker (2), Keech, Hardy, Hodgkin	1,500	Division Two
03.04.1899	Gainsborough Trinity (H)	D	0-0			Division Two

17.04.1899	Grimsby Town (H)	L	1-3	Keech		Division Two
22.04.1899	Glossop (A)	L	0-4			Division Two
29.04.1899	New Brighton Tower (H)	W	6-0	Allen (2), Pike, Keech, Tebbs, OG		Division Two

* Played at Walnut Street, Leicester

1898/99 Top Scorers

Leicester Fosse		Loughborough	
Tommy Gailbraith	17	Dick Pegg	12
Rab King	16	Horace Pike	7
Alf Watkins	13	William Keech	5

1899/1900
Football League Second Division

			HOME				AWAY						
		P	W	D	L	F	A	W	D	L	F	A	G Ave	Pts
1	The Wednesday	34	17	0	0	61	7	8	4	5	23	15	3.82	54
2	Bolton Wanderers	34	14	2	1	47	7	8	6	3	32	18	3.16	52
3	Small Heath	34	15	1	1	57	13	5	5	7	20	26	1.97	46
4	Newton Heath	34	15	1	1	44	11	5	3	9	19	16	2.33	44
5	**Leicester Fosse**	34	11	5	1	34	8	6	4	7	19	28	1.47	43
6	Grimsby Town	34	10	3	4	46	24	7	3	7	21	22	1.46	40
7	Chesterfield Town	34	10	4	3	35	24	6	2	9	30	36	1.08	38
8	Woolwich Arsenal	34	13	1	3	47	12	3	3	11	15	31	1.44	36
9	Lincoln City	34	11	5	1	31	9	3	3	11	16	34	1.09	36

10	New Brighton Tower	34	9	4	4	44	22	4	5	8	22	36	1.14	35
11	Burslem Port Vale	34	11	2	4	26	17	3	4	10	13	33	0.78	34
12	Walsall	34	10	5	2	35	18	2	3	12	15	37	0.91	32
13	Gainsborough Trinity	34	8	4	5	37	24	1	3	13	10	51	0.63	25
14	Middlesbrough	34	8	4	5	28	15	0	4	13	11	53	0.57	24
15	Burton Swifts	34	8	5	4	31	24	1	1	15	12	60	0.51	24
16	Barnsley	34	8	5	4	36	23	0	2	15	10	56	0.58	23
17	Luton Town	34	5	3	9	25	25	0	5	12	15	50	0.53	18
18	**Loughborough**	**34**	**1**	**6**	**10**	**12**	**26**	**0**	**0**	**17**	**6**	**74**	**0.18**	**8**

Leicester Fosse

Date	Opposition	Result	Score	Scorer	Attd	Competition
02.09.1899	Woolwich Arsenal (A)	W	2-0	King, Brown	10,000	Division Two
09.09.1899	Barnsley (H)	W	1-0	Wragg	6,000	Division Two
16.09.1899	Burton Swifts (H)	W	1-0	Ball	5,000	Division Two
23.09.1899	Luton Town (A)	D	0-0		4,000	Division Two
25.09.1899	Walsall (A)	W	2-1	Bradshaw, Brown	2,500	Division Two
30.09.1899	Burslem Port Vale (H)	W	2-0	Bradshaw, McMillan	5,000	Division Two
14.10.1899	Middlesbrough (H)	W	4-1	Brown, King (2), McMillan	8,000	Division Two
21.10.1899	Chesterfield (A)	D	0-0		7,000	Division Two
28.10.1899	Wellingborough (H)	W	3-1	McMillan, Bishop, Brown	4,000	FA Cup 3QR

Date	Opponent	Result	Score	Scorers	Attendance	Competition
04.11.1899	Bolton Wanderers (A)	D	2-2	McMillan, Dainty	5,000	Division Two
11.11.1899	Loughborough (A)	W	2-0	Wragg, Brown	5,000	Division Two
25.11.1899	Sheffield Wednesday (H)	D	0-0		12.000	Division Two
27.11.1899	Burton Swifts (A)	W	3-1	Brown (2), Swift	2,000	FA Cup 4QR
02.12.1899	Lincoln City (A)	L	0-2		4,000	Division Two
09.12.1899	Hucknall Portland (A)	W	6-1	King, Bradshaw, McMillan (2), Lyon (2)	2,000	FA Cup 5QR
16.12.1899	New Brighton Tower (A)	D	2-2	McMillan, Bradshaw	2,000	Division Two
23.12.1899	Grimsby Town (H)	W	3-0	McMillan (2), OG	5,000	Division Two
25.12.1899	Loughborough (H)	W	5-0	Bradshaw, King (2), Galbraith, Allen	7,000	Division Two
27.12.1899	Walsall (H)	W	2-1	McMillan, King	2,500	Division Two
30.12.1899	Woolwich Arsenal (H)	D	0-0		8,500	Division Two
06.01.1900	Barnsley (A)	W	2-1	King, Dainty	1,000	Division Two
13.01.1900	Burton Swifts (A)	L	0-2		2,000	Division Two
20.01.1900	Luton Town (H)	D	2-2	Allen, McMillan	6,000	Division Two
27.01.1900	Sheffield United (A)	L	0-1			FA Cup R1

03.02.1900	Burslem Port Vale (A)	W	2-0	Eaton (2)	600	Division Two
17.02.1900	Middlesbrough (A)	W	1-0	Brown	8,000	Division Two
24.02.1900	Chesterfield (H)	D	2-2	McMillan, King	5,000	Division Two
03.03.1900	Gainsborough Trinity (A)	L	0-3		2,000	Division Two
10.03.1900	Bolton Wanderers (H)	D	0-0		10,000	Division Two
24.03.1900	Newton Heath (H)	W	2-0	King, Brown	8,000	Division Two
31.03.1900	Sheffield Wednesday (A)	L	0-2		12,000	Division Two
07.04.1900	Lincoln City (H)	W	2-0	Mercer, King	4,000	Division Two
13.04.1900	Newton Heath (A)	L	2-3	Mercer, Wragg	10,000	Division Two
14.04.1900	Small Heath (A)	L	1-4	Lyon	6,000	Division Two
16.04.1900	Gainsborough Trinity (H)	W	5-0	Wragg (2), Lyon, Dainty, King	1,500	Division Two
17.04.1900	Small Heath (H)	W	2-0	Bradshaw, Lyon	6,000	Division Two
21.04.1900	New Brighton Tower (H)	L	1-2	King	3,000	Division Two
28.04.1900	Grimsby Town (A)	L	1-6	King	3,000	Division Two

Loughborough FC

Date	Opposition	Result	Score	Scorers	Attd	Competition
02.09.1899	Bolton Wanderers (H)*	L	2-3	Tebbs, Clifford	5,000	Division Two
09.09.1899	Burton Swifts (A)	L	1-3	Harrison		Division Two
16.09.1899	Newton Heath (A)	L	0-4		6,000	Division Two
23.09.1899	Sheffield Wednesday (H)	D	0-0		4,000	Division Two
28.10.1899	Hinckley Town	L	1-2	Parker		FA Cup 3QR
30.09.1899	Lincoln City (A)	L	2-3	Clifford, Tebbs	3,000	Division Two
07.10.1899	Small Heath (H)	L	1-2	Brown	2,500	Division Two
21.10.1899	Grimsby Town (H)	D	0-0		2,000	Division Two
04.11.1899	Barnsley (H)	D	0-0		1,000	Division Two
11.11.1899	Leicester Fosse (H)	L	0-2		6,000	Division Two
25.11.1899	Burslem Port Vale (A)	L	1-3	Allen	500	Division Two
02.12.1899	Walsall (H)	D	0-0		2,000	Division Two
09.12.1899	Middlesbrough (A)	L	0-3		3,000	Division Two
23.12.1899	Gainsborough Trinity (A)	L	2-4	Brown, Allen		Division Two
25.12.1899	Leicester Fosse (A)	L	0-5		7,000	Division Two
26.12.1899	Woolwich Arsenal (A)	Aban (fog)	0-4		7,000	Division Two

30.12.1899	Bolton Wanderers (A)	L	0-7		3,000	Division Two
06.01.1900	Burton Swifts (H)	W	2-1	Bailey, Tebbs	400	Division Two
13.01.1900	Newton Heath (H)	L	0-2		600	Division Two
20.01.1900	Sheffield Wednesday (A)	L	0-5			Division Two
27.01.1900	New Brighton Tower (A)	L	0-3			Division Two
10.02.1900	Small Heath (A)	L	0-6		2,000	Division Two
17.02.1900	New Brighton Town (H)	L	1-2	Rose		Division Two
24.02.1900	Grimsby Town (A)	L	0-2		2,500	Division Two
03.03.1900	Woolwich Arsenal (H)	L	2-3	Tebbs, Rose	800	Division Two
10.03.1900	Barnsley (A)	L	0-7			Division Two
12.03.1900	Woolwich Arsenal (A)	L	0-12		600	Division Two
24.03.1900	Luton Town (A)	L	0-4			Division Two
31.03.1900	Burslem Port Vale (H)**	L	1-2	Rose	1,000	Division Two
07.04.1900	Walsall (A)	L	0-1		2,000	Division Two
13.04.1900	Chesterfield (A)	L	0-1		2,000	Division Two
14.04.1900	Middlesbrough (H)	D	1-1	Hazard	800	Division Two
16.04.1900	Chesterfield (H)	L	0-4		500	Division Two
17.04.1900	Luton Town (H)	D	1-1	A.N. Other	300	Division Two
23.04.1900	Lincoln City (H)	L	0-1		100	Division Two

28.04.1900	Gainsborough Trinity (H)	L	1-2	Hodgkin	100	Division Two

* Played at Filbert Street, Leicester

** Played at the Vicarage Ground, Whitwick – home of Whitwick White Cross FC

Top Scorers 1899/1900

Leicester Fosse		Loughborough	
Rab King	14	John Tebbs	4
John McMillan	12	Allen	2
Tommy Brown	9	James Brown	2

Bibliography

British Newspaper Archive: www.
britishnewspaperarchive.co.uk

Foulger, N., *Farewell to Filbert Street* (Leicester City
Football Club, 2002)

Gibbons, P., *Association Football in Victorian England –
A History of the Game from 1863 to 1900* (Upfront
Publishing Ltd, Second Edition, 2002)

Kirky D., *The 'Luffs': Story of the Loughborough Town Football
Club, 1886–1900* (David Kirkby Sports Publications, 1995)

Smith D., Taylor P., *Of Fossils & Foxes: The Official,
Definitive History of Leicester City Football Club* (Pitch
Publishing, Fifth Edition, 2016)

Taylor P., *The Luffs Who's Who: Players of Loughborough
Athletic and Football Club 1889 to 1900* (Tony Brown
Publishers, 2012)

Wilford B., *The Athletic Grounds of Loughborough* (Panda
Eyes Publishers, 2014)

Also available at all good book stores

9781785317576

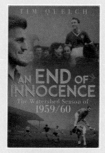

9781785317583

9781785317613

9781785318382

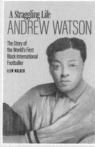

9781785318207

9781785318245

9781785316722

9781785317941

9781785318566

–The–

ATHLETIC GROUNDS

LOUGHBOROUGH

L. WATKINS

PROPRIETOR

GREYHOUND HOTEL